THE REALISATION OF CONCEPTS

THE REALISATION
OF CONCEPTS
Infinity, Cognition, and Health

W. M. Bernstein

KARNAC

First published in 2014 by
Karnac Books Ltd
118 Finchley Road
London NW3 5HT

British Library Cataloguing in Publication Data

A C.I.P. for this book is available from the British Library

ISBN-13: 978-1-78220-070-3

Typeset by V Publishing Solutions Pvt Ltd., Chennai, India

Printed in Great Britain

www.karnacbooks.com

World invisible, we view thee … World unknowable, we know thee

—Francis Thompson, *In No Strange Land* (1913)

CONTENTS

ACKNOWLEDGEMENTS

Dr David McCraney and Mary Stone provided me with the material, psychological and social support that I needed to write this book. The cats Johnny and Moshe were enthusiastic and close by throughout the project.

I have had good luck at finding extraordinary teachers throughout my career, including Mel Snyder (d. 1990), Robert Wicklund, Walter Stephan, Mark Davis, and Warner Burke. Unique guidance came from Dr Gerald Caplan (d. 2008) who was my psychotherapist for a few months while I was in college. After listening to my free-associations, Caplan communicated to me his understanding of my subjective understanding of myself. The precision of his analysis gave me a new feeling of freedom and happiness.

Being understood very exactly by Professor Caplan was a critical developmental experience for me. In addition to articulating how some invalid self-concepts limited me in life, he made sure I understood something about the psychological significance of the concept of infinity.

Finally, I want to thank Edythe Bernstein, my mother. Now 91, her life is nearing its end. Trained as a psychoanalyst, she taught me to read, and read, and become my own teacher. She has been an empathic, loveable, wonderful friend.

ABOUT THE AUTHOR

W. M. Bernstein trained in biology (Tufts University, BS); experimental social psychology (University of Texas at Austin, PhD); basic and applied social and organisational psychology (NIMH post-doctoral fellow, Columbia University); psychoanalysis (Massachusetts General Hospital, Harvard Medical School); and psychopharmacology (White River Junction VA Medical Center, Vermont, and New Mexico State University). Readers are encouraged to send comments to: info@mindbrainhealthcare.com

PLAN OF THE BOOK

Preface and Introduction

The Preface outlines three philosophical approaches to the *hard problem*. That is, how do the operations of the mind relate to those of the body? The Introduction surveys important changes in popular and scientific thinking over the last 100 years. Readers indifferent to philosophy may want to start reading at the Introduction.

Part I

Chapter One looks at scientific concepts and their role in human evolution, and stresses the importance of using very general concepts when attempting to integrate theories at multiple levels of analysis. Chapter Two considers the nature of organisations involved in building neuroscience theories. Chapter Three identifies psychological, social and philosophical barriers to theory integration. Chapter Four describes a growing consensus about brain structures and their related functions. An example of a general model from Panksepp and Wright (2012) is described. Problems with using affect concepts are spelled out. Chapter Five discusses the nature of general concepts and the autonomic nervous systems (ANS). Chapter Six recapitulates the arguments made so far in this book and in *A Basic Theory of Neuropsychoanalysis* (Bernstein, 2011). It also specifies assumptions that help to integrate biological and psychosocial theories.

Part II

Chapter Seven outlines the basic features of the polyvagal theory (Porges, 2011) and other biological theories of stress that use affect concepts. Chapters Eight and Nine discuss relations between stress, anxiety, and decisions to activate instincts and semantic concepts. Chapter Ten examines psychopathological conditions of the mind and brain in light of assumptions about the ANS and cognition.

Part III

Chapter Eleven looks at how parasympathetic control develops normally, and how abnormal development might be remediated using biofeedback during talk and drug therapies. A model of brain–mind information processes leading to cognitive competence and psychopathology is presented. Chapter Twelve considers authority, self-control, and metatheory. Chapter Thirteen describes brain states supporting non-ordinary experiences. L'Esprit D'Escalier describes a dream. The Conclusion considers the nature of concepts used in religion, science, and medicine for understanding mind-body relationships.

PREFACE

The *hard problem* in philosophy assumes that physical and mental phenomena are so different that they might never be related scientifically. How can a person's ideas and feelings arise out of the physical material of their body, especially the brain?

Three important philosophies are used by science to deal with the *hard problem*. One philosophy is Radical Behaviourism, a form of scientific reductionism. Another is Dual Aspect Monism used by psychoanalysis and neuropsychoanalysis. Reductionism assumes mental things such as an individual's subjective experiences of ideas and feelings are beyond the reach of scientific methods. So it solves the mind-body problem by ignoring study of the mind. Dual Aspect Monism imagines that physical and mental things are irreconcilable but that both should be of interest to science.

A third attack on the hard problem is made by writers who assume that ideas have ontological durability. Plato's *Forms*, *The Logos*, and Spinoza's ideas about infinity and cognition suggest that concepts constitute the unified, sturdy foundation of nature. E. O. Wilson (1998) imagines that ideas are connected in a systematic way he calls consilience, and when "instinct is … aligned with reason" a love of nature drives human development (Wilson, 1984, p. 2).

So, in contrast to reductionism and dual aspect monism, Wilson and more ancient sources suggest that physical manifestations of nature are born of ideas. Of course, the causal arrow also goes the other way. For example, seeing an attractive person can cause mental events such as friendly or sexual thoughts; reflexive reactions in muscles and organs of the body (e.g., pupil dilation); and, perhaps, overt muscular movements toward the person.

A distinction between material, physical objects and mental objects is the degree to which they can be registered by exteroceptive sense organs (eyes, ears, etc.). Concepts without physical representations outside the brain can only be observed by interoception. This involves registration of something going on inside one's own nervous system.

The invention of devices such as x-ray machines that extend the range of human exteroception has worked to change our thinking about what aspects of reality are amenable to scientific inquiry. Ideas once only imagined, such as going to the moon, can become manifest concretely and observed objectively. So, our ideas of a concept's objectivity and subjectivity change.

The most important determinant of a concept's potential to become realised physically is its validity. Scientific validity is a continuous, not a categorical variable. That is, scientific concepts are neither all true nor all false but rather, more or less true. Relatively invalid ideas might never be manifest in reality or only be capable of physical manifestation for brief periods. For example, a psychotic's idea that he is a king or a god can be manifest in bizarre physical, psychological and social forms, but usually for only a short time. This is because such ideas account poorly for the way the world works. Similarly, the concepts underlying Germany's Third Reich were realised, but only for twelve years. In comparison, more democratic and republican societies have lasted for centuries.

The process of evolution selects and encodes genetically the most valid concepts to operationalise in physical forms for promoting life in specific environments. Valid concepts are easier to operationlaise in nature and in science than less valid ideas. Concepts with high *construct validity* can be verified operationally in biological, psychological, and socio-economic experiments (cf., Campbell & Fiske, 1959).

Science is a social mechanism for selecting valid over invalid concepts. An idea's "amount of validity" is the important issue for science and for the individual person. The truth of concepts, including the knowledge of the conditions that promote and inhibit their physical manifestations, does not change. In contrast, an idea's degree of objectivity or subjectivity does change. Theories in neuroscience should be most concerned with concept validity. The boundaries of subjectivity and objectivity are altered over time by individuals, small social groups such as families, and large organizations like corporations, nations and scientific schools.

I think that the concept of *affect* gets in the way of seeing the underlying relationships between concepts and their physical instantiations. Here I present biological and psychological hypotheses without using affect concepts. This book is an extension of the ideas in *A Basic Theory of Neuropsychoanalysis* (Bernstein, 2011).

A Basic Theory coalesced over a few years. In general, the development of ideas is enhanced by the passage of time. The brain–mind operates constantly, unconsciously, automatically, and with conscious intention to find connections between its contents. These seeking processes are regulated by dynamic interactions of biological, psychological, and social variables. Some amount of energy must be used constantly to power information processes that maintain old connections and seek new ones between neurons and ideas. Otherwise, the person will fall apart.

A Basic Theory used ideas from three levels of understanding (bio-psycho-social) to explain the arousal and regulation of sensations, thoughts, feelings, and overt behaviours. I tried to connect well-made areas of biology and psychology with each other. Each linking attempt was gauged to be uncontroversial and based on reason and empirical evidence of the type that makes one fairly certain of something. To explain clinical and normal phenomena, I used concepts from behaviourism, psychoanalysis, neurobiology, and psychopharmacology, and from sensory, developmental, motivational, and cognitive social psychology. In the end, I had a general, somewhat comprehensive, theoretical framework.

Originally, I wanted to write a book about psychological depth. What is it? I think of psychological depth as the depth of a concept, which in turn is equivalent to its general validity. A valid, deep, general concept contains and explains many other concepts that are valid under relatively restrictive conditions. Maybe my book had been more broad than deep. I had gathered up ideas that were just lying in open view in the relevant fields and organised them together at the surface.

In order to evaluate scientific theories one needs a theory of theories. Attribution theory in social psychology concerns the theories of the typical person or *naïve scientist* (Heider, 1958). In other words, attribution theory and research attempt to understand how the typical person understands things. The hypotheses of professional scientists are subject to more rigorous testing than those of *naïve scientists*. But intuition or gut reactions stimulate thinking, feeling, and overt behaviour in all sorts of humans and other mammals.

If we try to explain formal scientists' explanations, we need a lofty perch (cf., Wicklund, 1990). General Systems Theories use general and more specific concepts that can be operationalised. To operationalise a concept is to represent and measure it in terms of its physical and temporal manifestations. For example, motivation to eat can be increased, in part, by food deprivation, with longer time periods usually causing stronger tendencies to seek and consume food. Operationalisation promotes theoretical clarity.

General Systems Theories consider cybernetics and information processing. Viewed from distant, general conceptual levels, a person might be appreciated in full, in the way that the entire Earth can be seen from outer space. And, by using optic, electro-magnetic, radioactive and biochemical methods, we can see in detail the specific, tiny surfaces of the person's nervous system, such as synaptic receptors.

This book tries to relate general concepts of the person to details about the operation of the nervous system. It includes ideas about the autonomic nervous system (ANS), which were mostly lacking in my former book. *The Polyvagal Theory* (Porges, 2011) was an ANS primer for me, illustrating the different regulatory roles of the phylogenetically older and newer parts of the vagal system. And, I have studied Panksepp and his colleagues' very important recent work (e.g., Panksepp & Wright, 2012; Solms & Panksepp, 2012).

Despite my admiration for the ANS specialists, I have a complaint about the affect concepts used to explain their findings. The term flummoxes all schools of basic and applied psychology because modern psychologies must make some assumptions about the relationships between brain and mind; and thoughts, feelings and motivations. These sorts of relationships have been hard to understand, and ambiguity about affect is a barrier to integrating brain–mind theories.

The term *affect* is used in explanations for almost every biological, psychological, and social phenomenon. The term connotes many things but what it denotes exactly is not clear, to me anyway. If centrally important concepts are unclear when examining a complex system, it is easy to become confused. The best way to keep things straight is to use the fewest number of general concepts needed to contain and explain other more specific ideas. Then it would be easier to see how the big picture and the little pictures are related.

It is understatement to say that body–brain–mind is a complex system. Shared understanding about the meaning of concepts, if not agreement on their relationships and implications, is very important in mind–brain studies. This is because we try to consider many variables, interacting constantly across multiple functional and structural levels of analysis.

I don't think affect concepts can grasp the nature of cognition. Nor will pure cognitive psychology ever understand motivational concepts. Motivational ideas are more general than cognitive concepts and clearer than affect concepts.

Motivational theories assume that bioenergetic forces are shaped by habits to produce overt behaviour. Habits of thought are controlled to a large extent by the same sorts of variables and processes described competently by the behaviourists. Moving a muscle is not very different from activating an idea (cf. Norman & Shallice, 1976). But the consequences of the latter can be much more far reaching.

Cognitive and motivational concepts need to be integrated in order to describe how the nervous system works to regulate subjective experience and overt behaviour. Integrated, deep theory has more potential to be an accurate predictive and explanatory device than any of its conceptual sub-parts.

Theories that can predict thoughts, feelings, and overt behaviours have many prosocial and nefarious applications. Governmental, political, military, commercial, and healthcare organisations want to help citizens, sway voters, kill enemies, defeat competitors, and promote the health of patients. Dominant groups are especially interested in generating conformity with laws to maintain social order. Social stability can promote the development of individuals, culture, science, art, and the uninterrupted production and consumption of a few essential and many inane goods and services.

Detailed concepts and methods useful for building a general, integrated theory of the person already exist within various scientific schools. Which general concepts might best promote integration of neurobiological, cognitive, and social methods and theories?

The most important, extant general integrative framework is the theory of evolution. Freud's most general concepts were Eros and Thanatos. Religions have gods and devils, and every group has something like liberals and conservatives. These traditional dichotomies have some utility for understanding the person. In comparison, evolution theory has great utility as a foundation and framework for cross-discipline theory integration. Darwin's ideas suggest that nature is good at deciding how to promote life over time in specific environments. Most scientists are reluctant to imagine that nature makes decisions. Or, they may hedge on defining what a decision is. This is due, in part, to avoid being identified with religious ideas such as *intelligent design*.

Religious fundamentalists openly use the verbiage of holy books to make decisions. But all individuals have some form of rule book containing standards that define ideal and forbidden thoughts and actions; thus, a typical person carries an implicit bible in mind.

Regardless of whether someone believes in a god or is an atheist, people generally understand the semantic concept of god. All known semantic concepts, including religious concepts, exist at least as structures in the brain–mind. Everyone is, at least, somewhat motivated to create a unique, self-authorised religion. "Rules for living" have been recorded on rock tablets, sheepskins, paper, electronic media, and, most importantly for us, in the brains of people.

Inevitably each person's story or theory of their own self involves a god-like actor of greater or lesser authority, and struggles with good and bad, right and wrong, pleasure and pain. The Bible emphasises that being good determines whether one will live forever in a pleasurable heaven or a painful hell. It also indicates that knowledge or awareness of some parts of reality is the original sin. The psychobiological system of self-concepts working to operate a Western mind, and maybe all types of minds, has to juggle the weird relationship between something like these two concepts. The most basic implication of this is that any theory of the person must account for conflicts between wanting and fearing knowledge.

Conceptual fashions

One hundred years ago psychoanalysis was the best medical treatment for a troubled mind. If successful, one was promised relief from neurotic anxiety and could look forward to a life of normal anxiety. Achievement of this goal may have seemed a small thing compared to the aspirations of people who wished for more from life, such as sublime aesthetic or spiritual experiences. After all, psychoanalysis was supposed to be a depth psychology. Was a reduction in anxiety the best it could offer?

Despite its limited aims, the absence of good alternative treatments ensured that customers would be numerous. But there were not many analysts. The training was long and the treatment periods sometimes longer. It was obvious that the method, which was often not effective anyway, could only be offered to a limited number of individuals.

The effects of psychoanalysis may have been most profound at the societal level. Knowledge of the theory was spread by its use in medicine, literature, cinema and common parlance (e.g., "He's a neurotic egotist!"). This promoted discussion of sexuality, unconscious processes, and the value of self-reflection. The accelerated liberalisation of sexual attitudes and the preoccupation with self-esteem in the 1960s were due, in no small part, to Freud's theory.

In the Sixties, clinical schools focused increasingly on social variables. Attachment schools were popular in psychoanalysis (e.g., Bowlby, 1969), and humanistic-transpersonal psychologies gained followers (e.g., Fromm, 1966; Perls, 1969). These movements were influenced by Gestalt perceptual and social psychologies. Unlike psychoanalysis, with its medical roots and focus on pathology, the Gestaltists were interested in good figures and wholeness. Ideas about self-actualisation and peak experience came from these groups (e.g., Maslow, 1954). They entertained a notion that one could be "better than well", and that life was an exciting journey of discovery.

In the same decade, states of consciousness became a legitimate area of study (e.g., Tart, 1969). Theoretical ideas and methods from social psychology were applied to resolve organisational, generational, racial, and gender conflicts (e.g., Deutsch, 1969). Modern intellectuals and hippies rediscovered hallucinogenic drugs that had been used for centuries by native cultures (e.g., Huxley, 1954; Leary et al., 1963). Eastern religions, mysticism, and Carl Jung became more popular in the Sixties along with the increased interest in consciousness and the Self.

Freud (1920) said he had never experienced anything like an oceanic feeling of limitlessness, or a feeling of oneness with nature. But in his last book, *Moses and Monotheism* (1938), he added some new ideas to this thinking about religion (see Chapter Twelve in this book). Perhaps psychological, social, and biochemical methods could do more than merely rid one of excessive anxiety. Could they promote something like peak experiences?

Of course, psychoanalysis had recognised the importance of social-developmental variables. But psychoanalysis was scorned in academic, scientific psychology. So, there was a curious contemporaneous relationship between the touchy-feely, transpersonal psychologies, and the no-feely, no-thinky behaviourists. Somewhere in that conceptual space were the psychoanalysts. During the isolation of the neuroscientifically relevant fields, marked advances occurred in developmental, social, and cognitive psychologies, ethology, neurobiology and psychopharmacology.

Seemingly at once, a whole host of perspectives were added to our description of the human being. There was no obvious agreement on big, general concepts that described, predicted or controlled the functions and purposes of the person. Relationships between useful theories concerning different levels of related phenomena were not apparent.

Concepts of minds, brains, and bodies were not in one whole piece. What did it all mean? Could we put Humpty Dumpty together again?

The 1970s saw the rise of computer science, cognitive psychology and, in psychiatry, psychopharmacology and descriptive diagnosis. The tumultuous cultural changes of the Sixties moderated. Psychoanalysis lost its dominance as a medical treatment. Cognitive therapy became popular. Racial and gender equality increased. Educators seemed better at teaching students to have high self-esteem than to read. Everyone was "above average". Aspects of hippy style were co-opted and commercialised. Members of Nixon's staff wearing wide lapels, polka dot ties, and long sideburns lied to us on TV (see Merle Haggard, 1979). When they changed their stories about Watergate or Vietnam, their previous versions of events were called "inoperative".

The nature of truth itself seemed to be changing in society at large. This change was related, in part, to the scientific acceptance of the importance of studying consciousness. It is hard still, I think, for many scientists to acknowledge that consciousness has something to do with truth. Formal science regards truth in a somewhat different fashion than does the typical citizen or naïve scientist.

In the Seventies and Eighties the reputation of truth was damaged by post-modern, deconstructionists. Truth, as my parents knew it, was dead. But "whenever deconstructionists required appendectomies, or bypass surgery or even a root-canal job, they never deconstructed medical or dental 'truth', but went along with whatever their board-certified, profit-oriented surgeon proclaimed was the last word" (Wolfe, 2000, p. 13). That is, concern with biological and socioeconomic conditions can work to bring down to earth the wildest theories of reality.

In the 1990s, there was a troubling shift in social norms concerning the good and the true. Intellectuals moved from a deconstructionist assumption that there is little concrete meaning or truth contained in words and behaviour, to an opposite position in which political correctness is demanded in speech and behaviour. Apparently it had become common for administrators at American universities to preside at programmes that aimed to ban any speech or behaviour they imagined might injure another's self-esteem (Lukianoff, 2012). One such programme operated from 1998 to 2007 at Michigan State University.

> Participants were shown a list of definitions of negative behaviours, which included using one's "white privileges" or

"heterosexual privilege" or "any action that is perceived as having racial meaning" or "any action working to change people's perceptions that result in your advantage and/or another's disadvantage"... When an audience member asked if it was appropriate to suspend a student for being unwilling to take part in this kind of thought reform [a university official] objected to the implication that the program was something students *had to do*. He reasoned that because the goal of the program was to increase accountability, students should recognize that they had the *choice* of taking part or being, for all practical purposes, expelled. (Lukianoff, 2012, pp. 120–121)

In 1960 I was nine years old. I thought I understood the broad outlines of the world I would enter as an adult. America was powerful, fair and good; children, adults, men and women, socio-economic, racial and religious groups, all had defined social roles; television images came in black and white; one's doctor knew everything; the earth's oceans and atmosphere were infinite and were to be conquered. But then I noticed that the air was not as pure as it had been; it was harder to find a quiet place; the light in the sky seemed different; sexual, religious and political talk was less private; smoking was bad for you; and it was difficult to know what was appropriate dress or speech. I had liked radio and found colour television disturbing. My hero President Kennedy was assassinated. And who the heck was Maharishi Mahesh Yogi?

What I was observing with distress was that every time I had learned the way things are or what was good and proper, they changed. This motivated me to worry more about what was true than what was good. If only because the underlying truth of things really never changes and, hence, worrying about the truth is much less wearing on body and mind than attempting to keep up with the fashions of the day.

During most of human history, any particular individual lived and died on a single cultural stage that rested on a stable earth, under a predictable sky. Now, instead of lasting for centuries or decades, common technologies, normative speech, social relations, and even the climate seem to change every year. Rapid environmental change within one's lifetime increases pressure on the person to change their learned habits of thought and behaviour. Their old habits are inconsistent with new environmental demands. This causes stressful internal conflicts (e.g., cognitive dissonance). If competent decisions are not made to resolve important conflicts, chronic anxiety ensues.

The individual must decide more or less consciously to conform, ignore, or resist the pressure of new expectations. Ideally, living in a fast-changing, stressful environment works to promote competence to know the difference between the contents and the processes of the mind. This is a necessary prerequisite for a theorist of reality. The naïve scientist notes that, "First it was like this. Now it's like that." And she asks, "What ideas can I rely on in this world?"

In other words, environmental changes pressure citizens and formal scientists to develop better explanatory concepts. For example, the validity of many people's concepts of themselves and others was challenged by the election of a "coloured person" as President of the United States. Barak Obama's election is the most salient example of countless other recent changes in normative social beliefs and expectations. More and less obvious social, psychological, and physical environmental shifts have been driven, in large part, by changes in communication and energy technologies.

Science is an evolved species of organisation

Neuroscientists are not post-modern deconstructionists who claim there is no truth. Hopefully, they are not enthusiastic supporters of any thought control efforts made by their university administrators. Ideally, science assumes truth exists and persists despite social fads: that some concepts are more valid than others; that it is possible to learn the conditions under which concepts are valid and not valid; and that events can be predicted most accurately, and controlled most effectively, when valid rather than invalid ideas are used to process sense data coming from the body and external world.

Science has evolved as a unique form of social arrangement. The evolution of social structures or species is not merely metaphorically similar to the evolution of biological forms. Social systems are integrated materially with biological systems (see Wilson, 1975, 1998) and with psychological systems (Burke, 2010; Katz & Kahn, 1973). Social cognition provides the developmental foundation of all thinking (e.g., Fiske & Taylor, 2008; Schore, 2003a, 2003b).

It is pretty safe to assume that semantic concepts (words) learned in social contexts provide the basic structure for the human mind, including the parts of the mind containing self-concepts. A concept about the self or not, is a collection of sensory attributes. For example, the semantic concept "lion" may contain sensory and social attributes such as large, yellow, roars, dangerous predator, powerful, king of the jungle, wise, kindly, and so on. A person's first conceptual system contains two items: self and other (most likely "mummy"). Depending on how flabbergasted the person was in making this basic distinction, he might spend the rest of his life asking (in a less formal manner): "How are my self-concepts differentiated from and integrated with my concepts for my mother, father, and others?"

All thinking depends on a biological substrate—the brain. The most central concepts in biology concern evolution. Evolutionary principles give concepts of biology, psychology and sociology their deepest, integrated meaning. The theories of each area of science represent the "meaning system" for understanding its particular field of study. These concepts reside in brains, minds, laboratories, classrooms, libraries, and computers around the world. Science has outlived many generations of individuals, tribes, and nations. Nature's big experiment in learning (evolution), and man's (science), have had time to grow. To develop the cognitive and biological meaning systems of the species, we have been creating new explanatory concepts or memes (Dawkins, 1975). A highly technical sub-set of these memes gives instructions on how to make new genes!

A curious feature of science is that one is permitted to know only what is not true. This may be a surprise to non-scientists. When research results are consistent with predictions based on one's concepts of how the world works—and when we can rule out chance as a likely cause of the results—we are able to reject the null hypothesis. This means we can say that the concept we tested cannot be proved false, and hence deserves further consideration. In the most formal sense, science is allowed to say, "This idea is most probably not wrong". But it can't say, "This idea is true".

Science holds the truth in such high regard that it assumes it can never be known. This may have something to do with the mandate given to science by society. That is, science, like religion, is authorised to be a referee of truth. One doesn't want to invest authority in a scientist or priest who can't delay gratification. The scientist can't be too committed to his favourite theory. Formal science is to have a higher standard of proof than that used by the average person. It should be "objective" when interpreting the meaning of data it gets from the eyes, ears, nose, and skin, and from numerous ingenious devices (e.g., x-ray machines) that register aspects of material reality that cannot be detected by the body's sensory devices.

In contrast, the typical citizen gets only raw sensory data collected by the body's exteroceptors (e.g., eyes, ears) and interoceptors to assess the truth of things. (We should think of sensory *and* associative neurons when talking about interoception). Naïve scientists, the term attribution theory uses for human beings, have gut reactions and other sorts of somatic and mental responses to sense data. Not only regular people, but also mystics and paranoids talk about knowing the truth. Feelings of knowing the truth are a bit more exciting and sexy on the face of it than knowing what is false. Of course, both types of knowing are useful. But life with few experiences of felt conviction can be a bit drab. One imagines a rigid, dorky scientist wearing belt *and* braces, who is reluctant to take anything on face value.

But face validity is often the first indication of the truth of something and, ideally, it works to promote more rigorous tests of some ideas by science. The subjective experience of face validity is determined mostly by in-born tendencies (instincts) to respond to sense data. Evolution has prepared animals to avoid dangerous environmental situations and to approach attractive ones. Animals crouch automatically when sights or sounds indicate the presence of a predator. People feel good when another's face forms a pattern of lines indicating a smile. If the pattern is a grimace, the observer may feel aggressive or afraid. We become aroused by sensing the secondary sexual characteristics of suitable mates. Visual, auditory, tactile, olfactory, or gustatory sensations of specific stimuli can release fixed action patterns, that is, instinctive behaviours. Animals are genetically predisposed to enact overt behaviours that have worked over time to protect or enhance the lives of their relatives.

Natural selection works via genetic mechanisms that have organised the brain and body to react to certain sensory arrays with specific overt behaviours. Genes give rise to neurological structures and processes that initiate useful, reflexive, gut reactions to things in the world. These are the face valid things. Animals with the most useful genetic inheritances live longer and hence mate more than those lacking the helpful genes. Gut reactions or instinctive tendencies represent responses to our first impressions of things.

Scientists are suspicious of first impressions. This is somewhat logical since instincts have been retained in genomes not because they always produce a useful behaviour, but because they have worked generally to promote safety and/or reproduction. Instincts have statistically important predictive validity. The shadow a mouse sees looming over the ground towards it may have been made by a falling leaf and not a hawk. But enough of the time the shadow has indicated real threats to safety. Accordingly, instincts to freeze, fight, or flee upon sensing a looming shadow have been conserved over evolution. Better safe than sorry.

Affect psychology (e.g., Ekman, 1973; Tomkins, 1962, 1963) is based on the idea of face validity. The body's reactions to external stimuli include stereotypic gross and micro-movements of the muscles in the face. Some facial gestures are reliably associated with various kinds of painful or pleasant reactions (affects). The focus on the face, and more recently the subcortical brain regions that regulate instinctive actions, is the strength and the weakness of the affect school. I will address this issue more extensively in Chapter Four.

Of course, scientists and regular guys can have a bias to discount the truth of what is obvious. For instance, I remember looking at a map of the world in primary school and thinking that the continents seemed to be like parts of a jigsaw puzzle that had once all been connected. The teacher told me sternly that geologists doubted that the continents were ever part of one mass. Soon after this episode, geologists accepted the validity of continental drift and plate tectonics. Such an experience could encourage anyone to take the obvious seriously (if not as the last word) and to doubt scientific authority.

So, it is important to understand the relationships between subjectivity and validity. The boundary between legitimate and illegitimate targets of scientific inquiry keeps changing. The locations and functions of the bodily organs only started to be known with some certainty within the last 300 years. Early on the heart was thought to be the location of the mind or soul. This was most likely due to the fact that one can notice that the heart's action changes in response to external events and thoughts in one's own mind. Understanding the mutual controlling relationships between vascular and respiratory systems, and brain–mind information processing, are centrally important for integrating biological and psychological concepts.

The mind found its way to the brain over time. The arcane operations of the brain, which looks to the naked eye very unlike a mechanism of any kind, have been represented by extrapolation from nuclear, magnetic, electronic, and biochemical data. What was once considered completely mysterious, subjective, or spiritual has now become the province of science (e.g., Walach et al., 2011).

I think that the degree of validity of concepts is, by definition, the bedrock of reality. Subjective appreciation of reality is more or less related to the way things are according to objective scientific measurement. And, of course, objectively measureable and subjective, face valid truths are not in zero-sum relationships. The continents can look on the surface to have once been connected; sophisticated research methods such as analysis of samples of the earth's core can produce results that are consistent or not consistent with the idea.

Instincts and executive functions

To get by in life, one needs a minimum number of good-enough concepts to explain reality. In our very social environments, the wisdom of the instincts needs to be controlled by semantic concepts represented in the neocortex of the brain. These concepts can specify numerous situational conditions indicating when instinctive actions are likely to help or hurt the person's chances of surviving and thriving in the world. The neocortex is largely an inhibitory organ. It shapes the instincts into sophisticated, cultural instruments. The high level of competence to remember, process, and reflect upon semantic concepts makes the human brain–mind unique. Compared to how evolution operates via genetic changes and selection pressures among other creatures, human viability is more dependent on the validity of concepts learned over the history of the species (cultural and scientific memes), and during the life of each individual.

In other animals, genes and the instinctual fixed action patterns that they promote determine mostly the survivability of individuals and species. With raw evolutionary forces operating as the "executive", the entire organism may be killed for being less than optimally competent instinctively. Changing mind–brain by learning and activating more and more valid concepts about nature and the self can delay complete organismic death.

The executive must be able to turn off ("kill") repetitive, non-helpful ideas. The experience of regulating the mind, that is, activating and deactivating ideas, may feel to psychotics like acts of murder or godlike creation. But for all people it difficult to stop 'habits of thinking'. We are familiar with our own ideas and come to love them after a fashion. But nostalgia for invalid ideas is perhaps the greatest barrier to human growth.

Cognitive therapy, begun in the Sixties, tries to increase the validity of the ideas the person holds about themselves and social life. Increased self-concept validity can have a salutary effect on a person's feelings (e.g., Beck, 1967, 1976). Since most people seeking psychotherapy think more negatively about themselves than is warranted because they have what Freud called a harsh superego, self-esteem tends to rise after cognitive therapy. But a person's degree of self-liking is related to many other variables in the complex brain–mind system. I assume that the more important cause of better mental functioning after cognitive treatment is not self-esteem increase, but the increase in validity of self- and non-self-concepts. That is, knowing explicitly what is true usually makes the person feel better and promotes the development of the mind (cf., Bion, 1962).

Knowledge of physical and social realities, such as gravity and social dominance hierarchies, works to shape thought, feeling, and overt behaviour. But such knowledge has a more limited effect on dreaming and imagination. People can fly in their dreams and imagine that they are a king or queen.

Over time, individuals and groups of people working together can devise solutions to formerly unsolvable problems. If augmented with valid principles of reality, instincts to attain immediate pleasure can be transformed into more effective action in the external world (e.g., Metcalfe & Mischel, 1999). We can now actually go to the moon after years of merely imagining it. Time was needed to develop methods to transform the concept into a physical reality. But technologies to produce metals, plastics, rockets, and navigation devices were not enough to land men on the moon. Social and organisational technologies were needed to coordinate the knowledge and overt behaviour of more than 400,000 individuals and 20,000 organisations participating in NASA's Apollo mission.

In the twentieth century, the boundaries between the realms of imagination and social reality started shifting quickly. Applications of basic knowledge of physics, chemistry, biology, and psychology worked to inform people of human potential. New knowledge led to telephones, radio, automobiles, cinema, intelligence testing, psychoanalysis, television, brain surgery, psychoactive drugs, small and then smaller personal computers in cell phones, and on and on.

If gadgets imagined in science fiction books and films could be made real, maybe one's own personal dreams could come true. Businesses that sell high-tech consumer items depend on such hopes. Members of the proletariat are now transformed nightly into stars on reality television. And I have had more than one non-psychotic patient tell me that science will soon discover a way for them to live forever.

Neuroscience was cooking in the background at mid-century. By the 1980s, the rate of acquisition of knowledge of the brain and mind started increasing dramatically. Basic research in physics and molecular biology were producing applications in medicine including real-time brain imaging, magnetic brain stimulation, and new drugs to treat mental illnesses.

Today, scientists and everyone else are a little overwhelmed with research results about the brain and mind. Every week a new neuro-chemical or imaging method is touted as a key for understanding and controlling one or another mental process. But theories to make sense of the increasing mountain of facts are in some disarray. This is not surprising. It is a complex affair to understand these things at various levels of analysis simultaneously. Lack of theoretical integration of biology and psychology makes it hard to understand the new findings. If we advance theoretical integration, individuals and cultures at large will probably benefit or, at least, change.

PART I

CHAPTER ONE

Scientific concepts and human evolution

The greatest achievement of neuropsychoanalysis has been to put biology in touch with depth psychology in the modern era (e.g., Kaplan-Solms & Solms, 2000). I assume a theory's depth is roughly equivalent to its generality, or its ability to contain and explain many less general ideas. The most general concepts are needed when attempting to integrate concepts at multiple levels of analysis. For a theory to be deep, the connections between the general, overarching concepts and ideas lower in the conceptual hierarchy need to be made explicit.

The relationships between theoretical concepts in neuropsychoanalysis and the psychobiology of the autonomic nervous system are central in the development of the deepest, most general concepts of body, brain and mind. We can validate empirically that particular levels and rates of change of physiological variables are correlated in time with both conscious and unconscious sensations, concepts and feelings. A patient and an "objective" doctor can each use valid concepts to explain, for example, the patient's blood pressure. They can observe via their eyes alterations in numbers or graphic figures displayed on a television screen, that represent moment to moment changes in the patient's blood pressure. The correlations over time between knowledge or, at least, data about events in the person's nervous system and the rest of the body had for most of history been the private possession of the person. They now can be made socially available in the form of objective, operational measures of the body's activities. The central interest of neuropsychoanalysis and affective neuroscience is how somatic and psychic things relate.

The aim of this book is to examine some of the problems bothering all integrative approaches to mind–brain phenomena. Neuroscience as a whole is vexed especially by how to think about cognitive processes and processes referred to variously as affect, emotion, arousal, and feeling. Points of agreement and disagreement between different models of mind–brain are not entirely obvious. Ambiguity about the meaning of terms is a problem. Unclarity is caused by at least two important factors.

First, various schools of thought are converging. This is the good news. The problem is that they bring with them concepts, terms, and methods from their own traditions. Sometimes the same terms, such as affect, are used by different schools with somewhat different denotations and connotations.

Second, some important concepts and terms from all the converging schools are outdated. The old concepts are like venerable whales on whose skin barnacles and other creatures have attached themselves and lived for decades. Every time a writer uses an existing term she may change its meaning somewhat to make it suitable for her purposes. The old concepts and terms have had utility but they are fuzzy. Reduction of conceptual ambiguity occurs when measures of concepts are operationalised. For example, stress levels of a person might be operationalised as changes in heart rate variability (HRV). Theoretical concepts that are complicated, vague, or adorned with many implicit connotations are hard to operationalise.

We are very interested in the interplay of many variables at many levels of analysis. If a concept is difficult to operationalise it is hard or impossible to understand what it means, let alone explain its relationships to other concepts. To promote conceptual clarity we need to look first at how theoretical concepts and terms are used by neuropsychoanalysts and affect theorists. I argue that the concept affect has outlived its theoretical utility.

Valid concepts

I assume that the motive to know reality is the greatest motive and that a fear of knowing reality is aroused to various degrees, at varying levels of mind and body, as knowledge changes (Bernstein, 2011, 2014). To know reality is to use valid concepts to interpret sensory information coming from the external world and the body. Using more valid concepts to interpret raw sense data causes greater pleasure in life than using less valid concepts. There is something about this pleasure that can activate strong resistance to creating and using valid concepts to experience pleasure and anticipate pain. I assume that better feelings indicate that one has used deeper than usual, valid concepts to interpret sensations or other concepts. This may or not seem like a radical idea (cf., Bion, 1962). But it is consistent with the somewhat remarkable fact that individuals learn and grow, and species and social organisations such as science evolve.

If knowing and using valid concepts were not more pleasurable than using false concepts, there would be no incentive to know the truth. The selective advantage of knowledge is driven by the feelings it causes. (For an opposite view, see LeDoux, 2000.) The pleasure of knowing truth is both a proximal and a distal cause of the development of individuals and cultures. For example, enjoyment of a Bach concerto depends, in part, upon having learned concepts to organise and give meaning to auditory sensations. On the basis of inherited preferences for certain auditory patterns (i.e., good gestalts), infants too might enjoy the Bach. But a person's potential to enjoy the music would increase with greater experience and learning of music.

Learning can sometimes allow one to glimpse briefly how nature is organized at large. This can cause great pleasure with intimations of knowing infinity. Infinity takes on a different colour when one is mired in an anxious, depressive or psychotic state. The fear is that the bad experience will go on forever. We might imagine then that at the deepest level of the mind, motives to both approach and avoid infinite pleasure and infinite pain are in dynamic, mutually regulating relationships.

Compromise concepts

Biopsychological tendencies to approach pleasure and avoid pain, along with simple ignorance of the truth, mean that most people's concepts of themselves and the external world are compromise formations (e.g., Brenner, 2006). Compromised thinking is the result of motivational and cognitive factors (e.g., Bernstein et al., 1979; Bernstein, 1995; Stephan et al., 1979). Compromise decisions are made more or less consciously to resolve conflicts between the desire to approach knowledge and the desire to avoid anxiety in general, and disintegration anxiety in particular (Kohut, 1977).

In the late 1960s, American cinema began to feature more and more gory, anxiety-inducing violence in films. By 1998, Spielberg's film *Saving Private Ryan* graphically depicted soldiers' viscera spilling out of their bodies. The most horrible aspect of this was observing the still conscious person viewing for the first time his own insides as he anticipated death. This kind of scene had been enacted for the English public during executions for treason starting in the fourteenth century. Prisoners were hung, often not to the point of death, and were able to witness their own evisceration. Almost certainly, the earliest ancient societies had staged similar events.

Such public displays were, at least, learning experiences that were imagined to deter crimes against authority. At some point in human history, the great majority of individuals had learned standards of good and bad behaviour. They could, therefore, police themselves to prevent overt enactment of antisocial behaviours, and avoid punishment by external and intrapsychic agencies.

The expectation of horrible pain and punishment for violating a moral standard (talion dread) is a common feature of the human mind. The efficacy of such a control system is so great that merely thinking of something one believes is antisocial can create guilt and anxiety. Freud (e.g., 1920, 1930) realised that this amounted to a form of over-control that worked not only to maintain social order, but often caused excessive anxiety and depression.

Methods for educating children and adults to control fundamental motives have varied over history. But to be effective, all such techniques must account for the fact that everyone is motivated to both approach and avoid "sinful" ideas and overt behaviours. Why forbid something if no one wants to do it? When one has an immoral thought, internal conflict arises. This causes stress in the body and mind. Then, in order to resolve the stressful conflict, the person must decide, in or out of awareness, to change something. He has either to change something overtly in the social or physical world, or something about how he thinks. If he does nothing materially, he must do something to something mentally.

Conflict-resolving decisions involve using existing ideas in new ways, or creating new ideas. Competent decisions based on more valid concepts of reality work to reduce stress and prevent anxiety better than incompetent decisions based on less valid concepts about one's self and the rest of the world.

Concepts about oneself or anything else involve a compromise with reality for two reasons. The first reason is ignorance. Unless one has perfect knowledge of everything, one's concepts will be incomplete, and hence by definition represent compromises with reality. But the validity of concepts can increase by learning from objective and subjective experience. The second reason is fear. Some aspects of external reality are so horribly threatening that people prefer to deny them. In place of valid conceptions of reality, distorted but less frightening concepts are borrowed or created. For example, normal children and adults tend to overestimate the ability of parents or other authorities to protect them from harm.

Having invalid ideas about oneself and the world exposes one to injury. For example, imagining one can fly can lead to immediate death. And, just as surely, believing falsely that one never had or will have an antisocial thought or feeling will cause stress and anxiety. Unresolved stress leads to concerns about one's ability to regulate body and mind. That is, acute and chronic stress can, and usually does, cause anxiety. Anxiety is in an inverse, linear relationship to longevity (e.g., Mroczek & Spiro, 2007; Russ et al., 2012). In common parlance, the more anxious one feels, the sooner one dies.

Psychoanalytic theory (e.g., Freud, 1912, 1924) assumed that moral standards forbidding incest and murder were the foundational building blocks of the human mind. If tendencies to enact such taboos became aroused, the person made an effort to deny them. Denial comes in many forms, the most extreme being repression—or complete blocking from consciousness of the taboo wish—and dissociation. In dissociation, conflicting ideas (e.g., "I depend on Daddy and Daddy beats me up") are experienced only one at a time in consciousness. Kohut (1977) called repression a horizontal split and dissociation a vertical split.

If one is forced to consider consciously an antisocial wish, one may simply negate its truth (e.g., Bernstein, 1984; Freud, 1925) or use humour to make light of a threatening condition (e.g., gallows humour). In the 1960s, it was a somewhat humorous habit in some Afro-American groups to call one's friends "mother fucker".

Cognitive dissonance theory (Festinger, 1957), validated by years of experimental research results, indicates that changes in self-conceptions occur when a person is induced, by means of the smallest amount of pressure necessary, to behave inconsistently with her usual ideas of herself (see Aronson, 1969, 1992; Metin & Camgoz, 2011; Wicklund & Brehm, 1976). For example, people tend to believe that they would only endure pain willingly for a good reason. This was demonstrated in a classic study by Aronson and Mills (1959). Subjects were induced to think they had freely chosen to undergo a painfully embarrassing initiation ritual in order to join a sorority. Compared to those who went through mild initiations, those suffering more painful hazing came to like the sorority more.

The dissonance theory reasoning is that enduring willingly the hardships of an initiation ritual is inconsistent with not liking the group. This arouses cognitive dissonance, described by Festinger (1957) as an "unpleasant form of arousal". I would define dissonance as a form of anxiety due to the unresolved stress of holding inconsistent ideas about oneself (Aronson, 1969). In order to reduce cognitive dissonance, the person comes to change her concept of how much she likes the group. Logically, this would involve adding positive attributes to one's concept of the group, or increasing one's estimates of the group's level of already presumed positive attributes. As a result, one's feeling of liking or attitude toward a concept of a group (or anything else) should become more positive. In the most general terms, the strength of the motive to approach such a concept in mind, and/or the thing the concept represents in the external world, should increase. This is entirely consistent with the findings of dissonance research.

The neural basis of cognitive dissonance reduction has been studied using functional magnetic resonance imaging (fMRI). Subjects induced to spend time "suffering" in an uncomfortable fMRI machine without pay came to like the experience more than subjects who were paid to participate. Activation of dorsal anterior cingulate cortex and anterior insular cortex was greater the more subjects reported liking the experience (Van Veen et al., 2009).

But, if the fear of suffering is extremely high, as it would be when anticipating being hung, drawn and quartered, the person's beliefs change less than if the fear is only mild. Aronson and Carlsmith (1963) demonstrated this effect in children. Their results are very relevant for how to get people to not behave antisocially. Specifically, they suggest that especially harsh punishments are not conducive to development of the self.

> If a person is induced to cease performing a desired action through the threat of punishment, he will experience dissonance. His cognition that he is not performing the action is dissonant with his cognition that the action is desirable. An effective way of reducing dissonance is by derogating the action. The greater the threat of punishment the less the dissonance—since a severe threat is consonant with ceasing to perform the action. Thus, the milder the threat, the greater will be a person's tendency to derogate the action. In a laboratory experiment 22 preschool children stopped playing with a desired toy in the face of either a mild or severe threat of punishment. The mild threat led to more derogation of the toy than the severe threat. (Aronson & Carlsmith, 1963, p. 584)

Dissonance-reducing changes in beliefs about the self are also called rationalisations. It should be apparent that rationalisation is a way to maintain the integrity or internal consistency of the self's system of concepts. It is a form of constant housekeeping that prevents disorganisation of the mind. This effect has been observed in monkeys as well as small children (Egan et al., 2007). The neurological processes underlying rationalisation take place very quickly without conscious deliberation (Jarcho et al., 2011). If some such processes do not operate regularly, the self as a whole set of meaningful concepts could disintegrate (cf., Kohut, 1977 on disintegration anxiety).

Compared to repression, rationalisation and humour are relatively better compromise solutions to conflict within the self because they do not block from consciousness what may, in part, be true. Not every man has a strong motive to commit incest or murder, but those who do use more extreme compromise defences than others. Logically, if one wants to do something but doesn't do it, whether it involves acceptable or unacceptable social behaviour, then the strength of the tendency to avoid doing it must have been, at least, just greater than the motive to do it (e.g., Bernstein, 1984). In general, biological control processes evolved to use energy very efficiently. The information to operate such systems is passed on to individuals by means of genetic material. But social and psychological regulatory systems develop mostly as a result of learning that occurs over the lifetime of a society or individual.

Cybernetic control processes

Social concepts concern macro-level processes and so, by definition, are nearer to the top of a hierarchy that subsumes biological and psychological concepts. At the same time, perhaps, the top of the structure of explanatory concepts resembles or recapitulates truths exemplified on the bottom of the structure of concepts. We can see the hierarchical parallel in the evolution and anatomy of the brain parts that specialise in primary information processing (subcortical areas) and in more advanced processing (neocortex). I use the term *initial information processing* rather than *primary processing*. The older term can cause confusion when discussing these sorts of things.

Remember Jung's famous axiom taken from alchemy: As above, below. The alchemists and other ancient scholars often assumed that specific and general processes have inherent similarities, and that they interact in a bi-directional causal manner. The conceptual top of the mind and the neocortex of the brain are in vital phylogenetic, anatomical and functional relationships with the subcortical parts of the mind and brain.

An individual's nervous system contains standards for operating physiological and mental systems. These standards are encoded in physical structures and activated by instincts and learned habits. Learned habits can be more or less valid in a scientific sense, and more or less consistent with social norms of behaviour. Standards are used, for example, by baroreceptors in the vascular system and brainstem for regulating blood pressure. In the neocortex, regulating thought, feeling and overt behaviour often involves moral standards. Both the operation of information encoded as standards for regulating physiological variables, and the standards for regulating feelings, thoughts and social behaviour, can be understood in cybernetic terms (e.g., Carver & Scheier, 1981; Miller et al., 1960; Wiener, 1948).

To regulate anything, decisions must be made. Having a common framework such as cybernetics to understand all forms of decision-making (e.g., somatic and mental) is probably a necessary condition for the integration of biological and psychological theories. As the kidneys' primary function is to make urine, the brain's primary function is to make competent decisions. All decisions involve registration of a current, real state of something and comparing it to some ideal state (the classic thermostat example). Sensory data are assessed automatically in brainstem and limbic structures as to whether, for example, a visual or olfactory stimulus is close enough to some internal standard to release a fixed action.

An information processing system decides, or tests, to see if a current state has reached some ideal threshold, or not. If not, operations may be initiated to bring the real state in line with a standard (e.g., turn on the heater). Then, another test is done to see if the operation worked. If so, the corrective operation is stopped and the decision-making process is exited. If the standard has still not been attained, the same corrective operation may be repeated, or a modified solution might be tried. If this next operation works, exit ensues. This is the so-called test-operate-test-exit (TOTE) process familiar from cybernetics or information theory.

The success and durability of individuals and groups is determined by the degree to which attempts to control biological, psychological and social processes approach ideal standards of operation. If these standards are not achieved to some satisfactory degree, old, instinctive, fixed action patterns and learned habits of body and mind tend to repeat.

Most generally, the mind–brain might be understood by means of three concepts: (1) Animals including humans are motivated to learn and use valid concepts; (2) Concept learning processes will repeat until they achieve some satisfactory standard of validity; and (3) The motives to approach knowledge and avoid it are in constant dynamic, mutually regulating relationships (cf., Freud, 1920).

The tendency to repeat ensures that some individuals will, at least by trial and error (Thorndike, 1913), hit upon a pleasure-increasing solution to their problem. If ignorance or motivated defensive operations stand in their way, they will mindlessly repeat some ineffective method. Eventually, such futile attempts cease when the person becomes depressed or dies. One can see why Freud's other name for the repetition compulsion was death instinct. Life without much pleasure from learning how to control sensation, thoughts, feeling, and overt behaviour will, sooner or later, make anyone wish they were dead.

A central dynamic in all individuals and societies concerns the motives to approach creative, pleasurable change and growth, and the motives to avoid change in order to preserve or augment security. From a logical point of view, growth and security operations need not be in zero-sum relationships. Change is usually not exactly death. But all animals with brains and minds are ambivalent about every object in mind and in the external world. This is another way to say that approach-avoidance dynamics are always controlling thought and overt behaviour. Double approach-avoidance conflicts (Lewin, 1936) occur consistently, consciously, and unconsciously at various degrees of intensity. Such conflicts are resolved more or less satisfactorily by cybernetic TOTE processes in the brainstem, limbic system and neocortex. Together, the tendencies to seek knowledge and to avoid it operate dynamically to regulate the body and mind.

Naïve science, formal science, and human evolution

Increasingly, writers are attempting to organise knowledge of the structures and processes of the body, brain and mind (see Solms & Turnbull, 2011). How do biological, psychological, and social variables operate together to explain the person? Integrated theories should be more powerful than those dealing with only one part of complex human phenomena. Scientific study of the body, brain, mind, and culture is a vast social activity, involving increasing numbers of individuals and organisations throughout the world. Technological advances in areas such as molecular biology, imaging technologies, and semantic priming methods have promoted integration by, for example, demonstrating that certain brain processes reliably occur contemporaneously with certain mental experiences. New, detailed information about brain–mind relations is accumulating rapidly.

Naïve and formal scientists are up to their ears in data and new findings. General theoretical concepts are needed to meaningfully relate phenomena occurring at multiple levels of analysis, that is, from the neurochemical and micro-neuroanatomical to the subjective experiences and overt molar behaviour of individuals and social groups. Without valid general theories it is harder to make decisions about what data to collect and how to interpret it.

> Scientists want to study the essential dynamics of objects and their evolution: they want to describe them for controlled time periods … this is a daunting task because the data generated is overwhelming …. Because the scientist is primarily interested in higher level phenomena, a workable solution to the data problem is to focus

on just those features [of the phenomena of interest] ... and extract and track them. This both reduces the amount of data and provides a crucial first step in understanding how these objects evolve. (Samtaney et al., 1994, p. 20)

If indeed "the scientist is primarily interested in higher level phenomena", it helps to have an ideal minimum number of valid general concepts, and to use unambiguous theoretical terms in order to reduce confusion between theoreticians, experimentalists, clinicians, and the general public. Out of necessity one must focus on a limited set of phenomena to do scientific work, especially experimental work. For example, behaviourists decided not to pay attention to subjective experience, so they didn't need any concepts to explain feelings or thoughts. Of course, aspects of reality persist despite being ignored by people. But the practical need for a limited focus in the laboratory needn't work to narrow the generality of cross-discipline theories.

The scope of psychoanalysis was enormous, and that of something like neuropsychoanalysis is even greater. How can we best capitalise on psychoanalytic insights of the mind by deleting, adding, and rearranging general concepts and terms in biology and psychology? Operations of mind and brain are today more observable than they were in Freud's day. In this book I examine how the most general theoretical concepts can contain and explain ideas from biology, psychoanalysis, and cognitive-social psychology.

Compared to the truth of general axioms (e.g., frustration causes aggression), the validity of less general ideas is qualified by detailed special conditions. For example, "adrenergic hormones and neurotransmitters are released in response to stress". Detailed ideas may be applied with less ambiguity than general concepts to make decisions in the clinic: "What drug might we give a person who is pathologically stressed, anxious, frustrated, or aggressive?" More general concepts can shape basic research and applied methods to diagnose and treat mental illness. For instance, Hebb's law (1949) is a generally valid axiom that contains and explains many other phenomena: "Neurons that fire together wire together". The general concept frames many other more specific, testable hypotheses concerning how particular variables interact under specific conditions to produce firing and wiring.

The importance of a concept can be measured by its containing and explaining capacity. Big, general concepts can help us decide whether and how to study links between any two or more sorts of variables pertaining to concepts lower down on a hierarchy of concepts. Lack of building methods and materials did not impede the construction of the Tower of Babel. Rather, failure resulted from deficiencies in communication among the workers. "Level of analysis" problems complicate attempts to integrate biological, psychological, and social theories. For example, "Are all parts of the brain and mind operating on a pleasure principle?"

Conceptual ambiguity and inconsistent use of terms makes it hard to understand exactly what a particular writer means. Variable understanding of words has muddled, and will continue to muddle, communications within the minds of individual theorists and between theorists. What does the other person mean when they use terms like affect, stress, or anxiety? And, one must ask oneself, what do I mean when I use these sorts of terms?

Conceptual ambiguity is reduced by operationalising concepts in experiments. For example, an experimenter might operationalise degrees of stress as intensity of electric shock; bodily reactions to stress might be measured by heart rate variability; and mental reactions, such as anxiety, can be operationalised by self-reports made on Likert scales. Concepts and their operationalisations are in dynamic relationships. The concept can be refined by the results of experiments using different measures of it. And the operationalisations will change as the concept's meaning becomes more explicit and refined. Ideally, we try to think both operationally and theoretically.

Psychoanalytic theory was beleaguered by ambiguity in its definition of terms (e.g., what exactly is the ego?). Freud wrote before there was a science of Human Experimental Social Psychology. Psychoanalytic concepts were imagined to be philosophical or meta-psychological, not scientific. The use of a couch in treatment was really the only fully operationalised idea in psychoanalysis (Bernstein, 2001). One can't blame the poor founders of the field. It was all so new. But we are still paying a price for this lack of precision in the form of descriptive taxonomies of mental illness, which are, in large part, overcompensations for the psychoanalysts' lack of precision.

Today, the most used descriptive "bibles" are the *Diagnostic and Statistical Manual of Mental Disorders* (DSM) from the American Psychiatric Association, and a very similar manual from the World Health Organization (ICD-10-CM). Attempts to describe overt manifestations of deeper mental processes were useful and important when the first DSM was produced in 1952. They worked to focus attention on the unreliability of some psychoanalytic diagnostic terms. But as reliability concerns became dominant, interest in validity disappeared. Instead, psychiatric disease entities multiplied on the surface, unconstrained by even the least controversial assumptions about common elements that might underlie symptom presentations.

But fuzzy ideas like affect, ego, and id are of some utility for the psychotherapist. They help organise what may be an hour's worth of verbal data coming from a patient each day. This, in turn, promotes the development of causal theories of how a particular patient's mind might work. Such theories are called formulations in psychoanalysis. Compared to invalid formulations, a valid theory of a patient will create more accurate predictions of their feelings, thoughts, and overt behaviours, and make change attempts more effective. Even ambiguous or invalid concepts help therapists to organise data about patients. At least they might work to keep therapists interested in their cases and, thereby, make it easier to remain in the consulting room. In other words, even invalid concepts can have a containing and comforting effect on the person who holds them.

While basic and applied psychologists have been working with ambiguous concepts, more operational ideas have worked to promote fast growth of specialised, well-bounded fields such as physics, chemistry, and molecular biology. We can hope to integrate discrete fields because the standards used to decide what constitutes proof of the validity of concepts are generally the same in all areas of scientific enquiry. But integrating the relevant fields in neuroscience is particularly complex. We are plagued not only by vague terms, and level of analysis problems, but also by philosophical questions about the nature of truth. Is subjective experience of reality inherently different from objective means of knowing? Are the body and the brain made of such different stuff that it is ultimately impossible to integrate body and mind sciences? Given such concerns, it makes sense to reflect upon current concepts of affective neuroscience and neuropsychoanalysis.

CHAPTER TWO

Theory-building organisations

Ideally, neuroscience is devoted to developing general theories that explain relationships between data and concepts from multiple levels of analysis (i.e., body, brain, and mind). How do neuropsychoanalysts, those concerned with both objective and subjective aspects of human experience, define their work?

> Neuropsychoanalysis is not (in our opinion) a "school" of psychoanalysis in the way that we currently speak of Freudian, Kleinian, Intersubjective, and Self Psychology schools … it is far better conceptualized as a link between *all* of psychoanalysis and the neurosciences. (Solms & Turnbull, 2011, p. 141)

Maybe neuropsychoanalysis is not a school, therapy, business, or religion, but it is a social organisation, a part of science. It has an official journal, conferences, fee-paying members, leaders and followers, and so on. It lives in a complex social environment of other journals, organisations, and individuals who might wish to join. When thinking about organisations it helps to know their expressed mission. What does an organisation say it attempts to do in the world? It helps to know the degree to which members are aligned and committed to the explicit mission and formal strategy for achieving it. Too much variation in the understanding of the organisation's mission and strategy can degrade productivity. There needs to be at least some minimal level of agreement, some common meaning system, for organisations to function (e.g., Bernstein & Burke, 1989).

Psychoanalytic ideas themselves can be used to study organisations (e.g., Bion, 1961; Levinson, 1976; Zaleznik, 1989). For example, we can analyse the relations between organisation members' explicit and implicit or unconscious understandings of the mission and strategy.

> [Neuropsychoanalysis] might be described as an attempt to insert psychoanalysis into the neurosciences, as a member of the family of neuroscience ... [by means of] ... studying the mental apparatus from the subjective point of view. (Solms & Turnbull, 2011, p. 141)

In Freudian terms, the aspiration to "insert psychoanalysis into ... as a member of the family" might be described as a derivative incestuous desire. I assume that Solms, a most proficient scholar of Freud, used this sexual imagery intentionally. In any case, from my point of view incestuous wishes are themselves derivatives of a more general, deeper motive to grow by means of associating familiar or proximal things with each other. Learning and using valid concepts to explain, predict, and control reality are the ultimate, intrinsic pleasures (Bernstein, 2011).

Logically, approach motives not acted on overtly must be constrained by opposing, avoidance motives that are, at least, slightly stronger than the approach tendency. The most forceful approach tendencies are aroused when the most pleasurable activities are anticipated. In psychoanalytic terms, the strongest antisocial, sexual and aggressive wishes arouse conscious or unconscious fears of severe punishment and pain for violating moral standards or taboos. These fears are usually just strong enough to block the overt enactment of the taboo behaviours.

I am assuming that putting formerly separate concepts together is a form of cognitive incest. Such thoughts can promote the deepest pleasures and, hence, arouse the greatest fears and resistances to action. Accordingly, the conflicts regarding the pleasures and pains of thinking represent a deeper, more general framework for organising the mind than do conflicts over the regulation of overt behaviours such as sex or aggression.

By definition, to conceive of reality differently than one had a moment ago is an alteration of consciousness. Theoretically we are better off considering the motives to change one's conscious, subjective experience as the most general sort of motives than tying mind–brain theory religiously to any particular kind of pleasure (e.g., sex, power, aggression, empathy). Andrew Weil made the same point in his great book *The Natural Mind*.

> The desire to alter consciousness periodically is an innate, normal drive analogous to hunger or the sexual drive ... and the sex drive is a special case of [the drive to alter consciousness]. (Weil, 1972, p. 32)

Usually, when the term "altered consciousness" is used, the writer is referring to some big, dramatic, or important change. But most simply, every change in consciousness from recalling a phone number to an experience of strong emotion, involves changes in the content of the person's focal awareness. The semantic priming literature (e.g., McNamara, 2005) and common experience suggest that the usual rate of alteration of attentional focus is on the order of milliseconds. And, since the mental control processes depend proximally on brain processes, we look naturally for neurological processes changing at similar rates.

Like all other somatic processes, information processes having subjective correlates of thought and feeling must be regulated, in order to maintain system stability or homeostasis. In the rapidly developing child and in vibrant adults, new concepts are added to the mind rapidly to increase the individual's fitness to operate in the world. Such changes are initially always destabilising to a greater or lesser degree. Over time, mind–brain accommodates to new ideas, and the ideas themselves will change somewhat in order to assimilate to the in-place mental organisation (e.g., Piaget, 1928, 1954). Important questions involve the relative effectiveness and efficiencies of various mind–brain control systems in both maintaining stability and promoting growth.

Forbidden cognition may occur when an individual allows his own sensations, thoughts and feelings to interrelate and interpenetrate too freely. By this logic, free association may be compared with incest. Jung (1948) recognised that the concept of incest, as compared to the relatively rare overt enactments of it, amounted most generally to the strongest desire of the person, that is, a desire for "self-fertilisation", or self-development. Self-development is the means to achieve the ultimate goal of self-realisation. To realise the self is to enact overtly in the objectively perceivable external world, more or less idiosyncratic ideas that the person has decided to use to resolve the foundational conflicts of his or her mind.

Competence at information processing, including the ability to free associate, maximises the chances that one can obtain the materials (e.g., sensory data, declarative concepts, procedural habits, feelings, etc.) needed to assemble the most complete, predicatively valid models of nature and, thereby, experience the greatest pleasures. Free association about ideas occurs within individual minds and between individuals in the social intercourse of science. And, of course, psychoanalysts interpret resistance to free association as indicating anxiety about violating moral standards. This is the central idea of Freudian depth psychology.

But I think the deeper idea is to see the process of thinking itself as the fundamental cause of anxiety and resistance. In other words, it is not so much the content of mind that causes anxiety and resistance. It is under-regulated or non-regulated conceptual processing itself that is most terrifying. "Where will it end?" One idea can lead to another, and another, and another, *ad infinitum*. The promise of infinite consciousness generates the greatest pleasures and horrors of the mind.

Nazi psychology and synesthesia

German culture has produced some of the greatest scientific, mathematical, and artistic achievements in history (see Watson, 2010). Nazism's brutal legacy has cast a shadow over German achievements ever since. A basis for German cultural achievements has been a high competence to think theoretically and to excel in the operationalisation or realisation of concepts. The manner in which German competences became perverted in Nazism is depicted with great insight in the documentary film *Undergångens Arkitektur* or *Architecture of Doom* (Cohen, 1989). Nazism was driven in large part by concepts, some wildly false and others with elements of validity. Nazi psychology, as exemplified by the personality theories of Jaensch (1938), provides an example. Jaensch postulated two basic sorts of personality.

> The J-type of personality characteristic of a good Nazi makes definite, unambiguous perceptual judgments and persists in them ...

By contrast, the S-type was someone of racially mixed heredity and included Jews, Parisians, East Asians, and communists. The S-Type was synaesthetic: one who enjoys concomitant sensation, a subjective experience from another sense than the one being stimulated, as in 'color hearing'. Synesthesia ... seemed to Jaensch to be a kind of perceptual slovenliness, the qualities of one sense carelessly mixed with those of another. (Dana et al., 2008)

The importance of this theory for us is that it concerns regulation of consciousness. But in contrast to theories concerning the regulation and meaning of semantic concepts, Jaensch focused on the regulation of raw sensory information. Synaesthesia involves translation of sense data into experience other than that dictated by the exteroceptors that had first registered the data. For example, odors sensed by the nose might create visual forms in focal attention.

The ability to exchange one form of sensation for another was imagined by the Nazis to be a dirty sin characterising the minds of hated groups such as Jews and communists. Jews, of course, were denigrated for their involvement with banks and money. Money can be exchanged for anything. It has the attribute of fungibility making it perhaps the most important conceptual innovation in practical economics.

Various neurological mechanisms have been proposed to explain synesthesia (e.g., Grossenbacher & Lovelace, 2001). It occurs with greater frequency than usual with the use of hallucinogenic drugs (e.g., de Rios, 2003). I think a logical prerequisite for synesthesia is that sensory data from all sensory modalities is subject to the same initial data processing operation—equipartitioning. This universal data form, like a flat file format in computers, makes all sensory data fungible or suitable for processing at any level or on any channel in the brain. The idea of equipartitioning is central to the work of Allan Snyder and his group in Australia.

Sensations and concepts

Snyder has demonstrated convincingly that either relatively raw sense data or concepts can be in conscious awareness at any one time (e.g., Snyder, 2009; Snyder et al., 2004; Snyder & Mitchell, 1999). Activation of concepts, which organise sensory details, effectively shuts off awareness of sensation. The control of concept activation is dynamic. One can either be aware of a sensation organising concept, or let the sensations flow. For example, one can be aware of a cat, or unrelated visual and auditory sensory attributes such as fur, purring, tail, etc. The competence to decide what to attend to—concept or sense data—is a fundamental aspect of mental control.

But the sense data we can be aware of is not entirely raw. Snyder's research with autistic savants indicates that compared to normal individuals, they have privileged access to sense data. This access underlies all their mental abilities such as lightning fast identification of prime numbers, perfect pitch, detailed memory and calendar skills. Snyder assumes the skills depend on the autist's access to raw sensory data that has undergone the first or *initial stage* of information processing. That is, raw sense data is automatically grouped into equal numbers of items. This is called equipartitioning. A sensory item that cannot be placed into a neat package with other items is, by definition, a left over bit of data. Such remainders cause a form of irritation that in normal people stimulates further information processing attempts. That is, semantic concepts are brought into play to make meaning of the sensory data that has not been made meaningful, or packaged automatically by the initial equipartitioning processes.

If raw sensory data modalities are fungible, the number of possible responses to sense data is enormous, if not infinite. Synesthesia is a process that violates norms of information processing. Such nonconformity was seen as proof of immorality by Hitler's psychologists, but also viewed as the most sublime form of aesthetic experience, or Gesamtkunstwerk, by Hitler's hero Richard Wagner. At the most general level, the fear of certain punishment for experiencing sinful pleasure, whether it involves synaesthesia, incest, or thoughts of infinity, has been historically the most common method used by society to regulate the minds of individuals.

We can somehow classify systems of beliefs on a continuum of general validity. The most generally valid theories of physics and chemistry are given a status as the truest truths, because the value system of science as a whole is reductionist. If instinctive, empathic, prosocial forms of subjective human reactions to others are discounted entirely, sadistic tendencies can become dominant. In the most extreme example, Nazism demonstrated the dangers of making something like radical reductionist values normative in a large social system. And, of course, science is a large social system. Affective neuroscience has been, in part, a correction to reductionist behaviourism that rejects subjective experiences of thought and feeling as worthy of analysis (Panksepp, 1998). As such, affective neuroscience works to expand beneficially our biopsychological concepts.

But every theoretical system has some problems built into it. Most modern psychology theories have what might be called sympathocentric biases when explaining biopsychological phenomena. In the old treatises on the relations between thinking, feeling, and overt behaviour, the person was often imagined as seeing a bear, being afraid, and running away (e.g., Bard, 1928; Cannon, 1927; James & Lange, 1922). Of course, environmental stimuli (e.g., the bear) and gross, overt movements of the body were, and still are, relatively easy to observe compared to the subtle workings of the brain and mind. So naturally the early emotion theorists focused on sympathetic arousal and its consequences, and not on the more arcane, parasympathetic, down-regulation processes.

Porges' polyvagal theory works, in part, to correct this bias. Competent, sophisticated conceptual activity, compared to sympathetically driven, overt fight and flight behaviours enacted by the muscles, depends usually on lower levels of arousal. This was recognised first by Yerkes and Dodson (1908) and has been validated and refined by years of research, including neurologically based work (e.g., Diamond et al., 2007; Lupien et al., 2007). The Yerkes–Dodson law states that on average, complex processes like thinking are performed most competently under moderate arousal, and can become incompetent in states of very low or very high arousal. In comparison, simple tasks like pounding a nail with a hammer are performed best under high sympathetic arousal.

Understanding reality most deeply depends on making sophisticated, valid concepts in the neocortex. Competent top-down regulation, exercised by neocortical functions, is dependent on parasympathetic braking, and is in a dynamic relationship with bottom-up brainstem signalling. A valid, general theory of mind–brain has to accurately differentiate cognition from motivation and specify how ANS processes influence brain and mind. I think cognitive and motivational concepts and their relationships are sufficient to explain the phenomena of interest to mind–brain theorists, and that affect concepts now work as barriers to a parsimonious, integrated mind–brain theory.

The person as scientist

Fritz Heider (1958) thought of the human being most generally as a naïve scientist. Heider's thinking became the basis of attribution theory, a branch of experimental social psychology that aims to discover the way the typical person comes to make causal inferences. The validity of the person's causal assumptions determines the accuracy of their estimates of the pain and pleasure likely to result from avoiding or approaching objects in mind and in the external world. For example, the naïve scientist asks: Why did my friend just step on my foot?; What are the risks of stepping on his foot? Why do I feel anxious? Why do I have a headache? Do I have brain cancer? Why did I do well in that chemistry test?

A very important result of using concepts to make causal inferences is probability estimates. Most generally, people generate expectations of the likelihood of success of different responses to sense data, and other concepts, on the basis of their interpretations of them. Such expectations lead the naïve scientist to decide what to do overtly. If one has and uses valid self and non-self-explanatory concepts for explaining things, she has the most potential to make competent responses to the world. Concept validity is a function of both cognitive factors (e.g., the use of data and logic to assess the validity of concepts about the world and the self) and motivational factors (e.g., the tendency to habitually use distorted concepts in order to protect and enhance self-esteem).

Discovering valid causal relations is the explicit task of the formal or sophisticated scientist. The formal attribution theorist asks: What might cause a student to attribute his success to "study efforts" rather than "an easy test"? The sophisticated scientist attempts to explain the explaining behaviour of the naïve scientist (e.g., Bernstein et al., 1979; Stephan et al., 1979). Formal scientists are humans; that is, they are also naïve scientists. Formal scientists are imagined to be more "objective" than the naïve ones, in part because they use sophisticated empirical methods that have evolved in a social context of intense communication. But everyone's cognitions are affected by the wish to approach pleasure and avoid pain, and the tendency to repeat information processing until the most valid concepts are discovered.

Associating formally separate ideas can have the quality of violating a deep taboo, and may be considered a kind of cognitive crime of incestuous proportions. Imagining the integration of ideas can be a cause and an effect of both pleasure and fear. And overt appetitive attempts to combine forbidden things is driven by such potent mental states.

Like Heider (e.g., 1958), I assume that the desire to understand reality by using the most valid concepts is the best, highest order, most general concept to explain the person (Bernstein, 2011). Similarly, Wright and Panksepp (2012) differentiate this sort of desire from other "affects" or "emotions" (cf., Panksepp & Solms, 2011). They elevate SEEKING, one of Panksepp's seven primary process emotions, to a special status over and above his other six primal affective processes. (Panksepp likes to write his primary process emotions in capital letters.)

> Ultimately the function of all primal affective processes is to better anticipate and cope with the future, each being molded through evolution to reflect the needs and best coping strategies of nature. But the SEEKING system stands out from the others because of its vast purview—its participation in practically all goal-directed mental and bodily activities. (Wright & Panksepp, 2012, p. 6)

SEEKING is the "foraging/exploration/investigation/curiosity/interest/expectancy system" (Panksepp, 1998, p. 145). That's a lot of stuff. SEEKING is a good, general description of the defining feature of the brain–mind system. More exactly, the most basic function of the brain-mind is to MAKE DECISIONS. The brain does not exist to RAGE, PLAY, PANIC, LUST, FEAR or CARE (i.e., Panksepp's other primary process emotions). SEEKING involves collecting and processing sensory data at varying levels of sophistication within and between various brain structures, in order to make a decision to RAGE or CARE or do some combinations of things. Learning and using valid concepts to make the best decisions is the highest order function in mind–brain. Panksepp says, perceptively:

> It would have been wasteful for evolution to have constructed separate search and approach systems for each bodily need. The most efficient course was for each need-detection system to control two distinct functions: a generalized, nonspecific form of appetitive arousal and various need-specific resource-detection systems. (Panksepp, 2010, p. 166)

Needs are motivating

Panksepp's SEEKING system is the most general part of his mind–brain theory. I prefer to express a similar idea this way: The motive to seek knowledge is the primary motive of the person, and the brain–mind's primary function is decision making.

The most general function of the kidneys is to make urine of a certain type under different conditions of electrolyte levels, osmolarity, blood volume, and so on. It fulfils this function sometimes by making watery urine and other times it produces more concentrated urine. The kidneys do not exist to DILUTE or CONCENTRATE but rather to make the best sort of urine needed by the person's body at a particular moment. And, of course, the functions of the kidneys and all the other internal organs are influenced by decisions made in the brainstem and, under certain conditions, higher regions of the brain.

There is a hierarchy of functions and a differentiation between means and ends in each organ of the body, and between each organ. Kurt Lewin's group of Gestalt psychologists (e.g., Ovsiankina, 1928; Zagarnik, 1925) identified a motive that qualifies as a sort of motive of all motives. After Wertheimer (e.g., 1923) and others, Lewin assumed that any incomplete task or object aroused a tension state and a subsequent urge to reduce such tension. Heider (1958), from the Lewinian school, went all the way to see the most general motive of the person or naïve scientist as a quest for knowledge or, we could say, more completely valid concepts of reality (see also Baumeister & Bushman, 2008; Wicklund & Gollwitzer, 1982).

Specific need states may activate attempts to seek knowledge of some sort from the general, problem-solving competence of neocortical brain regions. That is, body systems in need of important ingredients are begging, more or less urgently, for the brain and mind to make a decision of some sort to help them. If the need is water, decisions involving assessments of urgency, alternative appetitive plans, and overt execution of approach behaviours must be made. A system like Panksepp's SEEKING is general enough to possibly solve any type of appetitive problem. One needs water, food, sex, thermal control, directions to the pub, and so on. Of course, such a system needs the relevant data, valid enough interpretative concepts, and instructions on how and when to activate the concepts to, in turn, make good enough decisions.

Most of the time, we can delay decisions without much danger to life and limb. Regardless of the urgency to decide, all decisions might be described with concepts from cybernetic systems theories. Sensors in body, brain and mind test the levels of needed items. If a below standard level is detected, some operation is initiated to correct the situation. Once corrected, the decision-making process is exited: test-operate-test-exit (TOTE).

Brain–mind regulates the visceral plumbing of the body to learn about reality and to maintain physical and mental security. One attempts to make the best decisions in order to feel the most pleasure and the least pain. Mental Competence involves the brain–mind's ability to protect and care for the whole body and mind, including the lesser organs. Ideally, the person achieves their goals without being injured or killed. Relations inside the person between biological and psychological functions may be imagined to involve the same two tendencies that regulate social relations between people. Bakan (1966) called these tendencies communality or social concern, and agency or self-concern. These have been related to femininity and masculinity, respectively (e.g., Spence & Helmreich, 1978).

It is not merely a metaphor to say that the neocortical aspect of the brain is a ruler. It governs by being open to various degrees to information about the needs of the other organs in the body, and about its own condition. It is remarkable that Latin and Greek, and the modern languages based on them, ascribe a gender, or a classification of neuter, to all nouns. This indicates that during their early development, all semantic concepts were subject to a form of preconditioning. Ideas are more or less pre-authorised to represent first, before anything else, the level of masculinity and femininity of objects. Plato, of course, thought the human was originally an eight-limbed creature combining male and female attributes. This animal was somehow split in two, and spends its life trying to reconnect to its lost part.

Exteroceptors and biofeedback

Sense data about one's body coming from the external world and from the inside of the body can, by means of intensive information processing, work its way into explicit awareness. Data from the body is usually private and subjective. Certainly at first, the only social and somewhat explicit semantic concepts the infant has for capturing and understanding the workings of his own body came from his mother. The parent senses somehow the internal state of the child and then responds competently to help regulate the child's body and mind. The parent communicates in words and gestures her more or less accurate understandings and, thereby, teaches the child how to understand his body and mind.

If the mother is without much empathy and/or knowledge of how a human body works, the concepts the infant learns for interpreting sensory data from afferent, autonomic neurons are likely to be few and not especially developed. Most adults, not just the mentally ill, have relatively primitive theories residing in the neocortex to capture raw sensory data about their bodies. Accordingly, bodily sensations in awareness cannot be understood too precisely in regard to their origin or meaning.

But the private or subjective nature of concepts used to interpret sense data does not disqualify them from being judged as in or out of line with standards. It is just that most people are more able to use exteroceptors rather than interoception for discerning somatic events. This is because the exteroceptors are attached to very differentiated and integrated semantic concepts that were learned in physical and social contexts. Visual sensations are the type of data most captured in semantic concepts. For example, one can see a line on a screen indicating one's blood pressure in real time. The patient or research subject can have the same objective view of the phenomenon as the physician or scientist standing next to him who is also viewing the graph. The patient himself is also potentially aware of changes in his mind and body that are not necessarily in the mind of a social agent observing the patient.

People are somehow able to use efferent motor neurons to effect changes in autonomic functions such as blood pressure, heart rate, urine production, diaphoresis, body temperature, blood glucose levels, and so on. Representing sensory information so it can be registered by exteroceptors (i.e., providing biofeedback) can work to increase the person's competence to control body functions (e.g., Porges, 2011). Providing neurofeedback about the electrical activity of the brain itself can work to increase mental control (e.g., Thomas, 2012).

Without using sensory aids such as biofeedback, it is very hard for the person to know what is going on inside his body. Many people have probably more explicit, differentiated, valid concepts to understand what a Mars rover is doing 35 million miles away from Earth than they have for interpreting sensory data coming from organs sitting inches below their own skin.

The somatic systems operate automatically and out of awareness most of the time. However, it is possible to gain conscious control of usually unconscious autonomic functions. For example, expert yogis can control what are for almost everyone else completely autonomic functions like peristalsis and vomit reflexes (e.g., Weil, 1972, 1980). To do such things one must process sensory data from gastrointestinal areas, use TOTE processes in the neocortex to determine the state of the organs, and then operate efferent motor neurons to change the organs' operations. Using biofeedback to inform TOTE processes can give the average person control over autonomic functions in the manner of yoga experts.

Information about aspects of brain function itself from quantitative EEG (QEEG) is somehow indicative of how data from the body and the mind itself is processed in the brain. A person can use sensory information that resided formerly out of conscious awareness in combination with valid concepts of biology, to control what are typically autonomic processes (e.g., Obrist et al., 2009). Feedback of data to exteroceptors makes formerly subjective and unconscious mental activity objective and conscious. Compared to automatic control processes, consciousness and intentional regulation attempts use more energy (e.g., Gailliot et al., 2007).

The energy costs of conscious mental operations are 'worth it' when they work to supplant chronically ineffective and energy inefficient flaws in automatic processes with novel, better solutions to conflicts aroused by stressors in the external world and in the mind–brain. Eventually, the use of more valid control habits, learned with help from explicit conscious awareness, can become automated and energy efficient. I assume in this book that increasing control over sympathetic and parasympathetic processes is a key to increasing conceptual competence.

When invalid concepts are used repeatedly and habitually to interpret and control events, health and wealth suffer. The body, brain and mind have structurally encoded standards that when used in cybernetic feedback operations work to regulate and improve functioning.

How else would the autonomic and central nervous systems control things?

All material things represent manifestations of concepts. Not all valid concepts are represented in material, operational detail in any individual's brain or any social agency. But I tend to believe that such concepts have some existence, or ontological reality. Where do concepts exist before they are manifest in physical form? (I am confident that if you ask 100 people this question, many will respond with some version of "god knows".)

Evolution

Darwin's theory was nominally about biology, but its concepts and methods are of great importance to ethologists, animal and human experimental social psychologists, and religious fundamentalists. It is plausible to expect that human behaviour will soon start to depend increasingly on demands made by normal people to gain direct, immediate access to sensory data about their own bodies (e.g., blood glucose levels, brain states depicted in EEGs, changes in cortisol production by minute). Most of that sort of data is not processed using semantic concepts in the neocortex. In other words, most people, most of the time, do not intentionally attempt to make decisions about how and why to focus attention on particular sorts of sensory data coming from the body.

All the data needed to measure and regulate autonomic function is always in the brain. But most people have few, sparse, or no concepts to capture and explain such data. Accordingly, heart rate variability (HRV) data such as respiratory sinus arrhythmia (RSA) may be regulated mostly or entirely outside of conscious awareness. But such data can be provided to a person's exteroceptors and thereby put into focal awareness. For example, one can show a person a visual representation of heart rate variability as it changes moment to moment. Patient and doctor can both observe how the patient's fear, happiness, curiosity, headache, or memories of his favourite cat, the school bully, and his kindergarten teacher are correlated in real time with RSA changes. When changes in physiological variables are measured simultaneously with changes in the person's subjective state, somatic and mental variables can be organised into a model indicating the direction and potency of causes operating in the body, brain, and mind. When causal models are valid, effective methods to create changes in an underlying causal state of affairs can be developed.

Remember, if sensations are not captured or contained or explained by semantic concepts, the information value or the meaning of the sensory data is not understood. Valid concepts that may not have been known by the prior teachers or, at least, have remained unlearned by the patient can be taught to patients. Biofeedback is a prototype of a method by which a patient learns something new, or uses old concepts and habits in new ways in order to develop competence to control formerly out-of-control visceral functions such as blood pressure. Ideally, the nature of the relations between raw sensory data, concepts, feelings, and overt behaviour should be spelled out unambiguously in integrated neuroscience theories.

Today, the typical person constantly carries a powerful computer in his or her cell phone. These computers, when in communication with biosensors, allow people to display visual data about their own bodies in real time. When there is routine access to sense data that was formerly outside awareness, the validity of concepts held by individuals about their bodies and minds can increase dramatically (e.g., Green & Green, 1977). Access to interpretable feedback about the self and the rest of nature is necessary to create valid concepts of reality. If creating valid concepts is the most pleasurable thing, there should be a proliferation of such devices. Neurofeedback and biofeedback machines are increasingly available and sought after. These include applications for cell phones that monitor heart rate, overt physical movements, and sleep quality (see Edwards-Stewart, 2012).

Learning how one's body and mind work to cause conscious experience can help the individual differentiate his own self-concepts from all his non-self-concepts. How do I cause or control my own private thoughts and feelings and my overt behaviour? How do other people, like Mummy, control me? Who is in control? My brainstem? My self-concepts in the neocortex?

Self-concepts are related in a more or less complicated manner to each other and concepts of everything else. It is critical in psychotherapy, for example, to explain to patients the difference between the actual physical and social objects—like mother and father—from their own mental representations, their concepts, of the objects. Remarkably, people often do not make this basic sort of differentiation.

Biofeedback devices make data about somatic states salient to exteroceptors. This allows the person to notice how somatic states alter with changes in focal attention. It can help people differentiate and integrate self and non-self correlates and causes of mental and physical states. It is entirely possible that we will see a spurt in human development due to widespread use of small portable technologies that facilitate the person's ability to relate objective data about the body to subjective experiences of thought and feeling. Fast changes in species development may be more common in evolution than gradual change (e.g., Eldredge & Gould, 1972; Gould & Eldredge, 1977).

CHAPTER THREE

Barriers to knowledge and theoretical integration

Fear, ignorance, and lack of education are related systematically in social, psychological, and biological systems. Most people use valid enough concepts to interpret reality to be able to adequately control stress and fear. The person's competence to control mind and body determine her success at work and love. But we have the injunction against knowledge in the parable of Adam and Eve. Something like *original sin* is a good candidate for the person's deepest source of fear.

From cybernetic, biological, and evolutionary perspectives, having barriers to knowledge makes sense. In the first place, change of any brain or mind structures involves risk. The common clichés apply: "If it ain't broke, don't fix it" and, "The perfect is the enemy of the good". The dangers of change are maximal when experiments are conducted in a willy nilly, trial and error manner. Evolution theory assumes that trial and error is nature's method for initiating genetic changes. The religious, intelligent design school imagines that someone up there is planning all these experiments with a purpose.

Evolution proceeds in the manner of an old tree. Older trees are comprised mostly of slow-growing or dead tissues that lie behind a still active, relatively thin, growing outer layer. Evolution conserves the valid structures and processes it has learned over time and uses them in

33

many different species of plants and animals. By definition, at any one point in time, the changing parts of life represent only a small portion of all the change that has preceded them and become institutionalised in biological, psychological, and social systems.

Natural biology takes its time with changes, testing endless varieties of methods to perform this or that biological function, and tends to conserve especially good designs. This increases the odds that whatever knowledge is passed on in the genes is valid. To imagine that Mother Nature has seen to it, whatever it may be, is a variety of quiescent, conservative comfort. Conservative pleasures include nostalgia and, in the most fundamental religious and political groups, an avid anticipation of the end of the world. I sometimes enjoy escaping reality by listening to paranoid friends describe how the forces of man and the devil are conspiring to cause an apocalypse.

It is axiomatic that the neocortex is largely an inhibitory organ. All sorts of instinctive, reflexive systems are ready to activate fixed actions when sense data indicate the presence of environmental releasing stimuli. Neocortical regions and functions are called on to make final, executive decisions regarding which pending impulses to elaborate, and which to suppress. On average, any specific impulse will be suppressed at any particular time because it is not the best solution to the person's current problem. Or, it may play only a partial role in a larger plan to cope with stress. The mind, sitting in such a generally inhibitory brain, will also tend on the one hand to use concepts conservatively. Everything else being equal, "no" is, on average, the best executive response to any specific request made by an instinctive system.

But on the other hand, the mind—and we must assume the brain—can act quite liberally when deciding whether to, at least, entertain new and different concepts. Before the age of about three, and sometimes until old age, the person is not so good at differentiating concepts and their realisations. Freud described this tendency to overvalue thought compared to reality as *the omnipotence of thought*.

> The fact that it has been possible to construct a system of contagious magic on associations of contiguity shows that the importance attached to wishes and to the will has been extended from them on to all those psychical acts which are subject to the will. A general overvaluation has thus come about of all mental processes—an attitude towards the world, that is, which, in view of

our knowledge of the relation between reality and thought, cannot fail to strike us as an overvaluation of the latter. Things become less important than ideas of things: whatever is done to the latter will inevitably also occur to the former. Relations which hold between the ideas of things are assumed to hold equally between the things themselves. Since distance is of no importance in thinking—since what lies furthest apart both in time and space can without difficulty be comprehended in a single act of consciousness—so, too, the world of magic has a telepathic disregard for special distance and treats past situations as though they were present. (Freud, 1913, pp. 85–86)

As the child ventures outside the protected environment of the family, the conflicts between realised and unrealised concepts begin to intensify. One can decide consciously or implicitly to give up one's belief in the omnipotence of thought. To in effect say to oneself, "Well, this is the way it is for me. I will adjust my goals and plans so that I might achieve what is achievable by someone with my assets and deficits." Success in life depends on accurate estimates of one's competence, effort, and the difficulty of attaining goals. Otherwise, the person is involved in wishful thinking and "pushing their luck" (see Bernstein, 2011, p. 140, note 4).

Naïve and formal science

So ignorance can be caused by cognitive factors such as the difficulty of getting information lying under the surface of things, and the general tendency to focus on what is salient to exteroceptors. These sorts of problems respond well to technological solutions. Formal scientists use esoteric machines to gather data about the brain and body. The regular person, the naïve scientist, can use machines for this too (e.g., biofeedback devices).

Apparently, the subcortical brain has access to all the data the person needs to assess the state of each bodily organ. Decisions regarding whether or how to influence a target organ or organ system are made subcortically and can involve some neocortical, executive functions. But unlike trained yogis, most of us have little awareness or understanding of how our own individual bodies operate. Hence, we have a restricted range of functional competence to control body, brain and mind.

At least in my day, every school child had heard the expression, "The person uses only 10% of their brain". I am not exactly sure what this means, but it is consistent with the idea that *de facto* levels of mental competence around the world fall short of what is theoretically possible. I also like how the saying quantifies something about mental competence: on average, a person is 90% short of their ability to operate the mental equipment. Whatever nonsense this "fact" about the brain is based on, I still like it as a comical and rough estimate.

The tendency to pay attention to what is salient or obvious is well studied (e.g., Jones & Nisbett, 1971). The common sense psychologist observes what is obvious because much of what she cares about is obvious. "If I need a job and a guy gives me a job, I don't worry about his motivations." It is generally easier to pay attention to data and concepts that are just lying on the surface of things (e.g., only attending to what a person says literally without trying to discern why he is saying what he is saying). It takes effort and special skills to investigate under the surface to discern how overt behaviour including speech arises from arcane brain and mind events.

In short, there are often few incentives and usually many barriers to seeking deep knowledge. Seeking knowledge involves effort, risk, and maybe assumptions that wanting to know aspects of reality is a sin—the original sin. Fear of punishment for wanting or actually knowing some valid concepts about reality can lead to more or less extreme attempts to deny reality. Sometimes denial can be conflated subtly with philosophical, spiritual, or social concerns.

Philosophical barriers

From my way of thinking we might achieve great pleasure through theory integration. But great pleasure may be, or may be caused by, great sin. At some level neuroscience theorising has to be a somewhat risky enterprise. There just have to be strong resistances to making integrative theory, even inside the brain of the most successfully psychoanalysed neuroscientist.

The foundation of the human mind is, in part, comprised of standards of prosocial behaviour. This was Freud's idea of the superego. The strongest motives require the most durable and effective inhibitory systems. Universal anticipation of intense punishment (e.g., talion dread) works mostly to suppress the overt enactment of sexual incest and murder. But if attaining intense pleasure can occur from engaging in highly sophisticated activities such as theoretical science, control of such desires should also manifest in derivative forms. Instead of imagining castration for violating a taboo, the neuroscientist imagines a philosophical barrier to satisfaction. Which brings us to the interestingly named *hard problem*:

> The hard problem ... raises the question of how consciousness ... actually emerges from matter. Modern neuroscience is well equipped to solve the easy problem [how brain and mind events are correlated in time], but it is less clear whether it is capable of solving the hard problem. Science has few precedents for solving a problem that philosophers have deemed insoluble in principle. (Solms & Turnbull, 2002)

Are there any practical implications for theory integrators in neuroscience of an assumption that material and mental things are of an essentially different nature? The hard problem in physics is the relationship between relativity and quantum theories. But neuropsychoanalysis is not close to having two seemingly valid but non-integrable theories of reality. Isn't worrying about the hard problem "protesting too much" or, at least, too soon?

We can correlate some mind and brain phenomena in time. There is little need to worry now about what seem to be ultimate barriers to knowledge like a Heisenberg uncertainty principle. We are far from discovering the *unus mundus* from which everything emerges and returns. (See the correspondence of Wolfgang Pauli and Carl Jung edited by Meier, 2001.) The current, important barriers to developing more integrated theoretical systems include the tremendous complexity and difficulty of the task, and some deep-seated anxiety about doing it. As a practical matter I assume few neuroscientists are bothered, at least consciously, about the hard problem.

Freud and neuropsychoanalysis solve this hard problem via an assumption that brain and mind are fundamentally different, but that they seem to have something to do with each other (dual aspect monism). At least we are getting the brain and mind, the parent and the child, the originator and its offspring, on the same page. And having a hard problem is an excellent sort of security operation for a person who might fear that feeling pleasure from theoretical integration is a sin.

One is protected from doing what one wants because it is impossible, at least philosophically.

But the hard problem can be solved by being a sort of Platonist who believes that the most real things are some forms of information, or forms of truth. Specifically, nature at bottom is comprised of concepts in some relationships, and something resembling a consilience of ideas underlies diverse living and non-living manifestations of itself in the physical and mental worlds (Wilson, 1998). The classic problem of Plato's Beard gets at the idea. The beard exists both as an idea and a material mop of hair. They are not the same, but they both emerge from the same underlying thing—the idea of a beard. This is to say that ideas, not their concrete physical instantiations, are the most fundamental and durable stuff.

The idea that subjectivity and objectivity may represent two fundamentally different ways of knowing things is related to the hard problem. But this distinction is more apparent than real. Each person knows things objectively and subjectively, often at the same time. Subjectivity and objectivity are not in a mutually exclusive, inverse relationship but rather occur or exist simultaneously as do feelings of pain and pleasure. I assume that:

1. Subjective experiences of pleasure and pain, such as being happy upon learning that a rigorous scientific study confirmed one's own predictions, are most affected by the validity of the concepts one uses unconsciously and consciously to analyse sense data and other concepts. In the long run, and sometimes even in the moment, more truth leads to more pleasure.
2. All sense data, including objective scientific results, are experienced by a person whose mind–brain is somewhat different from the mind–brain of others. So, perceivers' reactions to the same data may vary subjectively. For example, a group of neurologists can view the same MRI image of a patient's brain. Ideally, they have some shared objective perspectives and interpretations of data due to their common knowledge of medicine. But one or more of the observers may have in addition to her objective, socially shared view, idiosyncratic reactions to the data. For example, a doctor may think, "My father seems likely to have a stroke". Ideally, this won't impede her ability to make a good decision about the patient based on the objective data.

3. In the twentieth century, experimental social psychology had validated and quantified many reliable cause and effect relationships between subjective experiences of thought and feeling, and objective biological and social variables (see Baumeister & Bushman, 2010).

In this context, one can understand the appeal of Spinoza for neuroscientists (e.g., Damasio, 2003). For me, two ideas from Spinoza are important: (1) He assumes "the necessary existence of an absolutely infinite substance" (Curely, 1985). I take that substance to be something like a consilience of ideas (Wilson, 1998) or the Platonic forms, or what Christians call the logos; and, (2) "Spinoza mainly saw emotions as caused by cognitions" (Bennet, 1984). Once we can reduce the rampant ambiguity about what we are calling emotions, affects, feelings, and so on, I think the relations between cognitions and energetic states of mind might be clarified.

Spiritual barriers

While writing *A Basic Theory of Neuropsychoanalysis* (Bernstein, 2011), I described to some colleagues my model of relations between conscious awareness, raw sensations, concepts, feelings, and overt behaviour. My friend Dr Mario Marquez commented that there was something missing from the model—spirituality. I remember wanting to say, "But spirituality is the invisible part of scientific models".

In college, I had learned in a phenomenology of religion course that sacred things, including the truest truths, were imagined to be ineffable, that is, inexpressible in words. For instance, Zen masters repeat to students who claim to have experienced the true Zen, "neti, neti" or "not this, not this". In other words, whatever the student imagined was the deep truth or spirit was not it exactly. Similarly, practitioners of Taoism say that the Tao that can be expressed is not the true Tao. So, by an Eastern mentality some part of truth—the true Zen or real Tao—seems beyond knowing or, at least, beyond what can be thought or spoken explicitly in words. Truth may be imagined to dissipate at a certain point of explicitness. In some contrast to this, we know now that dream-like mentation can occur contemporaneously with explicit awareness of rational concepts in lucid dreaming (e.g., LeBerge, 1999).

In the Western mind, if one is nearby or in the presence of truth, or its equivalent—god—one dare not name, approach, or look at it too closely without feeling sinful or guilty. One avoids guilt through small and large shows of fearful respect. Jews are reluctant to utter the name of God. In all sorts of religions, one must be profoundly humble when in the presence of a revered deity, that is, the truth. One must bow, make a sign with the hands, get on the knees, kiss a holy object, or wear some special hat before entering a temple, and so on.

In Judaism and Christianity, the barriers to knowing truth by means of explicit concepts are based less on a preference for the intuitive psychological state preferred in the East. Rather, having knowledge is imagined to be a sin—the original sin of Adam and Eve. They violated God's injunction to avoid the sensuous pleasure of the apple, sex, and self-knowledge. They had violated the laws of some ultimate authority. Their punishment was to be made self-conscious, ashamed of their nakedness. It is at least interesting that in this story the punishment for gaining knowledge is a kind of increase in knowledge.

In any case, it seems safe to say that in all religions the god is some knower of everything true and maybe also of everything false. (Or is that the devil's job?) The Christian logos describes complete knowledge. The logos is the perfect wisdom of the word of God. Dr Marquez had said that spirituality was left out of my model. But spirituality appears, by definition, ineffable. This has been more or less the attitude of all the world's religions regarding important unknown truths. The most important truths are somehow indescribable, but they can engender intense states of pleasure (awe, wonderment, bliss, ecstasy) or pain (guilt, fear, terror, horror, insanity).

I think that all taboos are derivatives of an underlying fear of explicit knowledge. In particular, the incest taboo is a derivative of the more fundamental, general resistance to explicit knowledge of the world and the self. Beliefs and feelings about the risks of being aware explicitly of some sensations and concepts operate habitually. This may lead to their being denied, negated, repressed, dissociated, projected, or defended against in countless other ways, and therefore blocked from focal attention. Ambivalence about knowledge, the love and fear of it, plus the defensive and creative reactions to the conflict, shape the theories and research of every naïve and formal scientist.

In science, true things not yet defined explicitly are the invisible parts of any model of natural phenomena. They are the truths not spelled out clearly in words, numeric formulae, or graphic images. They make up what we call *the error term* in statistical models. The unknown truth is the repository of the questions we attempt to answer by scientific methods and theory.

Dimensions of concepts

Concepts may be characterised as varying in three dimensions: validity, subjectivity-objectivity, and depth. The current theoretical debates in neuropsychoanalysis involve implicit and explicit assumptions about scientific validity, subjectivity-objectivity, and depth. How individual naïve scientists and formal scientists think about the relationship between these three dimensions has important implications for how they interpret reality. For example, I argue in Chapter Twelve that psychotic and mystical experiences both involve a change in the person's manner of differentiating these "three dimensions of truth".

Early science attacked the questions lying on the surface of the field of unknown truth. Succeeding generations, ideally, start to descend more deeply from the point reached by their predecessors. Obviously, a vast or infinite number of unknown truths exists for every scientific field, including neuroscience. Hopefully, over time, science will specify more and more of the intricate system of the causes of variation in sensations, thoughts, feelings, and overt behaviour. This will involve extensive transformations of the relations between the theories and methods of all scientific fields. Grander, more integrated, and pleasurable theories may come.

The motive to know the deepest truths is shared by science and religion. There is a rising trend to address the neuroscience of spirituality (e.g., Walach et al., 2011). The conflict between and within scientific and religious individuals and groups is due to implicit assumptions used to understand the nature of the repository of unknown truths. The assumptions concern whether the repository of unknown truths is infinite or not.

Some with fundamentalist religious beliefs behave as if they fear that when science discovers a truth, the wealth of unknown truths is diminished. They feel somehow robbed personally of the opportunity to learn the scientifically discovered truth through their own subjective experiences, for example, spiritual experience. This has to include an assumption that using objective, explicit scientific concepts is in a zero-sum relationship with the subjective sensing, thinking, and feeling going on in true spiritual experience. That is, as one increases the other must decrease in direct proportion. A subtractive operation must be performed for every additive operation. Logically, holding an assumption that as knowledge grows, the overall quantity of ignorance is shrunk, must involve an assumption that unknown truth is not infinite.

Religious and scientific fundamentalists or reductionists believe, at least implicitly, that one day everything will be known. I think the ideas that nature is limited and ultimately knowable, and infinitely deep and hence never knowable completely, both cause anxiety and pleasure within each individual to varying degrees. One can doubt the permanence of ineffability in one moment, and be sure of it the next.

This point is illustrated by certain patients who describe themselves as spiritual (see Masters, 2010). One such patient of mine, a man with bipolar disorder, complained that I seemed to deride or not take seriously his spiritual concerns. He refused further use of psychotropic drugs to treat his disorder. He acknowledged that the medicines, products of objective scientific research, had reduced greatly his symptoms. But he felt they somehow didn't allow him to follow a natural, spiritual path. He assumed implicitly that he would be injured if his subjective experiences of mania and depression were reduced by a product of scientific thought such as a drug. To him, scientific and spiritual truths were mutually exclusive. At any one time, one can (or should) only use scientific or spiritual truths, not both. This sort of thinking should be seen as a variation on the hard problem. It makes it impossible to integrate religious and scientific concepts, feelings, and sensations.

Science at its best assumes, like Spinoza, that truth is infinitely deep. But fundamentalist thinking also exists in science. Radical reductionists are intent on explaining all natural phenomena in terms of mechanics: physics and chemistry. But the human sensory apparatus does not register events occurring on a biochemical level as chemical events *per se*. Rather, the person knows of them via changes in the subjective experiences of sensations, feelings, and thoughts. For example, chemical changes in the body are experienced as changes in mood, not the bonding of a neurotransmitter to a neuronal receptor site. So a radical reductionist position diminishes the importance of subjective experience of sense data, feeling, and thought. But what must they assume will happen to subjective experience when everything is known in physio-chemical terms? Is reductionism a sort of phobia of mental experience? Reductionism has a Zen-like quality regarding thought. It values parsimonious thinking and it is, for my money, a religion.

So, should we posit the existence of a deep instinct to not know things explicitly? All instinct systems work constantly, and they can promote the most competent decisions to approach pleasure and avoid pain if they are somehow aligned with neocortical, cognitive processes. But instincts can also be co-opted in psychological defensive operations involving the exclusion of certain contents from explicit awareness.

If we assume that to learn is the most general motive of the person, and if we are committed to a dynamic view of biopsychological proc- esses, we have to assume that some strong, organised counter-forces are at work to regulate learning processes. This is consistent with the general idea that the neocortex functions as an inhibitor, or ideally a sculptor of action tendencies originating in the brainstem and limbic system.

Cognitive and social barriers

In the meantime, a major, proximal inhibitor of theory development in neuropsychoanalysis and affective neuroscience is ambiguity about the meaning of concepts. More distal inhibitors may concern hard prob- lems in philosophy. But conceptual ambiguity, by definition, obscures the explicit truth. The dialogue between Panksepp and Damasio (2011) is a good example of writers having trouble understanding what the other guy is talking about. Can we get clarity on some general terms and concepts to help organise bio-psycho-social theory?

Freud's (1920) most general concepts, Eros and Thanatos, have not been especially helpful in promoting theoretical integration within psychoanalysis itself, let alone between psychoanalysis and adjacent biological and social schools. Integration involves combining items that were once separated. Most modern cultures, governments, businesses, and scientific schools see value in the integration of ideas, people, technologies, and so on. But integration, like all forms of change, is always resisted. When progressives promoted racial integration in the United States, South Africa and other places, resistance took violent forms. More than a few people were murdered.

Arguing about the integration of scientific theories might seem to be a gentler process than promoting racial integration. But probably the most important idea in psychoanalysis, retained in neuropsychoanalysis, is that higher processes of the mind such as science, art and politics depend on a neocortex that is an evolved extension of subcortical brain-stem and limbic structures. Individual and social decision-making processes using words are similar in some fundamental ways to older decision-making processes occurring in brain areas that regulate metabolic equilibrium in the body, and regulate stereotypical destructive and creative behavioural responses to stressors in the external world.

In some sense, "argument is war" whether it involves killing on a military battlefield or challenges to the valued concepts of others (see Lakeoff & Johnson, 1980). People want to protect and expand their material and conceptual possessions. Who will be able to insert their bullets or ideas into the brains and minds of the others? In any case, it is safe to say that the relative degrees of destructiveness and creativeness involved in conflict resolution are a function of the imaginations of the combatants. Situations can seem to allow only for zero-sum decisions, e.g., my life or yours, my theory or yours, pleasure or pain.

If sensory data match well enough quantitatively some standard of an object (e.g., a representation in mind associated with a predator's shadow), *fixed action* avoidance behaviours will be enacted such as crouching. This sort of representation is called a *releaser* by ethologists (e.g., Lorenz, 1963; Tinbergen, 1951). But sophisticated, multivariate, scientific problems are not likely to be solved by simple yes or no responses.

The neocortex evolved to inhibit and elaborate immediate instinctual reflexive actions. Sometimes neocortical functioning works to create explicit awareness of "good reasons" for the inhibition of one action, and the enactment of alternative actions. Both naïve and formal theorists develop expectations or predictions of what might happen as a result of certain behaviours.

Compared to situations in which more than two options are salient, inferring that one has only two options (e.g., fight or flight) is more likely to evoke conflict, sympathetic arousal, stress, and anxiety. Statistically speaking, complex cognitive tasks involving many decisional alternatives are performed best usually under more subtle autonomic conditions than those characterising full-blown sympathetic fight-flight or parasympathetic imbolization. Most generally, high parasympathetic tone is associated with good decision making and, hence, competent biological, psychological, and social functioning (e.g., Porges, 2011).

CHAPTER FOUR

Recent consensus and longstanding problems

Despite all the social, psychological, philosophical, and spiritual barriers to our work, there is increasing explicitness and agreement about the structures and processes in the brain, and about their relations to mental processes. The things we argue about in neuroscience exist in such an open, relatively disorganised field that we are unlikely to encounter many questions calling logically for either/ or decisions.

An early conceptual battle fought by Hobson and Solms (e.g., Hobson, 2004; Solms, 2004) played out as if dreams had to be explained as meaningful or not. Hobson had claimed that dream experiences are produced as a by-product of brainstem activity involved in processing sensory data from the body (e.g., Hobson & McCarley, 1977); and that dreams were not meaningfully important indicators of the person's state of mind. Solms (e.g., 2000) presented evidence that dreams are excited from the forebrain—a phylogenetically newer structure with special information processing competences lacking in the brainstem. This is consistent with the idea that dreams are psychologically meaningful for the development of the mind.

In the meantime, Zhang (2004, 2005) had developed an explicit theory of how dreams are products of input from both lower and higher brain regions and processes (see Bernstein, 2011, Chapter Ten). One never really had to choose between "dreams are brain processes" or "dreams are mind processes". The whole debate seemed more about the politics of scientific theory than scientific theory itself.

More generally, a consensus regarding the hierarchal and mutually regulatory aspects of the three basic decision-making systems of the brain–mind is starting to be accepted. The biopsychologists (e.g., MacClean, 1990; Panksepp, 1998; Porges, 2011) have shown that a prototypical, fixed action response to stress sub-served by the reptilian brainstem is immobilisation. The reptile, or monkey, or human operating only on the basis of decisions made in a particular vagal, brainstem nucleus may be either immobile or mobile. Instinctive fight or flight behaviours, variously elaborated with learned behaviours, are inhibited or activated, in part, by decision-making processes in limbic structures. These decisions have a "go, no-go" quality, but potentially can function with more flexibility than purely reptilian brainstem structures. The neocortex evolved anatomically on top of limbic structures and is the third system of the brain associated with its own special sort of responses to stress. Conceptual processing can take place in the neocortex and promote a vast array of sophisticated responses to stressors.

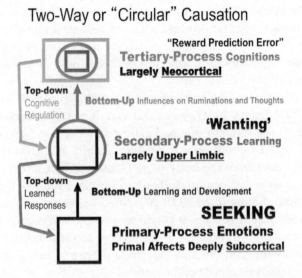

Figure 1. Mind–brain model from Panksepp and Wright 2012.

Most basically, the number of degrees of freedom for responding to stress and conflict increases dramatically as information-processing operations move from the bottom to the top of the brain. Figure 1 (Panksepp & Wright 2012) illustrates the general features of this mind–brain model.

Figure 1 depicts the rough anatomical relationships between the three different phylogenetic brain regions and includes some assumptions about the way that information is processed between and within the structures. I think most neuroscientists would understand and agree with the general assumptions of the model. And I imagine that many readers would not know exactly if they understood some terms and assumptions in the model. No scientific model claims to be perfect. We can use Figure 1 to illustrate some general problems with terms and concepts.

Depth

Estimating the depth of concepts, or what I call their general validity, is one criterion for evaluating theoretical models. The Panksepp and Wright (2012) model in Figure 1 has more depth than its predecessor, the Solms and Panksepp model (2012). This was achieved by elevating one of Panksepp's seven affects, SEEKING, to a higher level of generality than his other six affects: RAGE, FEAR, LUST, CARE, PANIC and PLAY. SEEKING is imagined to be the most general affect, in large part, because all the other sub-affects, operating in specific subcortical regions, make recourse to the general, problem-solving, conflict-resolving competence of the neocortex when necessary. This is reasonable and accords with how others think of functional hierarchies, affect, and motivational concepts.

> Multiple neural levels of function representation, with higher levels acting as the boss of lower levels, is the essence of a brain hierarchy … For motivation, the simplest and traditional hierarchical view is that the brain stem mediates mere reflexes, whereas the forebrain mediates controlling motivational functions. However, that view ignores the evidence that in a whole healthy brain, the brainstem elements contribute to causing true affect and motivational functions. (Berridge, 2004, p. 203)

But I think the new model also implies a related but different sort of theoretical change. That is, it is deeper than his former one because it represents a more valid characterisation of a hierarchy of explanatory concepts. A hierarchy of brain function is not the same as a hierarchy of explanatory concepts. But neither are the two sorts of hierarchies unrelated.

The assumption that functional brain hierarchies and hierarchies of concepts to explain the mind must be kept strictly separate was what motivated the creation of Freudian metapsychology. Metapsychology assumed that the central dynamic and structural concepts of psychoanalysis—such as pleasure principle, repetition compulsion, repression, and superego—were philosophical concepts and not amenable to scientific study. In fact, this assumption was wrong. Functional equivalents of the pleasure principle, repetition compulsion, superego, and other psychoanalytic concepts have been studied by experimental social psychologists for over fifty years. Rigorous experimental research has demonstrated that in normal and clinical populations, individuals change, distort, ambiguate, deny, and dissociate from concepts that are imagined to pose threats to the self:

1. People experience cognitive dissonance, a form of anxiety, when their overt behaviour is inconsistent with their self-concepts (Festinger, 1957). Monkeys also experience cognitive dissonance (Egan, 2007). Neurological correlates of dissonance reduction have been discovered (e.g., Jarcho et al., 2011; Van Veen et al., 2009).

2. Work on misattribution of arousal has operationalised the somatic and cognitive mechanisms underlying many psychoanalytic concepts including the cause of feelings and transference (e.g., Schachter & Singer, 1962; Zillmann, 1983).

3. Objective self-awareness theory and research demonstrated that self-focused attention works to make salient discrepancies between one's ideal self (ego ideals) and real self. Such gaps motivate attempts to achieve standards or avoid self-focus (e.g., Duval & Wicklund, 1972; Wicklund, 1975).

4. Attributional egotism research has convincingly demonstrated how people explain the causes of their successes and failures in order to protect and enhance their self-esteem (e.g., Bernstein et al., 1979; Snyder et al., 1978).

5. It has been demonstrated convincingly that people create and exploit attributional ambiguity, which works to obscure the causes of their behaviour and reduce stress and anxiety (e.g., Bernstein et al., 1983; Jones & Berglas, 1978; Snyder & Wicklund, 1981).

6. Symbolic self-completion theory and research (Wicklund & Gollwitzer, 1982) showed that people who have not yet realised, or completed attempts to attain self-defining goals, make compensatory displays of completion.
7. Freud's assumptions about negation of taboo wishes have been validated and modified by experimental studies (e.g., Bernstein, 1984).

In short, Freudian sorts of concepts *are* amenable to scientific inquiry. But both Freudian metatheory and reductionist behaviourism had assumed they were not. Tompkins' affect ideas (1962–1963) served, in part, as useful transitional containers or compromise concepts born out of a need to account for mental experience excluded from study by reductionist behaviourism. When the behaviourists threw the baby of subjective experience out of science, Tompkins' affect ideas put him back in. But the affect baby is not animated enough to swim (think) and so may drown.

The cruel reductionists from whom the affect theorists saved the baby, had in fact discovered general principles of motivation which are applicable to cognition and feeling. They had just restricted their focus to dependent variables concerning overt behaviour. Behaviourists operationalised convincingly the general determinants of motivation in all animal phyla, that is, habit and drive (e.g., Hull, 1943; Spence, 1956). The ethologists made important distinctions between instincts and learned habits (e.g., Tinbergen, 1972). Instincts are hard-wired habits or fixed action patterns that are released by a fixed set of evolutionarily important sensory arrays. Learned semantic concepts and habits to use them can involve a much larger number of standards to govern thought, feeling, and overt muscular behaviour than can hard-wired instincts.

In contrast to the clarity and generality of motivational and ethological concepts, the affect concept is ambiguous. This is indicated by some dictionary definitions (see Huitt, 2003):

> Affect: feeling or emotion as distinguished from cognition, thought, or action.

> Emotion: an intense feeling; a complex and usually strong subjective response, as love or fear; a state of agitation or disturbance.

> Feeling: sensation perceived by the sense of touch; an indefinite state of mind; an affective state of consciousness, such as that

resulting from emotions, sentiments, or desires; an emotional state
or disposition; non-intellectual or subjective human response.

The idea is no better clarified in the psychological literature. For
Zajonc (1980), the term affect is taken to indicate an instinctual reaction to stimulation occurring before the typical cognitive processes
considered necessary for the formation of a more complex emotion.
Zajonc suggests affective reactions can occur without extensive perceptual and cognitive encoding, and can be made sooner and with
greater confidence than cognitive judgements. Other writers (e.g.,
Lazarus, 1982) consider affect to be post-cognitive and elicited only
after a certain amount of cognitive processing of information has been
accomplished. Lerner and Keltner (2000) think that affect can be both
pre- and post-cognitive, with thoughts being produced by initial emotional responses, and further affect being produced by the thoughts.
Damasio (1994) argues that affect is necessary to enable more rational
modes of cognition.

Why make a special effort to differentiate an ambiguous concept like
affect, from clearer motivational concepts and associated axiomatic concepts from learning, behavioural, ethological, and evolutionary theories? Perhaps Panksepp considers higher order concepts as equivalents
to Freudian metaconcepts that were incorrectly thought un-testable.

> In sum, the brain contains no singular "motivational" process in its
> infrastructure. Thus, *motivational* structures should be recognized
> as higher order concepts that subsume the many factors that coa-
> lesce to guide desired actions. (Panksepp & Wright, 2012, p. 69)

Experimental social psychology has come the closest to integrating
mental and overt behavioural processes with the stimulus-organism-
response (S-O-R) model. That is, where behaviourism considered only
S-R (Stimulus and Response), Lewin and his students allowed that
something in the Organism mediated overt muscular responses to
external stimuli (the O in S-O-R). Cognitive-social psychologists have
studied explicitly cognition, motivation, feelings, and overt behaviour.

I think something like SEEKING is best understood as the highest
order motive. Its goal is to explain reality and, thereby, experience the
most pleasurable feelings by means of validly conceived sensations.
This idea contradicts one holding that subjective experiences of feelings

or thought are not a basis for the evolution of brain–mind systems (e.g., LeDoux, 2000, p. 131).

> Our hope is to gradually coax scholars to view human mental life from other than traditional human cognitive perspectives and to become more open to the powers of the primal affective faculties of human brains. (Panksepp & Wright, 2012, p. 67)

Certainly, brainstem events can exert urgent biological presses in the limbic system and in the neocortex to activate feelings, thoughts, and overt behaviour. The intention to underscore this point is at the centre of Panksepp's mission as a theorist. By focusing on the importance of the brainstem and "primal affects", Panksepp is trying to correct a current bias in psychology to favour cognitive explanations. In part, I agree with him on this. But I want to coax *him* into going all the way with his idea of the importance of SEEKING as a higher order concept to explain the entire person. I think people use the word affect because they imagine it brands their work as a more legitimate area for scientific study than motivation with its mysterious teleological quality. Thinking is too a spooky thing. What the hell is it anyway? Basic neuroaffect theory is almost completely devoid of concepts to explain cognition (e.g., Panksepp, 2010; Porges, 2011).

The idea that facial muscular gestures are causes and effects of subjective experience is of great importance (e.g., Ekman, 1973; Lanzetta & Orr, 1986). But I think the term and the concept of affect now serve to create confusion in neuroscience. We do not need affect theories *and* motivation theories. Motivational and cognitive concepts, and the relations between them, are sufficient to contain and explain the person. Affective neuroscience and its cousin neuropsychoanalysis can't yet quite conceive of cognition as a natural biological process driven by motivational forces. This is because affect concepts developed, in part, as a compromise to cope with the *hard problem*.

Today we consider the functions of the mind, including conscious experiences, as caused by the functioning of the brain. We can now correlate in time many brain and mind processes. But an idea that must underlie attempts to build an integrated mind-body theory is that natural forces more general than any specific brain or mind operations work to cause, in part, mental phenomena. The question of whether such general, deep concepts can be studied by scientific methods has been answered in the affirmative. This implies that making a distinction between metatheory and theory proper is superfluous (see Chapter Thirteen).

But the more general question raised by Freudian metapsychology is still relevant today: How do deep forces of nature, represented by general concepts, work as distal causes of all the specific, proximal causes of mind–brain phenomena including conscious experience? I have assumed, and I think Panksepp wants to assume, that the desire to seek knowledge of reality is the best candidate for the sort of overarching concept the metapsychologists were looking for. The validity of such an assumption can be tested by scientific methods.

Affect concepts and motivational concepts are hopelessly confounded

When I was an undergraduate from 1969 to 1973, my psychology professors were mostly earnest Behaviourists. But they seemed to accept the idea that the configurations of the muscles in the face might have some importance for psychology. They also believed more oddly that the configuration of the speech making muscles was equivalent to the meaning implied by an uttered word. Today, despite uncertainty about what *affect* denotes explicitly, there seems to be implicit uniformity among users of the term in regard to its most important connotation. That is, affect is a basic set of muscular gestures or instinctive reactions to stimuli, and more recently, some basic reactions in the brain. Somehow I think affect theories are incapable of recognising that semantic concepts might represent a feature of the natural world.

Psychoanalytically oriented writers now regularly use the terms affect, affect regulation, and mentalisation (e.g., Fongay et al., 2004). Clinical affect regulation theories and practices also include cognitive elements (e.g., Caplan, 1970; Beck, 1967; Beck et al., 1987). Slightly older psychoanalytic approaches also use the ambiguous term affect along with cognitive concepts (e.g., Brenner, 2006). At bottom, psychoanalysts want to understand how cognition gives a meaning and a tone to sensations or arousal. For example, there is Brenner's (2006, p. 24) definition: "Any affect includes (a) sensations of pleasure and unpleasure or a mixture of the two, plus (b) thoughts, memories, wishes, fears—in a word, ideas." Cognitive psychologists (e.g., Neisser, 1976) and cognitive-social psychologists (e.g., Schachter & Singer, 1962) believe that explanatory semantic concepts somehow combine with sensation or arousal to form a meaningful subjective experience of feelings (Bernstein, 2011).

The affect psychology position emphasises the reflexive nature of behaviour. But mind–brain theory integrations must indicate how reflex-like actions influence and are influenced by learning and using semantic concepts (see Lieberman & Eisenberg, 2004). Of course, Panksepp is attempting to integrate ideas. But if one does not recognise unambiguously that at some deep platonic level, all feeling and behaviour is related to universal concepts of some sort, there is a bias to emphasise more the differences between cognition, motivation, and overt behaviour, rather than their underlying integrated functions and purposes.

For example, Figure 1 differentiates between processes of seeking, wanting, and reducing prediction errors. It labels them respectively primary, secondary, and tertiary processes. The distinction between at least three levels of complexity of information processing in the brain–mind is valid. But using information in order to make decisions is similar, in important ways, at basic cellular and more advanced neocortical levels. Learning takes place throughout the nervous system, and all decision making, including deciding to learn or change decision-making habits, uses something like cybernetic TOTE processing. In defence of their use of the terms primary-process emotions and primary affects, Panksepp and Wright (2012, p. 69) say:

> The way Freud originally developed primary and secondary processes … was fundamentally a[s] a form of thinking. We use the same terminology in a different way, for two reasons: (1) As a consequence of evolutionary theory and modern neuroscience advances, the optimal way to restructure primary-process concepts needs to be renegotiated. (2) It may be important to view the dynamic unconscious to be largely a mix of basic learning as well automatized cortical thinking processes.

Panksepp's concepts describe things that are sort of like Freud's primary and secondary thinking? The important thing is to indicate how a new concept is an improvement on an old one. Why not give a new, better concept a new name that is uncontaminated with unwanted connotations? A term that might cause less confusion is *initial processing*. That is, Freud and Panksepp are trying to describe the first phases of information processing of raw sense data. Other mental states can "regress" to primary processing in, for example, psychosis or sleep. But most basically the change is to revert to basic, initial, data processing operations like equipartitioning. All data processed by all individuals must undergo such processes initially.

The central problem for body–brain–mind theory is to integrate cognitive and motivational principles. I think that affect concepts function now more as barriers than aids to such integration. The term and the concept have been used as containers for things sort of like emotions and feelings that had been excluded from psychological inquiry by behaviourism. Affect has served, in part, as a useful transitional, compromise concept, born out of the need to account for mental experience and at the same time adhere to the reductionist bias of science. But affective neuroscience and neuropsychoanalysis are still bedevilled by the *hard problem*.

Perhaps science's resistance to mentalistic concepts has reduced over time as brain–mind correlations have been found. But the compromise term affect is not merely still in use, it dominates mind–brain theorising. In order to form therapeutic relationships with patients, we often have to collude with their defensive compromise formations. Do we have to go along with compromised scientific theoretical concepts?

> Motivational concepts are needed to understand the brain, just as brain concepts are needed to understand motivation. Motivation concepts can aid behavioural neuroscience to live up to its potential of providing brain-based explanations of motivated behaviour in real life. Without them, neuroscience models would remain over simplified fragments, removed from the behavioural reality they purport to explain. Trying to explain how the brain controls motivated behaviour without motivational concepts is like trying to understand what your computer does without concepts of *software*. Erich von Holst, an important early behavioural neuroscientist, emphasized that we need what he called *level-adequate concepts* to understand how brains control behaviour. Level adequate means an explanation that adequately matches the level of complexity of the thing we are trying to explain. Concepts of hedonic reaction, incentive motivation, homeostatic reflex, hierarchy, heterarchy, etc., are all level adequate in the sense that they are the simplest possible concepts to adequately capture the crucial corresponding aspects of

what brains actually do … Good concepts of motivation are vital to
reach that goal. (Berridge, 2004, p. 205, italics added)

A focus on the causes and effects of the activation of semantic concepts to contain and explain sense data is the key to developing level
adequate motivational explanations of mind–brain phenomena. What
Berridge (2004) misses is the lack of parsimony in neuroscience theories
that use affect concepts *and* motivational concepts. I think this occurs
because of the history of the development of ideas in psychology, and
not for any logical reason. For example, in the following passage I can't
see the theoretical advantage of using affect and motivational concepts.
Can you?

> Epstein (1982) suggested that real motivation is always accompa-
> nied by affective reactions to the goal itself. By affective reaction,
> Epstein meant behavioural, autonomic, or similar physiological
> responses that indicated the presence of some hedonic or emo-
> tional state. As Epstein put it, "What I mean by affect is discern-
> ible patterns of somatic and autonomic-glandular responding
> that are expressed as integral aspects of appetitive-consummatory
> sequences of behaviour." His point was that motivation is directed
> toward hedonically laden goals, and if a goal is hedonic, it should
> elicit an affective reaction. Thus, the presence of hedonic reactions
> confirms that the behaviour was truly motivated. (Berridge, 2004,
> p. 188)

If one assumes that all goals, including goals of thinking and overt
behaviour, are hedonically laden, and if one accepts Epstein's point of
view that hedonically laden goals evoke affect, then affect concepts are
superfluous. All we need are concepts from motivation theory and cognitive theory.

And, it is centrally important to distinguish between goals and
the processes aimed at achieving them. Not all mind–brain processes
aimed at goal attainment produce equal degrees of pleasure. The repetition compulsion is a regular, durable, fundamental brain process. It
serves to increase the odds of learning the most pleasurable solutions
to conflicts between tendencies to approach pleasure and avoid pain.
When repetition is serving this purpose it may not be itself especially

pleasurable. Repetition of ineffective conflict resolution operations can cause frustration, aggression, and mental illness.

Open systems and evolution

In addition to a model's hierarchy of concepts, we can also consider if it depicts an isolated or an open system (e.g., Burke, 2010; von Bertanlanffy, 1956; Wiener, 1948). Open systems models refer to those that spell out as explicitly as possible, answers to three sorts of questions: (1) How do particular items in the environment enter a system like the body, mind, brain, or New York subway? (2) How are the aspects of the ingested environment processed to be destroyed, preserved, or made into something new? (3) How do these processes create waste products and more valued items which are variously transported back into the environment?

> An open system is a system which continuously interacts with its environment. The interaction can take the form of information, energy, or material transfers into or out of the system boundary, depending on the discipline which defines the concept ... The concept of an open system was formalized within a framework that enabled one to inter-relate the theory of the organism, thermodynamics, and evolutionary theory. (Luhmann, 1995, pp. 6–7)

Today, systems thinking includes information theory (e.g., Rieke et al., 1997). In the natural sciences an open system is one whose border is permeable to both energy and mass. When considering mind–brain systems, we must consider the informational value of sensing changes in the energy and mass of objects.

Figure 1 leaves unspecified the nature of the mind–brain system's relationships to its environments. Of course, these relations are implied in the figure. But to enhance communication, it helps to describe things explicitly. Heider (1958), Bernstein (2011), maybe Wright and Panksepp (2012), and many other writers, assume that brain and mind have evolved to process sensory data with more valid, deeper concepts in order to make the best decisions.

The primary function of the brain, its *raison d'être*, is to make decisions. Good decisions are its valued output. Biological energy is used to make and enact decisions. Sometimes decisions are made to create new concepts or standards to decide on actions. Decision quality is promoted by learning and using the most valid general and detailed explanatory concepts. Accordingly, it makes sense to organise a model of the human mind and brain on the basis of the most general assumptions about the person. The model should include explicit assumptions about the relations of the mind and brain to their environments.

Feelings and meaning

I like the term *feeling* for a simple reason. Ordinary people, naïve scientists in Heider's terms, rarely if ever say, "I have a negative affect" or "My emotions are good today". Rather, the word feeling is most used in common parlance to describe a subjective experience whose meaning is more or less validly represented by concepts in and out of awareness. It does not connote an entire literature that has been less than clear about what it is talking about. The essential feature of *feeling* as I use the term is *meaningful sensation*.

Meaning comes from semantic concepts in the neocortex used to interpret raw sensory data and other concepts. Meaningful sensations are what psychoanalysis cares about. Affect is one of those words that promises to explain more than it really does. It is like using a fancy medical term with a patient who comes in sweating profusely for no obvious reason. "It's diaphoresis, Bobby. We see this often in medicine. Don't worry, you'll be all right." This manner of merely describing the surface characteristics of a symptom without any explicit hypotheses about its causes is the style of the diagnostic and statistical manuals used in psychiatry. "This is just a slight case of dysthymia, Mrs Fields. These pills will help you."

This is not to suggest that there is not important, meaningful information contained in the subjective experience of relatively raw sensory data at the initial stages of information processing. Rather, the meaning of sensory information in the earliest stages of processing is determined by comparing it to inborn and learned standards of correct or ideal body, brain, or mind functioning. This leads to decisions to activate or inactivate particular somatic and mental processes in attempts to change something about the body or mind. The sensation of *releasers* in the environment like the shadow of a predator or the secondary sexual characteristics of a potential mate, work to promote overt behavioural responses involving fleeing, fighting, freezing, sex, nurturing, and other hard-wired, fixed action patterns.

Instinctual, fixed actions are triggered by zero-sum, or go, no-go decisions. When sensory thresholds exceed standards, somatic responses ensue in the viscera and the muscles. Do the stimuli match closely enough a sensory array encoded in the brain and, hence, call for corrective action? For example, does a low glucose level cause a decision to release insulin, and/or an overt food-seeking behaviour? I think fixed action patterns should be understood to include not just overt, instinctual movements of the voluntary muscles of the body but also the reflexive activities of the autonomic nervous system such as release of insulin; or in the case of hypotension, beta-adrenergic vasoconstricting neurotransmitters.

Using the term fixed actions rather than reflex adds the more general perspective of information processing to the debate. The mind–brain makes go, no-go decisions, and decisions with perhaps an infinite number of degrees of freedom. At bottom, the elements of the most complex nuanced decisions are probably the result of organising multiple, binary decisions. That is, qualitative differences in experience are due most likely to the results of innumerable, quantitative decisions made by meaningfully organized binary elements (see Miles-Brenden, 2013).

As the nervous system developed and more was happening in a neocortex, data deriving from interoception of the brain's workings itself came to be processed increasingly by the brain. Instinctive, initial decision making is different from decisions made in the neocortex that use learned semantic concepts to make attributions for explaining sensations. Usually, instincts are more strongly stimulated by raw sensory patterns than they are by the semantic concepts used to interpret such patterns (see Pavio, 1971). For example, standing close to a real bear is more sympathetically arousing than hearing or thinking the word "bear".

Panksepp would consider making attributions a tertiary process. Concepts about what caused what can go on to affect decisions regarding behavioural, cognitive, and feeling responses to the sensations. Activation of instincts based on initial information processing is a meaningful event in as much as it uses a standard for decision making. But decisions to activate fixed action patterns use only one or relatively few standards. Does the sensory array match closely enough the representation of an evolved releaser stored in the brain? If the answer is yes, the instinct is enacted. If no, it is not enacted overtly.

Neocortical, tertiary decision-making processes involve many more degrees of decisional freedom than brainstem decision-making. Panksepp uses the term secondary processes to indicate decision-making processes with more potential degrees of freedom than primary processes, but fewer than tertiary processes. I'm not sure that the assumption that there are three categorically different processes is useful. Should we, for now, think more in terms of a continuum of decisional freedom from the bottom to the top of the brain?

In any case, if decisions to go are made at the go, no-go stage, one of nine (Tompkins, 1962), or seven (Panksepp, 2010) affects, or twelve instincts (MacDougall, 1908) will be enacted overtly. The variability in the imagined number of basic affects is due to the fact that affect writers have to squeeze the entire panoply of human responding capabilities into a set of instinctive mechanisms operating individually or together.

The exceptionally detailed work, including single cell stimulation by biopsychologists, has located brain structures and neurochemicals that regulate something like six basic sorts of behaviours that have given organisms selective advantages over time. But there are problems with the idea that there are specific neurons or neuron systems entirely dedicated to the regulation of specific behaviours.

> The reemergence of motivated behaviour during recovery after a brain lesion meant that motivational control must be partly distributed elsewhere in the brain, not entirely contained in the destroyed center ... [There are also problems with] the idea of a dedicated drive neuron itself, no matter where in the brain it might be imagined to be. The most dramatic evidence against dedicated drive neurons came from studies of motivation elicited by electrical brain stimulation, which discovered that, sometimes, the activation of one single brain site could elicit much different motivated behaviour, depending on environmental situations, individual predisposition, and experience. (Berridge, 2004, p. 201)

A solution to these sorts of problems is to build mind–brain theory on the most basic, general differentiations. A most useful general axiom is that biopsychosocial systems approach pleasure and avoid pain phenomena. The subtle and not so subtle interactions between these biological, psychological, and social systems give rise to the vast range of human feeling, thought, and behaviour.

Panksepp's SEEKING concept describes appetitive, approach motives. Compared to using a finite number of specific affects, a general characterisation based on the spatial and temporal asymmetries in approach and avoidance motives might best promote theoretical integrations of concepts concerning thought and feeling. The concept of affect is not especially amenable to explaining higher cognitive processes. This is due, in part, to confusion between general motives and their specific control systems.

In contrast to brainstem and limbic structures, the neocortex can use many more concepts, including those learned and stored in memory and those developed "on the fly", as standards to determine the deeper meaning of raw data. Hence, it can enact more than just a few sorts of fixed actions in response to stressors. Deeper meaning here comes from the neocortical processing of raw data involving multiple variables and, in turn, the development of models of relationships between the variables. Such models should specify conditions regulating the causal relations. For example, I have observed and heard from others that serotonin reuptake inhibitors are more effective at reducing depression in younger than in older patients. Why might that be so? Well, multiple variable systems are involved. Consideration of variables at multiple levels of anatomical and functional levels can work to produce better predictions about the consequences of interacting with objects in the world than can consideration of subcortical, instinctive systems alone.

This is not to say that *fixed action patterns* do not represent valid responses to reality. The validity of the standards and operating procedures of the brainstem has been extensively tested over the course of evolution. It is just that the Standards used to activate fixed actions consider sense data in terms of their immediate, initial meanings for the biological system: pain avoidance and pleasure approach. This was Tompkins' most important idea regarding affects. That is, there are good affects regarding pleasure and bad affects related to pain. These basic tendencies can quickly potentiate instinctual, fixed action patterns in response to sensation of evolutionarily important releasers.

If there is conflict between approach and avoidance motives of equal strength, individuals will experience stress. If one or the other motive dominates, security operations (e.g., fighting, fleeing, or immobilisation), or appetitive and consummatory behaviours involving overt attempts to regulate temperature, oxygen, glucose, parenting, and so on, will prevail. Overt performance of such instincts can be totally inhibited, partially inhibited, or redirected (e.g., sublimated) by semantic concepts activated in the neocortex.

CHAPTER FIVE

Controlling sensations, concepts, feelings, and overt behaviour

Five terms are important for explaining the workings of the mind, brain and body: (1) *sense data*, (2) *semantic concepts*, (3) *feelings*, (4) *expectations* or *predictions*, and (5) *overt behaviour*. Focal attention alternates between sensations and concepts (see Snyder et al., 2004). Concepts contain and explain the multiple sensory attributes of objects in the world and in the mind itself. Concepts work to generate expectations or predictions about the likely pleasure and pain consequences of approaching or avoiding objects in the mind by changing attentional focus and in the world by means of overt behaviour. Feelings indicate, in part, the amount of validity of concepts used to contain sensations and other concepts.

The ability to regulate the switching of attention between concepts and raw sensory data is the key process variable that affects the person's competence to regulate the mind and brain. The key structural variable is the degree of validity of the concepts that are activated to interpret sensations and other concepts. That is, concepts must be encoded and stored in memory in some brain structures involving information processing. Such processes might remain inactive, or they may be used in or out of focal attention to interpret raw sensory data and more complex thoughts and feelings. I think the use of the most valid concepts for interpreting sensation and other ideas can produce the most sublime feelings.

I use the term *concept-activation complexes* to describe a switched-on concept, the operation that gives rise to experiences of thoughts and feelings (Bernstein, 2011, p. 183). People learn habits in and out of conscious awareness to activate particular concepts that work to contain and explain sensations. These habits are procedural habits akin to those regulating muscular behaviour. The strength of habits to activate any particular concept in any particular situation can vary from weak to strong. And the validity of the concept activated can vary from low to high. Feelings are sensations explained by concepts that may or may not appear in conscious awareness. That is, concepts in mind can be: (1) not operating; (2) operating under the control of automatic habits; (3) the focus of conscious attention; (4) perhaps used intentionally.

In mental illness, invalid concepts may be activated often to explain sensations coming from the body. For example, a paranoid person, unconscious of what is making him anxious, may use concepts that indicate he is in great danger from an external agent, while in truth he is afraid of thoughts and feelings coming from his own mind. Paranoid concept-activation complexes work to contain and explain sensations of danger and anxiety, albeit invalidly, and in turn, can partially reduce disintegration anxiety (e.g., Kohut, 1977). Paranoid defences represent a very regressed position in which the person "knows" there is only one cause for his anxiety. "They are out to get me. If they weren't, I wouldn't be anxious." This is a fruitless, frustrating, repetitive, defensive cycle of information processing.

Paranoia, caused by anxiety, is a type of defensive regression in mental competence occurring in the neocortex. It is an example of zero-sum thinking occurring at a level of the brain and mind that evolved to augment the initial stages of information processing. Functionally, paranoia and other defences against anxiety represent states in which the neocortex acts like a subcortical structure. Such structures have evolved to detect with exteroceptors threats in the external environment, and to react with fixed action patterns of the musculature. This simplifies mental operations for the nervous person by reducing the complexity of mind and brain. It is easier to operate a two-part brain than a three-part brain. Paranoia, of course, involves a projection. This involves an invalid assumption that internal threats are coming from the outside. In projection, subcortical processes are called into play when neocortical processes should probably be dominating. Psychotherapy with paranoids is useless until the projections are withdrawn.

So one's advanced brain can become functionally equivalent to a more primitive decision-making system, like those of the brainstem, when defensive operations are aroused. In severe mental disorders, defensive concepts working to distort the meaning of sense data will be repeatedly activated until a more valid concept is used. But motivations to avoid reality are not the only motives causing repetitive use of invalid concepts. More commonly, people use invalid ideas because they never learned better ones. If the person is taught more valid ideas and is able to use them, she is not mentally ill. But some people cling to their treasured delusions regardless of what we tell them.

Implicit procedural habits, including psychological defensive operations, can become known explicitly or declaratively by means of talking therapies, hallucinogens, eye movement therapy, and biofeedback (e.g., Bernstein, 2011). Presumably, all psychotherapists have witnessed how a patient's use of a more valid concept than, for example, a paranoid defence to explain sensory data from the social world or the body, can work to improve cognitive functioning and reduce experiences of negative feelings.

Paranoid thinking represents a condition of presumed, chronic emergency and, hence, can cause sympathetic arousal. Usually sympathetic arousal arises first in subcortical areas. Then cognitive operations decide how to cope with the arousal. This works mostly by means of inhibition or modification of instinctual impulsive tendencies. In paranoia, advanced information processes of the neocortex become limited to seeing things in black and white terms. While many paranoids develop elaborately organised methods to avoid the plotting against them, underlying it all is a single decision regarding whether or not "they are out to get me". Subcortical decisions to initiate sympathetic arousal can be ordered to participate in neocortical follies as well as more useful projects. Such neocortical incompetence arising from fear or ignorance is, I would wager, the largest cause of physical illness and, of course, stupid behaviour.

Mental competence depends, in large part, on which system has the most power to control things. The paranoid, after interpreting the shadow of a potted palm as a policeman, is unable to inhibit a tendency to run away, or more generally avoid the presumed danger. Now, subjectively, paranoids report ruminating anxiously or angrily about the dangers. This indicates that their theory of what is bothering them is less than valid and doesn't really reduce stress or anxiety too much.

Conscious paranoid thoughts represent *misattributions of sympathetic arousal* (e.g., Schacter & Singer, 1962). *A standard of correctness* such as "I should love daddy and other authorities" comes in conflict with a wish to put a stick in daddy's eye. The conflict increases physiological arousal and a need to explain its source. Somewhere along the line, the anxious patient made an assumption that "when I feel threatened it is always because something outside of me, something with authority like Daddy, presents a threat to my security". This habit of thinking is very reinforcing because it reduces anxiety. At least the person can believe: "There is not something in me that is dangerous to me. That would be infinitely worse. I could never get away." But sooner or later, a habit to categorically fear authority figures creates a lot of stress, anxiety, physiological arousal, and its attendant wear and tear. This is because subcortically based instincts respond to imagined dangers in the same way they respond to real ones.

Animals without much neocortex do not have to be too afraid of their own thoughts. Compared to humans, the external world is more salient and important as a cause of behaviour in other mammals. The individual's neocortex must be large and developed enough to create internal states powerful enough to command the focal attention of a mammal.

Instinctive decision making is different in this regard from some decisions made in the neocortex that use learned concepts chosen from a large range of attributions for explaining sensations. In turn, these concepts about "what caused what" can be used to decide between a large number of behavioural, cognitive, and feeling responses to the sensations. Activation of instincts based on initial information processing is a meaningful event in as much as it uses a standard for decision making. But the decision to activate the raw instinct or reflex uses only one standard: does the sensory array match the representation of an evolved releaser? If the answer is yes, the instinct is enacted. If no, it is not enacted.

Decision-making processes below the level of the neocortex tend to involve decisions in which only one binary set (1/0) is used to define decisional options. But decisional options can be specified by use of multiple sets of binary operators. For example, learning encoded in the brain can direct that certain decisions be enacted only under precise conditions. Each variable determining a decision can be coded with binary language. For example, decision x is made if and only if a = 1, b = 0, c = 1, d = 0, e = 1. There are more standards or conditions used to make decisions about the meaning of stimuli when information processing goes from brainstem to limbic decision-making structures. And the number increases dramatically in the neocortex.

Panksepp's primary, secondary, and tertiary levels of processing correspond most simply to what must be a vast number of levels of difference between subcortical decisional processes regulated by one or few standards and neocortical decision making which can be based on multiple standards or criteria for determining meaning. His scheme, or his use of Freud's scheme, raises an important question for brain–mind researchers and theorists: what is the number of variables processed by the brain and mind needed to define decision making as a form of initial information processing? And, how many variables qualify thinking as a secondary or tertiary process? Attempting to answer such questions theoretically and operationally would promote integration of body–brain–mind theories.

Triune brain, affect theory, and cognition

The centre of the human information processing system is, roughly, a triune brain. The brain processes information with increasing intensity as it moves from brainstem to limbic system to neocortex. The capturing of relatively raw sensory information in the neocortex can produce feelings, that is, meaningful sensations. I think the subjective experiences arising out of the brainstem are activated by raw sensations or perhaps slightly more processed protoconcepts. There is very credible research indicating that raw sensory data from all sense modalities are processed into packets containing equal numbers of bits of information (e.g., Snyder et al., 2004).

Often, all the sensory data about an object cannot be placed in an equipartioned package. These leftover bits of information are, I think, always the stimuli for conceptual activity. The function of conceptual thought is to understand sensory information that cannot be neatly packaged by subcortical areas. "Don't wake up the boss unless you have a problem you can't handle yourself."

A theoretical problem for affect writers is how to get the brain to do anything new. As far as I know, sophisticated behaviours represent some unique mix of affective responding. By this reasoning, no person has likely had a new thought or feeling since the human brain achieved, through evolution, its current, stable neuroanatomical configuration.

Importantly, affective gestures of the face can be enacted without any felt sense of meaning as in cases of pseudo-bulbar affect. Pseudo-bulbar affect is a disconnection syndrome, where neuronal connections between the neocortex and pontine brainstem structures are disrupted by stroke, muscular sclerosis, tumours or other disease processes. Patients with this neurological disorder might laugh or cry or become enraged for no apparent reason. When asked why they are happy or sad or mad, these patients tell you they are not happy or sad or mad but that they feel normal, not especially anything.

This suggests that if we want to understand meaningful subjective experiences of thought and feeling, and how the whole brain works to promote and inhibit them, the concept of affect is insufficient. This is because it does not explicitly recognise how sensations and energy combine with semantic concepts to produce meaningful sensations, that is, feelings. I can't imagine that the neocortical brain is less important in all this than the configuration of the facial muscles.

Autonomic and cognitive processes influence stress levels

As noted in Chapter Two, early writers attempting to understand stress, feeling, and behaviour tended to study instances of high sympathetic arousal. Seeing a bear was the prototypical situation that Bard (1928), Cannon (1927), and James and Lange (1922) analysed. What happens first? Is it the feeling of fear, the thought, the overt fleeing? We know now that instinctive fixed actions are fast, and that the raw sensory representations of threats registered subcortically can go on to be more or less extensively processed all the way up to the neocortex, resulting in conscious experiences of thought and feeling. The thoughts and feelings, in turn, can come back to regulate subcortical activity and overt behaviour.

Sympathetically aroused, overt flight and flight behaviours are much easier to observe than the private conceptual processes occurring in the brain and mind. A real bear and overt running away are much more obvious than avoiding the thought of a bear. Before fMRIs and other technologies could reveal brain processes in real time, behaviourists and psychobiologists studied what they could see. So, psychological theories have tended to be sympathocentric, or focused especially on how the arousing, sympathetic branch of the autonomic nervous system regulates overt behaviour. In contrast, *The Polyvagal Theory* (Porges, 2011) illustrates how less obvious, parasympathetic operations importantly moderate sympathetic responses to stress.

Since Selye (1936), numerous theories and countless studies have been devoted to understanding the causes, effects, and regulation of stress. As a practical matter, all anxiety patients we see for talking or drug therapy can be described as overly stimulated by sympathetic, adrenergic hormones and neurotransmitters. They are under a repeated stress caused by unresolved conflicts about whether to approach or avoid objects in the world and in their own minds. Anxiety is a result of unresolved conflicts that generate stress. This is consistent with the idea that unconscious conflicts produce stress, and then signal anxiety (Freud, 1926). Anxiety, in turn, works to activate compromise formations, or concepts that regulate approach avoidance tendencies in something of a chronically suboptimal manner.

Sense data from social and physical situations are constantly stimulating or priming ancient tendencies to enact fixed action patterns involving freezing, fleeing, fighting, and appetitive behaviours such as seeking sexual mates or predation. The general tendency of the brain to activate concepts of what the body and mind need has to involve something like spreading activation (e.g., Anderson, 1983; Collins & Loftus, 1975; Crestani, 1997; Damian et al., 2001; Marcel, 1980; McNamara, 2005; Meyer & Schvanevelt, 1971; Najmi & Wegner, 2008; Neely, 1977). The thresholds for activating concepts associated with recently sensed words are lower than if a closely associated word had not been registered in the brain–mind. Internal need states prime concepts related to what the person needs whether it be food, social affiliation, or sex (e.g., McClelland, 1955; Clark, 1956). Priming enables the body to communicate its needs to the brain.

Anxiety

The anxious person lacks concepts to decide how to effectively manage conflicting approach and avoidance tendencies. This can be due to poor education, or because the person is afraid to activate the potentially helpful idea. Without more valid concepts to interpret sensory arrays, the neocortex is not fully functional. It is no surprise that a person fears being urged to take either one of two options—execute a fixed action or not. One is automatically goaded by the brainstem. The stress often involves unresolved conflicts between desires to obtain pleasures of one kind or another, and fear that satisfying such desires represents a violation of deep moral standards and is certain to be punished. Unresolved stress causes anxiety. Without valid semantic concepts in the neocortex to help resolve conflict, a person is always somewhat afraid of her subcortical brain.

Tendencies to enact forbidden behaviours stimulated first in the brainstem and then, working by spreading activation to promote forbidden sensual thoughts and feelings based in the neocortex, are channelled into fruitless repetition of doing and undoing. This often manifests as obsessive thinking and compulsive rituals. These repetitive defences neutralise subcortical impulses to action. This is the prototypical compromise formation of the anxious person. The most anxious patients are those who had suffered physical and/or mental trauma in the past. They feel, think, and behave as if they are in constant danger. They are more or less consciously always seeing a bear and wishing to flee *and* fight. Anxiety disorders always involve simultaneous processes that turn up the throttle and push hard on the brakes. This wears out the body and mind.

Chronic unresolved conflict usually results in depression with cognitive and somatoform symptoms. These sometimes regress to psychosis and bipolar disorders. Unrelenting stress, sympathetic arousal, and anxiety exhaust adrenergic hormonal and neurotransmitters systems. Then psychomotor retardation, guilty feelings, and sadness start to dominate the clinical picture. Problems with memory and attentional focus also emerge, and appetitive curiosity and seeking of food, sex and learning decrease.

Anxiety disorders, anxious depressions, bipolar depressions, and psychoses can be treated with tranquillising drugs. Most tranquillisers work by raising the threshold for neuronal firing. Benzodiazepines and other anti-seizure medicines such as valproic acid, oxcarbamazepine and lamotrigine alterthe permeability of neurons to chloride or calcium ions. This hyperpolarises the cells and makes all-or-none firing less likely. Accordingly, the person becomes more relaxed. Conflict is still stimulating the brain, but the brain and then the mind become less reactive to stress effects.

One can also lessen conflicts by blocking the stimulating effects of dopamine. This neurotransmitter potentiates the appetitive tendencies.

When dopamine antagonists are introduced into the synapse, anticipatory pleasures drop. So, this is the other way to reduce stressful conflict. This strategy is usually reserved for anxiety that is so high it may induce psychotic reactions. The older antipsychotics such as chlorpromazine and haloperidol, and the newer drugs such as quetiapine, work to block particular dopamine receptors (e.g., D2 receptors).

Anxiety can also be lessened by increasing adrenergic stimulation. Amphetamines are dopamine and norepinephrine agonists that potentiate sympathetic arousal. I assume this strategy reduces anxiety by tilting the balance in conflict situations towards the approach of desired things. This can lead to conflict resolution, reductions in anxiety and depression, and enhanced cognitive functioning.

Conflict

The tendencies to approach pleasure and avoid pain are activated in an asymmetrical manner in all animal species. This was demonstrated convincingly by Miller (1944), Miller and Dollard (1941), and the experimental conflict school. In the classic example, mice developed a strong habit to run down a ramp and receive a food reward. Then the area in front of the food tray was wired to give the mouse an electric shock. This created experimentally an approach-avoidance conflict.

Depending on the incentive value of the food (tastiness), the individual's state of need (time without food), and the intensity of painful electric shocks, the mouse approach and avoidance behaviours can be manipulated. Sometimes the mice dithered right before the ambivalent region. Sometimes they ran backwards up the ramp. And sometimes they decided to endure the pain in order to obtain the food. Most generally, we learned from these experiments that compared to avoidance tendencies, approach motives activate at a further distance from an ambivalent region, and increase gradually with distance to the region. Avoidance behaviours are activated more sharply at closer distances to the problem area, as illustrated in Figure 2.

Importantly, Miller and Dollard (1941) found that mice in the conflict situation learned quickly to avoid shocks by turning a small wheel next to the food ramp. That is, they found a way to expand their range of decisional options to cope with stress. Such learning, by definition, involves the formation and use of new concepts. They could get the food *and* avoid shock. They were not reduced to deciding between the mutually exclusive options: no food/no shock *or* food/shock.

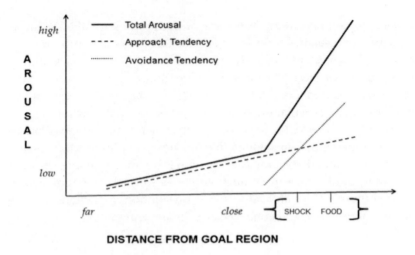

Figure 2. Approach and avoidance of an ambivalently charged region. Miller and Dollard (1941).

This classic understanding of the differences in approach and avoidance behaviour has been supported by research indicating that evaluations of the rewards of approach and evaluations of its dangers (i.e., decisions that would promote avoidance), are processed in different parts of the brain under the control of different sets of neurotransmitters. And that, "acute stress enhances selection of previously rewarding outcomes but impairs avoidance of previously negative outcomes, possibly due to stress-induced changes in dopamine in reward-processing brain regions" (Mather & Lighthall, 2012, p. 36).

The stressful nature of zero-sum decision making was illustrated famously by Brady (1958). Brady placed monkeys in restraining chairs and conditioned them to press a lever. They were given *electric shocks* every twenty seconds unless they pressed the lever during the same time period. This study came to an abrupt halt when many of the monkeys died from *perforated ulcers*. Was the ulcer due to decision making, stress itself, or the pain of shock?

To answer this question, Brady used a yoked *control* monkey. He placed an executive monkey in the restraining chair, which could press the lever to prevent the electric shock. The yoked monkey had no control over the lever, leaving only the executive with control. After twenty-three days of six hours in the stress situations followed by a six-hour rest period, the executive monkeys all died, but the non-deciding monkeys did not. He tested the stomachs of the executives and found that their stomach acidity was greatest during the rest period. When the sympathetic arousal stopped during the rest period, the stomachs of executives were flooded with digestive hormones. This is called a parasympathetic rebound associated with the hypothalamic-pituitary-adrenal axis (HPN axis). In all the variations of the Brady experiments, no yoked control monkey ever developed an ulcer. This suggests that the ulcers were a symptom of the excessive stress induced by having control.

In systems control terms, parasympathetic rebound can be considered a closed-loop transfer function. That is, parasympathetic rebound occurs because the arousing and quiescent functions behave as parts of a closed system. For example, in panic there is no controlling input from neocortical centres sub-serving conceptual processes. This may cause syncopal reactions, and parasympathetic rebound can be a cause of pleasure. For example, the little death or *la petite mort* experienced often after orgasm (cf. Beach & Jordan, 1956).

Without central nervous system input to regulate the body and brain, the two autonomic systems are functionally in a zero-sum relationship. That is, arousal goes very high and then rebounds to a very low level in an otherwise unregulated sequence. Subsequently, many studies have shown that control can reduce feelings of stress (e.g., Langer & Rodin, 1976; Marmot et al., 1979) and improve immune system function (Creswell et al., 2009).

For example, in the classic Glass and Singer studies (1972) some but not all subjects had a button to turn off stressful noise. Subjects in the perceived control condition were asked not to press the button if they could otherwise tolerate the noise. Even though these subjects rarely exercised overt control attempts—that is, they didn't push the button—they did not suffer from post-stress symptoms such as decrements in cognitive functioning. But subjects without a button exposed to the same amount of stressful noise did develop post-stress symptoms. So, perceived control was thought to inoculate the person from stress effects.

Apparently too, the type of attributions people make about why they are enduring stress-causing conditions can inoculate the human from the negative effects of stress (e.g., Foushee et al., 1981; Peterson et al., 1988). We know now that stress and the sympathetic, neuro-hormonal responses to it can both impair (e.g., Lupien et al., 2007) and aid cognitive function:

> Stress effects on prefrontal connectivity may be adaptive in the short term, to the extent that they bias processing in favor of a single, salient stimulus, in a manner that reverses after a period of reduced stress in healthy individuals. When susceptible individuals are exposed to repeated, chronic stress, by contrast, impairments in PFC-mediated flexibility may persist, counteracting short-term benefits in a way that may ultimately contribute to the diverse symptomatology of chronic stress-related neuropsychiatric diseases. (Liston et al., 2009, p. 917)

It is not that having decisional control *per se* causes stress. Rather, I think negative reactions are due to having to make decisions based on few or one single, salient stimulus, and not being able to change the focus of attention. There is a sense of horrifying infinity in that.

Anxiety control

Taken together, research on stress, control, and cognition suggests that if the individual uses concepts to imagine decisions involving more than two options, the concepts can operate as regulators of stress. Concepts contain and explain the meaning of sensations from the body. Sensations that cannot be packaged easily into protoconcepts, or equipartitioned groups of sensory details (e.g., Snyder et al., 2004), cause stress of various levels of intensity. Remember that ideas have structural and process correlates in the brain. The strength of habits to use particular concepts to contain stress varies. One might consider ideas, including old habits and new creations, as organs of the body or organelles. The concepts built in neocortical brain regions operate to somehow inhibit or regulate the actions of the subcortical brain and the entire body.

In the Glass and Singer (1972) noise experiments, we can assume that the subjects who chose not to press the button to turn off noise had to be using some concepts that let them contain stressful sensations. This, in turn, prevented post-noise effects such as impaired cognitive functioning. These concepts may have involved ideas of conforming with authority, and the feelings of security that conformity produces.

The moral, conforming subjects likely transformed the endurance of otherwise meaningless, painful sensations into meaningful sensations or feelings of pride. The feelings were indicators of their competence to be good citizens who did what the authoritative experimenter asked of them (see Milgram, 1963). Apparently, the nature of one's beliefs, especially about religion, which one applies to make meaning of stressful sensations, can work either to mitigate or intensify post-traumatic stress disorders (e.g., Fink, 2010; Lior et al., 2010; Oren & Possick, 2010).

Generally, the person is best able to cope with stressors if regulation of the autonomic nervous system can be influenced by the central nervous system, especially the semantic concepts residing in the neocortex. It is possible and, from an evolutionary perspective, very desirable in emergencies to be competent to perform both complex cognitive processing, for example, thinking of an escape plan, and simple, brutish tasks that may be instrumental in executing plans, for example, smashing down a locked door (see Bernstein, 2011, Chapter Four). But usually, high sympathetic arousal tends to promote high performance on simple tasks and reduce performance on complex tasks. From a statistical point of view, the best cognitive functioning occurs in moderate arousal states (Figure 3). This is the classic finding that arousal

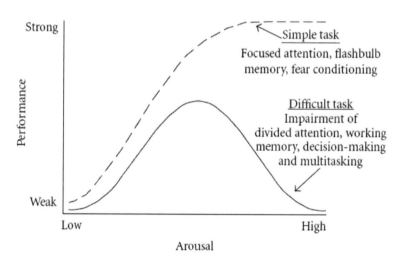

Figure 3. Cognitive competence and sympathetic arousal. Yerkes–Dodson law (From Diamond et al., 2007).

and performance of complex tasks are related in an inverted U curve (Yerkes & Dodson, 1908).

Modern neurobiology findings are consistent with the Yerkes–Dodson law. For example, there is a lawful relationship between stress hormones levels (glucocorticoids) and human memory performance paralleling the inverted U. Long-term potentiation, the process of forming long-term memories, is optimal when glucocorticoid levels are mildly elevated. But significant decreases of memory are observed both at low glucocorticoid levels, for example, due to adrenalectomy, and at high levels induced by exogenous glucocorticoid administration (see Lupien et al., 2007).

CHAPTER SIX

Recapitulation of axiomatic assumptions and their connections

Of course, I should be ashamed to base my thinking on so many kinds of ideas from all over the place. Nevertheless, we need about ten sorts of axiomatic assumptions from biology and psychology for this current project. Such general axioms can help integrate concepts from the sub-fields that focus on particular parts of the mind–brain system such as psychopharmacology (e.g., amphetamines change how adrenergic neurotransmitters are processed at the synapse) and psychoanalysis, (e.g., signal anxiety derives from unresolved conflicts).

The first nine ideas below have been described in this book so far. Most have been treated more extensively in Bernstein (2011). I derive the tenth idea from *The Polyvagal Theory* (Porges, 2011). I think each is a generally valid concept about mind and body.

1. The brain's primary function is to make decisions. All decisions, whether they involve attempts to regulate visceral functions, conceptual processes, or overt behaviour, can be thought to involve cybernetic, test-operate-test-exit processes (e.g., Carver & Scheier, 1981; Miller, 1980; Wiener, 1948). Having a single, general concept that subsumes all sorts of decision making (somatic and psychic) obviates the so-called hard problem. That is, the assumption that

mental and physical processes in the body are of such a different nature, that one can never integrate mind–brain theories.[1]

2. Decisions can be based on valid concepts concerning how things work in the world. For example, if one's self-concept included the attribute "can fly", one might make poor decisions when in high places. Learning and using the most valid concepts to interpret the meaning of sensory data and other concepts is the most pleasurable feeling. Conceptual discovery is motivated by more or less urgent curiosity. If one's life doesn't depend on making a decision to answer a particular question, thinking is play. Thinking is using concepts to contain and explain raw sensory data. The result of the explained sensation is a feeling. The more valid the concept used, the better the feeling. Thinking is intimately involved with sensation. It is sensual. Thinking valid thoughts is an intrinsic pleasure, and using valid concepts as instruments to obtain other pleasures is extrinsically rewarding (cf., Ryan & Deci, 2000). The truest concepts lead to the best decisions and, in turn, to overt success in the social worlds of love and work. A proximal cause of pleasurable feelings is particular combinations of neurotransmitters interacting dynamically in the brain.

3. Decisions to approach pleasure and to avoid pain are made more or less competently, by some combinations of sympathetic, parasympathetic, endocrine, subcortical, and neocortical control systems. Raw sensory data can activate subcortical processes that can set in motion fixed actions patterns of overt behaviour (e.g., Tinbergen, 1951). Also, sense data reaching neocortical areas can stimulate habitual use of old concepts to explain sense data and sometimes new concepts may be formed and used. Such neocortical processing may or may not cause overt behaviour. Apparently, information in the form of electric and chemical signals travels regularly between body, brainstem, limbic structures, and neocortex (see Figure 1 in this book from Panksepp & Wright, 2012).

4. The multiply determined approach and avoidance processes tend to operate in two distinct (asymmetrical) ways in time and in space, in all species of animals (see Figure 2 in this book from Miller & Dollard, 1941). The best decisions regarding approach and avoidance are based on the most valid concepts of how the self and the world work. ("You mean I can't jump over that eight-foot wall? I will have

to go around, I guess.") Valid concepts permit one to locate sensory objects accurately and determine their meaning. The concepts are used to decide whether sense data, delivered to the brain via exteroception or interoception, indicate that one should expect pain and/or pleasure from approaching or avoiding a thing in the external world, or a feeling or thought in one's own body or mind.

5. Based on pleasure and pain expectations, the individual may respond to physical, social and intrapsychic objects with avoidance and/or approach operations.

- Overt physical avoidance may involve fleeing, crouching, or freezing.
- Overt physical approach can include grooming, play, sex, fighting, or cooperation.
- Mental avoidances or psychological defences are attempts to reduce anxiety caused by particular sensations, concepts or feelings. The more pathological defences tend to support unrealistic wishes to eliminate anxiety completely or perfectly. Recognised defences include: projection, dissociation, compromise formations, obsessive thinking, and so on.
- Mental approach involves fewer defences against sensations coming from inside and outside the body. Approaching involves free thinking, relatively unconstrained by anxiety-causing conflicts (e.g., Bernstein, 2001; Lewin, 1936). Low anxiety promotes competent thinking by lowering defensive barriers to (1) shifting of attentional focus between sense data from extero- and interoceptors, feelings, and semantic concepts; (2) searching memory; (3) playing imaginatively with concepts and feelings. This can take the form of thought experiments designed to make valid inferences about the causes of a sensation, thought, or feeling. The causal arrow also goes the other way: competence in shifting attentional focus, searching memory, and imagination can reduce anxiety.

6. The general, higher-order learning and decision-making competencies of the brain involve the use of semantic concepts located in the neocortex. These operations can be enlisted by subcortical parts of brain to help in decision making (e.g., Bernstein, 2011, p. 44; Panksepp, 1998, p. 166). This is consistent with the assumption that learning, or SEEKING, is the highest order, most general, valid characterisation of the brain's function.

7. The need and desire to approach learning are supported by the nervous system's automatic tendency—spreading activation—to lower the activation thresholds of neuronal elements representing concepts that are proximal in time, space, or semantic meaning to recently activated or primed concepts. That is, the brain is always automatically likely to make connections between related concepts. This tendency is regulated dynamically by other opposing or inhibiting brain and mind processes. Semantic priming effects, discovered thirty-two years after Freud's death, validated his ideas about the importance of free association for understanding mental dynamics (see Barratt, 2013).

8. Frustration of goal attainment causes tension, and tension will persist if goals are unattained (e.g., Lewin, 1936). Repeated attempts to achieve completion will be made in and out of awareness (e.g., Zagarnik, 1927). If attempts to reduce tension are incompetent, aggression may ensue (Dollard et al., 1939). Processing of information about whether to approach or avoid a particular goal object will repeat in brain and mind until a concept is developed and used to resolve the conflict.

9. High sympathetic arousal improves performance of simple overt behaviours, but can disrupt the performance of more complex physical and cognitive tasks (See Figure 3 in this book from Yerkes & Dodson, 1908). Specifically, there is a curvilinear relationship between levels of adrenergic neurotransmitters and glucocorticoids and mental competence. Mental competence varies not-monotonically with arousal, but in a more complex fashion. Yerkes–Dodson is a statistically valid law. But for some people in some arousing situations, cognitive competence may change more linearly than curvilinearly, that is, it is better at higher arousal levels. Similarly, the model of asymmetries in approach-avoidance dynamics is valid statistically (see Figure 2 in this book from Miller & Dodson, 1941). For example, stimulants often improve the cognitive performance of people with attention deficient disorders and some dementias, presumably by raising levels of norepinephrine and dopamine in the brain to more normal, moderate levels (e.g., Lupien et al., 2007).

Countless biological, psychological, and social variables affect the relationships between arousal and performance and between approach and avoidance tendencies. We have to add new variables to our models to predict and explain more of the variation in mind–brain phenomena. It may help to think of axiomatic psychobiological laws such as Yerkes–Dodson, as behavioural phenotypes that can be caused by different, underlying brain–mind operational states or genotypes (see Chapter Nine, Figure 4).

10. The polyvagal theory (Porges, 2011) is consistent with the idea that parasympathetic tone promotes conceptual competence. Many variables affect mentation in addition to sympathetic arousal levels. Norepinephrine, dopamine, glutamate, and glucocorticoids do not act in a closed, sympathetic system. Rather, they operate in the context of the parasympathetic system, the neocortex, the rest of the brain and body, and the external social and physical environments. Arousal levels are affected by "inhibitory neurotransmitters"; immobilisation instincts; cardiovascular variables; learned habits to activate more or less valid explanations (attributions) for sense data coming from exteroceptors (e.g., eyes) and interoceptors (e.g., autonomic afferents); social conditions, and many other variables.

Linking assumptions

If the assumptions above are valid, we can go on to ask how these lawful relationships might relate (lawfully) to each other. As a start, it helps to think of approach motives as more or less equivalent to the desire to learn about objects in the external world, the body, and the mind (Bernstein, 2011). Panksepp's idea of SEEKING is most easily understood as representing the most important, overarching approach motive of the person. That is, to seek knowledge of how the world works. The other affects are enacted via specific, subcortical structures that all use the general problem-solving competencies in the neocortical learning centres. Developing general valid concepts, regardless of the sort of sensory data the concepts explain, can be intrinsically pleasurable, and instrumental in obtaining extrinsic pleasures such as food, sex, money, and prestige (e.g., Benabou & Tirole, 2003; Deci, 1975).

Approach motives involve curiosity. Somehow, the unknown is incentivising. Mystery draws us to understand it. Animals approach slowly and steadily objects and areas they want to learn about. Approach motives are activated far from objects of curiosity (Figure 3). One is unlikely to be harmed or killed at a good distance from unknown objects that might prove dangerous. Approach involves collecting raw sensory data about objects and then attempting to devise valid concepts to explain the data.

Vision is a good sensory modality for the curious because it can collect data at a distance. And semantic concepts are mostly populated by visual attributes. Words are used for advanced information processing. Sensory data from all modalities are most likely coded as integers (e.g., Snyder et al., 2004; Snyder & Mitchell, 1999) and some remaining fractions. This makes raw data from all the specific senses amenable to the same general conceptual processing operations and is consistent with the idea that one can have synesthetic experiences (see Chapter Two).[2]

Avoidance motives work to help us avoid pain and injury. They are activated closer to objects of curiosity and rise more quickly in intensity than approach motives (see Figure 3). This helps us react fast in emergencies. "Now that I have come closer to inspect this thing, I see that it is a poisonous snake (or a land mine). Better back up fast." Ideally, in safe environments, approach motives dominate more of the person's conscious experience and overt behaviour than avoidance motives. Compared to approach operations, avoidance tendencies are more associated with unpleasant sensations, concepts and feelings like anxiety and dread. All animal species have conserved the temporal, spatial, and energetic asymmetries of the pleasure-approach and pain-avoidance systems (e.g., Rind et al., 2008).

In mental illness, inability to resolve approach and avoidance conflicts causes conscious and unconscious repetitive, non-productive, energy-draining churning of information. This is often accompanied by feelings of anxiety, and thoughts of having violated moral standards, that is, guilt. Incompetence in making valid decisions to resolve conflict inhibits the ability to know the difference between what is good or acceptable and what is dangerous. Anxious people often confuse the perfect with the good. Hence, they have problems living life as a whole, true experience. Instead, they may have a *false-self personality* (Winnicott, 1960b) and experience sensations tentatively, in an "as if" manner.

Competent conceptual processing tends to involve moderate levels of arousal (Figure 3). One can be overwhelmed by curiosity, but it is experienced typically as a moderately intense, pleasant feeling. An historical tendency to concentrate on the sympathetic, arousing elements of the autonomic nervous system puts us at a disadvantage when trying to understand the pleasures of thought. Seeing a bear can cause freezing, or arousing, energy demanding, emergency fleeing, or fighting. This is not usually experienced as too pleasurable. Painting a picture of a bear or writing a story about one would be more fun for most people. That is, playing with the idea of a bear is usually more pleasurable than being confronted by a proximally threatening, real bear.

Regardless of whether one likes to get up close to a bear to kill or photograph it, or would prefer only to read about bears in books, being close to a real bear will cause high sympathetic arousal in most people. Visual, auditory, and olfactory sense data about the bear (sensory releasers), coming from an actual bear or a concept of a bear, will work to lower the threshold for activating proximal neuronal and neuromuscular elements in the "avoid bear meaning system". This potentiates fix action responses, and potentially novel responses to the situation. The word "bear" will prime recognition of related attributes of the concept bear (e.g., fangs, claws). And, to a milder extent than would a material bear, the word will prime instinctive actions that are unlikely to be expressed in overt behaviour.

The varied reactions people have to risk in general can be explained by combining differently a large number of neurochemical and cognitive factors. That one person might find closeness to bears pleasurable or exciting, and another reacts with anxiety or horror, is certainly plausible given the number of multiple neurochemical changes caused by such an encounter. In other words, raw sensations received by exteroceptors may give one more of a thrill than merely thinking about a bear.[3] Endogenous chemical responses to looming risks include adrenergic agonists, glutamate, vasopressin, glucocorticoids, endorphins, and many more.

Cognition, feeling and play

In any case, hunting animals today is done mostly as a form of play. Play hunting and more overt serious hunting can be intrinsically motivating (e.g., Panksepp, 1998; Porges, 2011). In play, instinctive responses, plus old and newly learned habits of mind and body, are practised in a low-risk situation. Pain avoidance thoughts, feelings, and behaviours are not especially needed, and the pleasures of approach can dominate.

Child's play is the model for the more sophisticated work of adults, such as scientific research, theory making, and art.

Learning self- and non-self-concepts, and when and how to use them, occurs over development and involves play. These concepts are involved in producing expectations of pleasure and pain that work to inhibit full enactment of overt aggressive and sexual fixed action patterns. That is, murder, rape, cannibalism, and other taboo behaviours are inhibited by concepts in most social situations and, by definition, in play. Social taboos that form part of the foundation of the mind are played out in theatre and the other arts (e.g., Freud, 1912). This allows for conceptual resolution of conflicts that might otherwise result in material injury to one's own or others' bodies and brains.

Play is especially prevalent and pleasurable in humans in the latency period, which begins at about six years of age and ends with puberty. If early caretakers have been good enough, the child has enough concepts with which to play (e.g., Winnicott, 1975). Since a child's play is not too much driven by hormones or full exposure to serious risk, even flimsy, essentially fanciful ideas are durable enough to allow her to participate in games. The stupidest kid in the gang may play the role of general in a war game, because choosing the wrong leaders in play usually has less gruesome consequences than in real war.

Empathy and social behaviour

Role taking and perspective taking are types of cognitive empathy. As such, they involve neocortical inferential processes including making causal attributions. In general, one can think of cognitive types of empathy like perspective taking as distinguishable from responses to others involving mostly feelings (e.g., Davis, 1983, 1994). The reflex-like tendency to adopt the posture of others and respond to them is mediated, in part, by mirror neurons (e.g., Gallesse, 2001) and autonomic connections to the facial muscles (e.g., Ekman, 1973; Lanzetta & Orr, 1986). That is, the body and subcortical parts of the brain play an important role in empathic feeling.

But the inferential thinking involved in cognitive empathy is a more neocortical affair. We have demonstrated that a cognitive habit to adopt another's perspective (e.g., trying to look at things from the other's point of view) increases accuracy in observers' inferences of what others think about themselves. But a tendency to experience tender concerned feelings about another's pain does not seem to increase accuracy about the other person's semantic self-concepts (Bernstein & Davis, 1982).

The way role taking promotes play was explicated convincingly by the social psychologist George Herbert Mead in *Mind, Self and Society* (1934). Social organisations can be thought of as systems of roles in which expectations are sent from the occupier of one role to one playing another role in the system (Katz & Kahn, 1973). Expectations of oneself and others stimulate and regulate overt behaviours.

Violation of social taboos by overt behaviour or merely antisocial thoughts, generate conscious and unconscious expectations of severe punishment and feelings of talion dread. Self-concept systems rest upon these sorts of grave social responsibilities. In other words, they are at the bottom of the top of the neocortical mind. The energy and neural circuitry developed over evolution to support instinctual action is borrowed to support all the cultural behaviour of people. And, of course, the same systems can be co-opted in defence against the stress and anxiety stimulated by the same underlying instinctual tendencies. The psychoanalytic term sublimation describes the more creative, social effects of co-opting the neural systems and the body's energies (e.g., Freud, 1930).

Notes

1. The word cybernetics was used by Plato in *Alcibiades* to refer to the study of self-governance. Remember, the hard problem for dual aspect monism is that material and mental phenomena are essentially different and, hence, not explainable by a single set of natural laws. The hard problem goes away if we assume with Plato that (a) universal forms or concepts underlie all of manifest reality; and (b) that all forms of auto- or self-control involve universal processes of information processing, decision making and cybernetics (e.g., Palensky, 2008).

2. Theoretically, we could base our thinking more on auditory data, which can be collected at great distances too. Then we would be more dependent on sound, as are dolphins (e.g., White, 2007). Olfaction is also a distance sense. But like audition, most people have fewer concepts to differentiate and integrate olfactory sensations than they have to interpret visual sensations. There are more semantic concepts (words) for things seen, than for things smelled, tasted, or sat on.

3. Sports involving killing a primitive creature with a modern weapon are so unfair on the face of it that they must involve some suppression or distortion of prosocial, empathic concepts in order to be experienced as pleasurable. Primitive, less technically sophisticated hunters may have had more empathic feeling for their prey than their modern counterparts. With less powerful weapons, one needs to get closer to a thing to kill it. This involves having lots of raw sensory data about one's prey that is contained in accurate concepts, which in turn increase the accuracy of predicting the prey's behaviour in order to not only kill it, but avoid being killed oneself. One comes to like sensory objects with which one is familiar (*The Mere Exposure Effect*, Zajonc, 1968, 2001). Primitive hunters' knowledge of and feelings for their prey were deep and intense. For example, American Plains Indians worshipped as a god the buffalo they killed and ate.

PART II

CHAPTER SEVEN

Parasympathetic systems and affect theory

Traditionally, the medical student learned that the parasympathetic nervous system promotes the somatic functions of an old man, sleeping after eating dinner. Vegetative functions of digestion, restoration, and tissue building were seen as the province of the parasympathetic system. A deeper, more general characterisation of the function of the parasympathetic system is that it promotes the digestion or processing of information in order to form concepts. Parasympathetic processes are centrally involved in making meaning, which is the focus of depth psychology (e.g., Brenner, 2006).

Porges (e.g., 2011) has helped illuminate part of the complex role played by the system of vagal nerves in the overall regulation of the individual's social behaviour, and arousal levels affect cognitive competence (see Figure 4). But terms such as cognition or concept are used rarely by Porges. He uses the term *social engagement system* for what gets regulated by myelinated vagal nerves from the brainstem's nucleus ambiguus (NA). Social engagement might be operationalised in terms of overt muscle movements, especially of the face. It is a term more amenable to behaviourism and affect theories than to cognitive psychology or psychoanalysis.

Porges' social engagement system does not include explicitly neocortical information processing such as social cognition (e.g., Fiske & Taylor, 2008). Subjective experiences of semantic, causal concepts (attributions) function to give meaning to sensations and, in turn, feeling, other concepts, and overt behaviours including social behaviours are generated. Sensations, concepts, and feelings are the most important proximal causes of overt behaviour (Bernstein, 2011).

Porges points to "the paradigm building research of Ainsworth" (Porges, 2011, p. 188) regarding infant responses to separation (e.g., Ainsworth et al., 1972). He notes that Ainsworth relied, in part, on affect regulation theorists such as Bowlby (e.g., 1969). But affect theory became problematic for Porges when it tried to include subjective reports as useful data.

> Tomkins (1962, 1963) developed a theory of affect that emphasized the importance of the face not only as a structure of communication but also as a structure of self-feedback. Following Tompkins, Ekman (1978) and Izard (1979) developed detailed coding systems for facial affect and have used these methods to study individual differences, developmental shifts, and the cross-cultural consistency of human facial expression ... *However, they later used subjective reports to label these facial expressions.* (Porges, 2011, p. 163, italics added)

For 80 years social scientists have made objective measures of subjects' overt behaviours including their "self-reporting behaviour". People are asked, for example to rate how anxious or happy or sad they feel by choosing a number ranging from 0 (not at all sad) to 4 (very sad). These types of measures (e.g., Likert, 1932) are reliable and they have face, predictive, and discriminant validity. There is no reason at all to imagine that these sorts of operationalisations are inferior to other sorts of measures such as those used by biologists to quantify somatic variables like heart rate or blood pressure.

Of course, a person may report that they don't smoke pot, for example, but engage in pot-smoking behaviour. This does not make the verbal report meaningless. It merely points out that public utterances and even private thoughts are not always in line with overt, publicly discernable behaviour. If they were, there would be no need for cognitive psychology, affect theories, or psychoanalysis. Behaviourism would suffice. Self-report measures, like most scientific variables, represent a composite of causal influences that can be differentiated reliably and objectively by multivariate statistical methods (e.g., Bernstein, 1984; Bernstein et al., 1979; Bernstein & Burke, 1989).

In any case, Porges' polyvagal theory is an important contribution to neuroscience. Working with human infants, he found that myelination of particular vagus nerves was incomplete until late in gestation. Compared to babies born after a full nine-month term, infants born prematurely have greater difficulty regulating bodily movements, including heart rate (e.g., Larson & Porges, 1982; Porges, 1983).

Infants, like animals, have relatively few semantic concepts in their brains that might provide a basis for social communication of subjective states of mind. This makes infants and animals ideal subjects for behaviourist and affect theorists. Before vagal tracts to the heart originating in the brainstem NA become myelinated, there is inadequate braking of the heart's intrinsically fast electrical rhythms, and other problems with somatic control. This is why premature infants must be kept in incubators that tightly control environmental stressors (e.g., temperature, sound, light). The infant will be incompetent in auto-regulating somatic functions until vagal myelination increases.

The polyvagal theory is based on the differentiation of the phylogenetically older, vegetative parts of the vagal system from the newer parts. The older vagal nerves originate in the brainstem nucleus tractus solitaries (NTS), they are unmyelinated, and they function, in part, to activate the old reptilian instinct to freeze or become immobile in response to stress or threat. Phylogenetically newer vagal nerves originate in the brainstem NA, they are myelinated, and they function, in part, to regulate the action of the heart. In particular, myelinated vagal efferents from the NA can inhibit the intrinsically rapid electrical pacemaker of the heart (sinoatrial node), promoting parasympathetic tone and social engagement. Porges' primary measure of parasympathetic tone is respiratory sinus arrhythmia (RSA).

> RSA is a naturally occurring rhythm in the heart rate pattern that oscillates at approximately the frequency of spontaneous breathing ... By quantifying RSA and the relation between RSA and heart rate during various challenges, it is possible to measure the dynamic regulation of the myelinated vagal brake to study the responses of

infants and young children to people and to objects. (Porges, 2011, p. 122)

A wide range of RSA indicates that the myelinated vagal tracts from the nucleus ambiguus to the heart can produce a large array of cardiac arousal levels via parasympathetic braking and a large number of subtle differences in somatic arousal intensity and quality. Porges assumes rightly that competent control of these states promotes social engagement competence. Inability to control the parasympathetic brake causes problems.

A lack of polyvagal tone in the heart is related to poor regulation of movements including facial expressions, causing dysregulation of affect and social engagement. According to Porges, the full extent of the social engagement system of the brain includes cranial nerves V (trigeminal), VII (facial), IX (glossopharyngeal), X (vagus), and XI (spinal accessory). These nerves, of course, are critical for controlling muscular movements in the face and speech, the affect-making areas. Keeping with the affect theory melody, three of the five nerves in Porges' social engagement system derive from the brainstem (VII, IX, and X).

But we know that speech making neurons have close ties to neocortical, association regions involved in using semantic concepts to think (e.g., Schwartz et al., 2009).

> The cerebral cortex is the chief controlling entity of the human central nervous system ... . The primary fields of the neocortex are the point of departure of neocortical evolution and, as such, they command the most space in the cerebral cortex of lower mammals and early primates ... With growing distance from the primary fields and increasing proximity to the allocortex [hippocampal-entorhinal areas], the association areas of the neocortex and anterior mesocortex exhibit greater features of structural immaturity ... . Myelination represents the final step in brain maturation. (Braak & Braak, 1996, p. 197)

Porges (2011) reports a study in which subjects were made anxious by frightening videos. Compared to normal subjects, those diagnosed with borderline personality disorder or who had histories of childhood abuse were less able to quickly re-establish parasympathetic tone (high

RSA range) after withdrawal of the frightening stimuli. The obvious implications of such a study are that mental health might be improved by increasing a person's ability to control RSA or, more generally, heart rate variability (HRV).

In fact, it has been demonstrated that RSA can be influenced by providing a person with data about his contemporaneous RSA range (e.g., Zucker et al., 2009). Subjects are shown a visual representation of RSA (biofeedback) and instructed to time their breathing to match the oscillations of the visual representation of RSA range. This procedure works to expand RSA range and alter other heart rate variables. Increased RSA range was associated with decreased PTSD symptomology in Zucker, et al., (2009). Neuropsychoanalysis suggests that doing research to correlate, at least in time, measures of somatic variables with measures of subjective experience of normal and pathological thought and feeling, is the way to build a depth psychology.

Affect concepts as barriers to theoretical integration

Overt behaviour, including social behaviour is regulated proximally by social cognition. Autonomic influences and subcortical information processing provide distal pre-conditions for variously competent thought and feeling based in the neocortex. Having and using valid concepts consciously and unconsciously works to generate accurate predictions of pain and pleasure likely to ensue when approaching objects in the world and the mind. The accuracy of predictions determines the competence of the person's overt behaviour in the physical and social worlds.

These sorts of assumptions are part of the growing consensus in neuroscience depicted in Chapter Four, Figure 1. But affect theory biopsychologists tend not to discuss explicitly cognitive dynamics. Psychobiological affect theories do not quite work to differentiate adequately, and integrate convincingly, central concepts from psychology concerning sensation, feeling, cognition, overt behaviour, and motivation.

An example of the problem comes from a recent *Nature Reviews* paper by Ulrich-Lai and Herman (2009) called "Neural regulation of endocrine and autonomic stress responses". They indicate implicitly that there are commonalities between somatic and mental decision making. (We have assumed here that all decision-making systems use universal cybernetic processes like TOTE.) But Ulrich-Lai and Herman (2009) don't quite go all the way in this regard. Note how the word decisions is adorned with quotation marks.

> The vast majority of 'decisions' regarding the initiation of physiological stress responses seem to be made at the level of limbic structures, which communicate information to subcortical sites positioned to interface with ongoing homeostatic feedback ...
> (Ulrich-Lai & Herman, 2009, p. 406)

I would rather say that initial aspects of the processing of raw sensory information in the limbic system and other subcortical areas could lead to decisions to initiate stress responses. Subsequent processing of stress-related information can occur in the neocortex where semantic concepts are activated more or less habitually.[1] Psychobiologists working mostly with small mammals in an affect theory tradition, focus on subcortical processes. Accordingly, they locate the critical barrier to theoretical advance as that between autonomic processes (ANS) and those of the hippocampal-pituitary-adrenal axis (HPN).

> Future growth of the stress physiology field will need to include more work that bridges the proverbial HPA versus ANS divide, thereby providing a more complete picture of how an individual learns to anticipate and otherwise cope with stress. Whereas the effector circuits that control stress are probably hard-wired, *the overall weighting of information is subject to considerable individual variation*. It is likely that dysfunctions of information processing across these circuits, resulting from environmental adversity and/or genetic factors, lie at the root of maladaptive stress reactions that can culminate in affective disease (for example, depression and post-traumatic stress disorder) and physical infirmities.
> (Ulrich-Lai & Herman, 2009, p. 406, italics added)

The more critical divide, at least for general mind–brain theory, is between the neocortex and everything else in the brain and body. But the role of advanced conceptual processes in the neocortex is only hinted at by these authors. Such processes are referred to obliquely as "subject to considerable individual variation". In contrast, some physiologists have more openly considered psychological causes and effects of stress. For example,

> In many areas of potential disease significance, there exist emerging bodies of literature that relate psychological parameters to relevant physiologic processes and elucidate the neuroendocrine mechanisms that mediate these relationships. In a sense, this work extends to the primary organ systems of the body our growing understanding of the physiology of "stress"—where stress is now also construed more broadly to include related personality and socio-environmental factors pertinent to individual adaptation ... It is in this endeavor to discover what pathophysiologies may lie within the psychosocial domain, moreover, that we believe behavioral physiology ultimately becomes behavioral and psychosomatic medicine. (Manuck et al., 1995, pp. 281–282)

I think the reluctance to address cognition explicitly, and the related tendency to consider them individual differences not amenable to nomothetic scientific inquiry, is due in part to the sort of spiritual barriers or primitive superstitions against the explicit expression of important truths described in Chapter Two. Such superstitions are somehow embedded implicitly in the historical compromise formations of affect theories. One must not say these things out loud. Perhaps the theorist should "knock on wood" when engaged in writing.

Of course, not all compromised thinking is due to defensive motivations. To assume so would be to repeat a bad psychoanalytic habit of attributing almost every aspect of human thought, feeling, and behaviour to motivational causes. Rather, the most important cause of not knowing the truth is unmotivated ignorance. In other words, the person using a compromise formation to interpret reality usually has just never learned some relevant valid concepts that would help her make more competent conflict-resolution decisions. Some valid concepts may be known by science but unknown to any particular individual, perhaps because she didn't go to school. And, of course, much of what is true about nature is not known by anyone.

In any case, compromise affect assumptions lead to limiting the scope of responses to stress to a social engagement system (Porges, 2011). The term works to marginalise consideration of the most important proximal causes of social engagement—social cognition.

Affect concepts prevent Panksepp from describing SEEKING as a motive or desire. Instead it is labelled as "the most general affect" (Panksepp & Wright, 2012). In my view, Panksepp's SEEKING is the motive to approach the learning of valid concepts because it leads to pleasurable feelings.

At all levels of body, mind, and society, people are more or less intensely looking for valid semantic concepts or truths about how the self and world operate. The seeking of truth is driven largely by expectations of experiencing highly rewarding feelings that come with deep, valid understanding of sensory data and other valid concepts. Formal scientists might resist characterising the person as motivated primarily to know the truth because it might lead to being labelled religious or unscientific.

Many writers are converging on mind and brain questions at once. Naturally people bring their own funds of knowledge and viewpoints. This project is gigantic, greater than any other prior scientific tasks. By definition, collaborations across traditional sub-field boundaries are required to create integrative theory. Hopefully it doesn't seem too batty to mention that collaboration can be fun, productive, and meaningful on many personal and scientific levels.

Note

1. All information processing might be considered stress related. Snyder has argued that all sensory information is pre-processed into groups of equal numbers of objects (e.g., Snyder & Mitchell, 1999; Snyder et al., 2004; Snyder, 2009). This is called equipartioning and it happens automatically, somewhere outside the neocortex (and maybe something like it happens in the neocortex too). I have assumed that there is no need to think if all sensory data can be neatly contained in some protoconceptual structure such as "groups with equal numbers of items in them" (Bernstein, 2011). In such a case, the peripheral parts of the nervous system and the subcortical parts of the brain have worked completely to reduce stress. If some sensory attributes cannot be contained by a protoconcept, that is, if something is left over, a semantic concept proper is needed.

    Snyder argues that unlike most people, autistic savants have awareness of very raw sense data at the initial stages of information processing including equipartitioning. But they have problems using or creating semantic concepts to contain raw sensations. If sensory items can't be partitioned into equal numbered groups I think a sort of irritation occurs in the person. Because of their privileged access to minimally processed sensory data, autists are more sensitive to and, thereby, more stressed by "left over sense data" than are non-autists.

I assume that all stress can be defined as a reaction to approach-avoidance conflict. The competence to learn and use concepts evolved to solve conflicts that the part of the body below the neocortex could not solve. For any individual at any one time, if there is no conflict, there is no higher-order thinking. Why waste the energy? Since no person or thing is completely good or completely bad, being conscious means to be bothered, to at least a minimal degree, by conflict (cf., *Cognitive Dissonance Theory* by Festinger, 1957).

CHAPTER EIGHT

Autonomic nervous systems I: stress and anxiety

Undeterred, if not emboldened, by my own ignorance and superstitions, I have diagnosed and treated thousands of people seeking help for psychological problems. My clinical experience, and no doubt that of others, suggests that many functional psychopathologies represent a condition in which sympathetic arousal systems are chronically over-excited. This may be a result of attempts to compensate for chronic parasympathetic over-braking. In other words, many patients come in with one foot pushing hard on the sympathetic accelerator and the other pushing hard on the parasympathetic brake.

Using the vagus only as a hard, chronic brake means it cannot realise its functional potential to dynamically control sympathetic arousal. The brain's competence is limited by strong mental habits to operate the brake in a restricted, static manner. I assume, like Freud (1923), that the chronically anxious person is engaged constantly in a largely unconscious, exhausting effort to control himself. He wants to approach something he expects will bring him pleasure such as a person, a place, or an idea in mind. At the same time, he expects that obtaining the pleasure puts him at risk of some terrible pain or punishment.

Guilt about masturbation is universal, at least at certain stages of development. "Masturbation represents the executive agency to the whole of infantile sexuality and is, therefore, able to take over the sense of guilt attaching to it." (Freud, 1905, p. 189) The feelings of guilt and shame are correlates of parasympathetic braking (e.g., Siegel, 2012).

An individual's concepts about reality, the belief system sitting in the neocortex, will mostly conform to the normative belief system of the culture the person lived in during youth. An enormous effort is made by society to train individuals to live in social groups. People were once wild animals and each infant is born a wild animal. Parents and other social authorities instil strong expectations of pain in most citizens should they have immoral, illegal, or even non-fashionable ideas, or worse, act on such ideas. Some government authorities continue to organise public whipping, stoning, and execution of law breakers, witches, minority group members, and just about any disapproved-of individual.

In addition to the pain of guilt feelings, cultures use anticipated pleasures as means of influence. There are rewards of status and money for those who have sublimated or co-opted biological instincts into economically useful personal and social habits. Importantly, the techniques of animal trainers have shifted over time to employ pleasurable rewards rather than painful punishments to shape animal behaviours (e.g., Shapiro et al., 2003). Such methods have been shown to be much more effective and efficient, not to mention less horrifying, than the older forms of training.[1] But social agents and the moral systems of most individuals still use pain and fear to excessive degrees to stimulate motives to avoid sinful pleasures.

Some degree of stress is generated by decision making. All decisions involve conflict at some levels since they involve giving up the positive aspects of forgone options. One may experience the unpleasant arousal of cognitive dissonance (Festinger, 1957). From my perspective, cognitive dissonance is a form of anxiety. I use the term anxiety to refer to a feeling caused by holding a low expectation of being able to make an effective stress-reducing decision or being able to enact it. The best decisions are based on valid concepts of reality or nature. The worst decisions are based on under- or over-estimations of the number of degrees of decisional freedom that exist in nature for one's self.

Sometimes, especially when deciding between overt motor behaviours, we may only have two options. For example, "I could say something to Joe or say nothing." But activity in the world of imagination and play with ideas is less constrained than activity in the three-dimensional world. One can imagine things like flying that are impossible for the unaided body. But since thinking is a function of a bodily organ, perhaps this is not exactly a true statement. More exactly, it just takes more time and energy to realise concepts in the overt, material world than it does to think them.

Anxiety is only an illness if the person imagines that a solvable problem is unsolvable or if they perceive a looming threat to health or wealth where none really exists. The most graphic examples I have seen of anxiety caused by an assumption of mutually exclusive decision options have come from male homosexuals who were committed to religions that they believed prohibited homosexuality. Holding strong, unshakable, religious convictions in such situations seems so absurd in a way that one tends to assume that the person is getting some secondary gain, such as sexual pleasure from masochistic fantasies.

In social psychology, cybernetic terms have been used to characterise anxiety. That is, anxiety or a generally unpleasant feeling is correlated in time with recognition or awareness of a discrepancy between some real condition of the self and some ideal self-standard (Duval & Wicklund, 1972). For example, one experiences an unpleasant state when aware that one's self-concept regarding current reality contains the attribute: "I smoke four cigarettes a day", and one's self-concepts regarding what one would like to do, one's aspirations (or, ego ideal) contain the standard, "I should smoke no more than one cigarette per day". Moral standards regulating thought, feeling, and overt behaviour are learned early on, and form an important part of the foundation of the person's self-concepts. Self-concepts define who we are and what we will do and will not do to reach our aspirations.

Stress, anxiety and exhaustion result from being sympathetically driven to gain ones favorite pleasures; while simultaneously being inhibited or "braked" by some agency that is "sensitive" to the idea of being punished for appetitive success, that is, getting what one wants. As we know, the agencies in brain and mind that regulate tendencies to approach pleasure are distinct from those in charge of avoiding pain (see Figure 3). In the body, the sympathetic system drives and controls urgently sought pleasures such as drinking, eating and sex. The parasympathetic system is involved with more or less dynamic braking of sympathetic impulses.

The sympathetic nervous system is more arranged to make simple binary, go, no-go decisions. The newer, myelinated parts of the parasympathetic vagal system are seemingly more involved in making complex decisions involving many criteria. The brainstem nucleus ambiguus, served by myelinated nerve cells, is anatomically connected to the white matter of the brain which interconnects neocortical regions with each other. The parasympathetic system's relationship to the neocortical areas involved in processing self-concepts is like that of the mother to the infant. It is an agency that manages to more or less competently shape and control sympathetic urges. The parasympathetic mother can be accurate or not about the pleasurable objects the baby wants right now. And she can be competent at teaching him valid principles of reality that will enable him to operate autonomously over time.

Repetition and learning

Freud (1912) felt the strongest desire was sex, and the universal fear was an expectation that one would certainly be punished for enjoying sexual thoughts, feelings, or overt behaviours. Kohut (1977) called the general fear *disintegration anxiety*, or a fear of the mind going to pieces. Most generally, all chronic anxiety disorders involve high approach motives frustrated by strong avoidance motives.

I think a common proximal cause of anxiety is imagining not having enough time to learn how to resolve a pressing problem (Bernstein, 2011). At the most general level, normal feelings of time urgency may be a derivative of the father of all reasons to worry about time—death. Ernest Becker (1975) said death was the big fear and people's behaviour in general was motivated by a wish to deny death.

The big fear is more like being unable to know with conviction the answer to the question: "What do I do in life?" Erikson (1973) made a similar point. He imagined that if in old age, one was not able to look back and understand the meaning of one's life's successes and failures, one would fall into fear of death. There is empirical support for this idea (e.g., Jarvis, 2004). Ideally, the process of evaluating the meaning of one's life is unencumbered by defensive operations.

Repeated, automatic attempts to solve conflicts are a feature of the normal mind–brain (see Bernstein, 2011, and *The Repetition Compulsion*, Freud, 1920). Repetitive attempts to apply a futile method to reduce stressful conflicts are pathology. Most people at least use trial and error methods to find an effective solution to their problems. This is The Law of Effect (Thorndike, 1913). Some search in a more programmatic way, guided by previously learned, valid self- and non-self-concepts. One way or another, most people are successful enough at conflict resolution to avoid constant anxiety.

The solution to any conflict imagined to have only two mutually exclusive decisional options is to add at least one more concept into the equation. This may involve inventing or leaning a new concept or using a concept already in mind. Learning habits to activate concepts that are more valid than old ineffective concepts is the criterion of successful change in psychotherapy. Adding at least one new idea to neurotically constrained decision-making processes adds an extra degree of freedom to thinking.

Short-term reductions in anxiety can come from almost any distraction of attention from the conflict or its derivatives. Working at a job, watching television, physical exercise, and taking drugs can alter a very anxious person's thinking for a time. Ideally, the person can make or use new valid self and/or non-self concepts to decide how to resolve the stressful conflict. But to durably resolve conflict is to suspend the strong habit to apply an ancient compromise concept and use a better one instead.

The prototypical defensive operation is seen in panic disorder. The person has a habit of activating anxiety-generating ideas upon sensing any relaxation. It is a perfect zero-sum system. Usually, the greatest pleasure achievable by people with severe panic disorder is the cessation of anxiety. They do not gain pleasure from approaching desired objects in and outside their own minds. They can get temporary relief by avoiding almost any idea emerging into awareness. The more severe the disorder, the more likely the emerging ideas are relatively close derivatives of the underlying conflict. This suggests that their entire pleasure-pain regulation system is operating with low ability to imagine joyful experiences. In short, they are missing important aspects of reality on a consistent basis.

This sort of failure of imagination occurring in very anxious people reduces the accuracy of their expectations and leads to incompetent approach avoidance decisions. This is due, in large part, to the corrosive effects of high sympathetic arousal on the ability to perform other than simple tasks (see Yerkes–Dodson curve, in Figure 3). The highly aroused nervous person can only manage simple control tasks. For example, they might repeat a sequence in which they experience pleasurable sexual thoughts and feelings. This, in turn, activates feelings and thoughts of painful punishments. Once one has been suitably punished, sex thoughts again come to mind, then thoughts of punishment, and so on.

Under high sympathetic arousal, over-learned, ineffective cognitive routines are easy to run, albeit unlikely to resolve fundamental conflicts. Easy repetitive tasks, like rocking back and forth, obsessional thoughts, and compulsive rituals can produce some comfort and give people something to do with their time. This is important because many of the most anxious cannot obtain a job or maintain durable social relations. At some point they may be judged unable to work by a government agency or the family. This is a huge social problem. Patients with conversion or somatoform disorders manage to experience mostly physical pain, instead of anxious feelings generated by unresolved conflicts.

> Patients with somatization have overall healthcare expenditures nine times that of unaffected persons, and over 82% [of such patients] stop working because of their health problems. (Shaibani & Sabbagh, 1998, p. 2486)

Eventually, fruitless, repetitive information processing drains energy and gives rise to frustration, aggression, and anxiety. At a certain point the person gives up the active, repetitive defence against anxiety. This is in part due to sympathetic exhaustion signalled by a drop in levels of sympathomimetic hormones (e.g., glucocorticoids, epinephrine) and adrenergic neurotransmitters (norepinephrine, dopamine). This causes mechanisms in the neuronal nucleus to direct increased production of post-synaptic adrenergic receptor sites to catch the increasingly scarce stimulating molecules (e.g., Friedman, 1975). When things get to this state, depressed mood and somatoform illness will occur and there can be further regression to bipolar illness and psychosis (e.g., Bernstein, 2011, 2012).

Most generally, the overall competence of a person to make effective decisions to resolve stressful conflict can be understood to vary, in part, with different combinations of sympathetic and parasympathetic influences. And, of course, advanced, conscious and unconscious information processing in the neocortex involves use of concepts that interpret sense data from extero- and interoception. Self- and non-self-concepts work to form the bases of expectations of pleasure and pain regarding objects in the world and in mind. Concepts and expectations are used in planning overt behaviour to approach and/or avoid pleasure and pain.

Competent thinking depends on feeling curious yet calm enough to suspend immediate judgements or action. Remember the Yerkes–Dodson law (Figure 3). For most individuals, most of the time, performance of complex cognitive tasks is better under conditions of moderate arousal than under low or very high arousal. The sum total of organismic arousal or energisation is, in part, a function of the interaction of parasympathetic brakes and sympathetic fuel. The sympathetic system responds urgently to sensations indicating wants and needs. It activates fast, fixed, reflex-like responses when dangers (e.g., predators) and pleasures (e.g., sex partners) are close in time and space. In contrast, the newer, myelinated parts of the parasympathetic vagal nerves help regulate sympathetic arousal and its correlated subjective sense of urgency.

The parasympathetic brake can be applied dynamically, on and off, with varying intensity within the time it takes the heart to beat once (about one second). Seconds and milliseconds are roughly the order of magnitude of rates of change in attentional focus. High RSA range is caused by signals carried by vagal efferents emanating from the nucleus ambiguus in the brainstem. Such signals increase parasympathetic tone which, in turn, can increase the person's ability to reflect upon the costs and benefits of decisions made in the brainstem with the aid of logic and concepts developed over life.

A dynamically changing heart, sensitive to respiratory processes, increases the brain's agility to activate concepts associated with many different memories and feelings. Good parasympathetic tone is associated with a calm feeling and curiosity. One is not always in an emergency, anxious about running out of time. This promotes consideration of the validity of multiple concepts to explain the meaning of raw sensory data. Valid causal concepts lead to the best predictions and control of the person's overt behaviour and subjective experiences (see Bernstein, 2011, Chapter Four).

High parasympathetic tone can be operationalized as a wide RSA range. Compared to low RSA range, high RSA range indicates that more dynamic changes in the frequency and force of attempts to modify sympathetic arousal are occurring. RSA varies moment to moment, allowing for fast variation in the extent of braking. These changes are a result of alterations in the firing of the myelinated vagal efferents stemming from the brainstem's nucleus ambiguus. The key point is that one somehow has the ability to vary the signal rates by means of a more or less intelligent decision-making process. It is very exciting that researchers are starting to operationalise measures of autonomic variables affecting conceptual processes, and are learning to manipulate the processes (e.g., Zuker et al., 2009).

Note

1. The deepest depictions of horrifying social control attempts I know of are:
    - The novel *1984* by George Orwell (1948) and the film made of the book in 1984 with Richard Burton. He plays the role of a government torturer using a sophisticated model of mind to cause intense mental suffering in a dissident. It was Burton's last film before dying.
    - The films made of the book *The Island of Dr Moreau* by H. G. Wells (1896). The last of the three films from the book had Marlon Brando as the perverse doctor who attempts to give wild animals such as goats, lions and bears, human-like bodies and minds. In a modernisation of the book's technologies, remotely controlled electrodes are implanted in the animals' chests to punish forbidden thought and action. It was Brando's last film before dying.
    - *The Origin of Consciousness in the Breakdown of the Bicameral Mind* by Julian Jaynes (1976). Not a shocking mass entertainment, Jayne's marvellously titled book is one of the best attempts to relate the history of social governing efforts to the formation of the Western mind.

CHAPTER NINE

Autonomic nervous systems II: thinking, feeling, and overt behaviour

Mental competence is decreased by unpleasant, intrusive thoughts and feelings of aroused anxiety due to unresolved, stressful approach-avoidance conflicts. Anxiety can be reduced by containing and explaining the conflict with good ideas. One can then think and plan behaviour designed to cope with the problem. Or, anxiety can be deferred by defence mechanisms (e.g., A. Freud, 1946). All defence mechanisms work by distorting really. The best defences represent relatively good trade-offs between anxiety avoidance and, for example, a need to know when you are being conned in a business deal.

Good defences achieve good anxiety control with a minimal distortion of reality. Humour makes light of things: "Life is a cosmic joke that no ordinary person can comprehend, so why worry?" Sub-clinical, obsessive-compulsive tendencies can be co-opted for the pursuit of valuable goals. It helps to be organised. Freud's idea of sublimation involves learning to channel the energy from one's foundational self-conflicts into creative work in art, science, business, and all other prosocial activities. Sublimation was Freud's attempt to describe the best one could do in response to reality.

The bad defences like psychotic dissociation and paranoia represent last-ditch strategies to not know something. If persistent, unresolved conflicts are the source of the worst mental pain and suffering, we might predict that denial mechanisms operate in close cooperation with truth-seeking mechanisms. An information system can only defend against knowing something specific if, at some level, it already knows what not to know.

In any case, we all distort reality somewhat to avoid anxiety and we are usually able to get away with it. The effectiveness of all cognitive operations including defence mechanisms depends, in part, on different states of the autonomic nervous system. The ANS determines in large part conditions affecting the neocortical ability to regulate stress and anxiety. Competent anxiety control depends on an ability to use good rather than bad defences. In other words, mental competence is increased when the person uses more, rather than less valid semantic concepts stored in the neocortex to make decisions

The ANS can initiate reflexive, instinctive stress responses that have survival value. The most primitive response to stress is immobilisation or freezing. This action works, in part, by increasing the difficulty of detection by predators. It is harder to notice a well camouflaged, unmoving lizard in the reeds than a frenetic creature, noisily running for its life. Even if the individual is noticed, playing dead can decrease predator, if not scavenger, interest in a meal of already dead reptile or opossum.

The pure, primitive immobilisation instinct can be either all on or all off. One may perform or not perform the fixed action selected by evolution as the best, statistically valid response to important stimulus arrays or releasers in the external world. This is the kind of decision involving the nucleus tractus solitaries (NTS), a source of older, unmyelinated vagus nerves that deliver signals to initiate immobilisation of the body. Zero-sum decision making is the hallmark of the initial stages of sensory data processing.

Early in the development of the individual's brain and mind, instinctive decisions about external objects are always based on face validity. This is because infant mammals, and people with forms of autism, have few or no concepts in mind to augment subcortical decisions about the meaning of sensory data.Instead, raw or minimally processed sensory data dominates attentional focus. When sensory arrays resemble closely enough an inherited representation of something that can threaten or enhance life, fixed actions may be executed.

With development of the neocortex, semantic concepts work to make decisions that can inhibit or promote overt enactment of instinctual tendencies. People with functional mental illnesses resemble infants, animals, and autists in that their ability to make and use semantic concepts is small relative to normal adult humans. By definition, functional mental illnesses such as chronic anxiety are due to habits to use invalid concepts to understand the self and the world. In mental illness, difficulty at learning and using better concepts is not usually due to gross neuropathology, or being merely a few days old.

The meaning of concepts

The semantic differential of Osgood et al., (1957) indicates that the meaning of all words (semantic concepts) can be understood generally as having three dimensions: evaluation (good-bad), potency (strong-weak), and activity (mobile-immobile). These are the things one wants to know about sense data representing objects in the world and the mind: (1) Is it good or bad? That is, can it cause me pleasure or pain? (2) Is it strong or weak? Or can it overpower me? (3) Can it move? In other words, can I escape it if necessary? Osgood determined that about 60% of the variation in the meaning of words concerns the evaluative, good-bad dimension. The question of the general meaning of words is still an important focus of psychological inquiry (e.g., Heise, 2010).

Maybe go, no-go brainstem decisions are based on summing the evaluations of objects on each of Osgood's meaning dimensions. Compared to using only one aspect of meaning, use of three decision-making elements should increase the accuracy of expectations of the relative amount of pain or pleasure likely to result from approach, avoidance, and freezing strategies. In any case, decisions to activate an instinct—all or none—without neocortical consultation must, by definition, be based on decisions about the obvious, salient aspect of the releasing stimulus.

But with learning and development, the neocortex becomes functionally competent to use semantic concepts to explain sensations. As the mind becomes a dynamic system of concepts, it starts to react to itself and the external world in a new manner. The person learns that things are not always as they seem and that there might be more to this than meets the eye. Ideas, images, and feelings start to appear in mind somewhat independent of the sensory information streaming in from the external world. If a person tends to interpret safe situations as dangerous ones, the emergence of innocuous sensations or thoughts into focal attention will activate some of the approach-avoidance machinery in subcortical areas that can initiate freezing, approaching, and avoiding external things.

Simple yes or no decisions can work to simplify subsequent information processing. Once the decision is made, one is less bothered by any concepts and concept usage habits associated with the not-chosen option. For example, "I will stay in bed where it is safer than going outside. I needn't worry about freezing, fleeing, or fighting. I can sleep." But problems can occur if the simplification process deprives the person of acting on information that might help to define reality more exactly.

From the neuroanatomical perspective, the neocortex might be able to learn the nature of one's situation using a deeper model of reality including multiple perspectives that were left out of subcortical binary decision process. Taking the information upstairs allows the boss to more thoroughly contemplate the situation. Executive decision making involves considering many decisional options. The neocortical executive has many degrees of decisional freedom. One need not pick option X or Y. There might be options from A to Z that could work in this situation.

Experimental research indicates that when the mind's eye turns to the self (after seeing one's image in a mirror) the discrepancy between one's real and ideal standing on some dimension of self-functioning becomes salient (e.g., Carver & Sheier, 1981; Duval & Wicklund, 1972; Silva & Duval 2001). This causes sympathetic arousal and results in attempts to either reduce the discrepancy or to avoid self-focus. In effect, the surface of the self, like the surface of physically realised concepts, contains information that is used initially mostly to evaluate whether it is more or less good or bad. (Osgood's evaluation dimension accounts for over 60% of the meaning of words.)

One tends to feel good if self-ideals have been met or exceeded, and not so good when falling short of ideals. By definition, most people hold self-ideals that are consistent with the normative ideals of their culture. In that sense, initial reactions to self-focus do not reveal much about the person's uniqueness. Rather, this is the sort of self-consciousness associated with embarrassment or shame. After initial evaluation of items in focal awareness, thinking about concepts one knows a great deal about, such as oneself, is different from other types of thinking. This is because single concepts in expert systems are nodes in relatively large networks.

Infants do not have many semantic concepts and no expert conceptual systems. Such systems develop with learning. Likewise, an adult who knows nothing of geology, for example, has no system of concepts about rocks. But when a learned geologist sees a bit of granite rock, or the word granite, thresholds to activate neurons that encode concepts related to granite are lowered. That is, compared to not thinking of granite, being primed by sensing a physical bit of the rock or by the word granite, makes it more likely the trained geologist will become aware of concepts like igneous rock, quartz, feldspar, and so on. This is the reliably researched process of spreading activation discovered in semantic priming experiments by cognitive psychologists (e.g., McNamara, 2005). Non-expert geologists have either never learned associates of granite, or the structure of their system of concepts in memory does not link granite to, for example, silicon.

Most generally, using self-concept words (I, me) can produce strong negative or positive feelings (e.g., Rude et al., 2004; Pennebaker & Chung, 2011; Mairesse et al., 2007). The psychoanalytic ideas of free association describe the subjective correlates of unconstrained spreading activation of neurons encoding concepts in some meaningful relationships. Self or ego defensive operations inhibit spreading activation, and these neuronal processes are very amenable to experimental observation (e.g., Bernstein, 2011, Appendix III).

Depending on the nature of one's own system of concepts about the self and the world, the emergence of concepts and feelings into mind can stimulate curiosity, fear, or some mixture of both. Immaturity and mental illness predispose the person to interpret sensations, concepts, and feelings emerging from the unconscious or the social world as emergencies (e.g., the child's fear of the dark). Reflexive instincts or learned habits to avoid or aggress may be enacted in imagination or overt behaviour.

For the more competent person, materialisation of thoughts and feelings within consciousness are welcomed as curiosities. For example, a patient told me that as a young child he had repeated dreams of a lion that terrified him. He prayed to God each night at bedtime to spare him from such dreams. But with increased self-understanding in adulthood, he came to regard the concept of the lion as containing valued attributes of his self-concept. Instead of wishing to avoid lion dreams, he began to long to have them.

Immobilisation reflex

The bottom of Figure 4 indicates that immobilisation reflexes are controlled by the phylogentically older, unmyelinated vagal nerves. As noted above, feigning death may work to increase an animal's chance of survival (e.g., the opossum's prototypical behaviour). The reptilian ability to shut down somatic activity is sometimes activated in young infants or children who have drowned, especially in cold water (e.g., Modell et al., 2004; Bickler & Buck, 2007). Remarkably, they can often be rescued after 30 minutes underwater with no brain damage. This is because the immobilisation process works to lower metabolic demands and, hence, the usual large demand for oxygen.

This instinct has varied functional uses. But immobilisation can have pathological and fatal consequences. For example, too much slowing of the heart and respiration can lead to death (e.g., Brady, 1958). Individuals in psychotic states, presumably terrified by some thought or feeling, can regress into ridged, catatonic postures for hours or days.

Affect theorists might imagine that something less than the complete enactment of more than one basic affect can be added together to generate the entire range of human behaviour. But when instincts or affects are executing their basic function, for example as a defence against threat, initiation decisions have a zero-sum nature. In contrast, the newer, smart vagus from the nucleus ambiguous produces signals ranging from low to high ranges of intensity. The braking operations' intensity, and the rate of change of the signals can change multiple times within a second.

Porges (2011, p. 172) notes that parts of the immobilisation instinct might be co-opted to promote effective social engagement including play and sexual intercourse. Being in close proximity to unknown individuals of one's own or another species can cause initially sympathetic arousal (e.g., Zajonc, 1968, 2001). Neurochemical and neuroanatomical aspects of a protective immobilisation instinct could work to keep anxious partners close enough to enact social and sexual intercourse. Neuropeptides such as oxytocin (e.g., Carter & Keverne, 2002) and vasopressin (e.g., DeWied, 1971) may play critical roles in the modification of instinctive fear and avoidance tendencies so that they work to promote social and sexual engagement.

Parasympathetic tone and sympathetic arousal

Figure 4 identifies nine body-mind states that tend to occur with particular combinations of sympathetic arousal and parasympathetic tone levels. These are not entirely distinct entities but have connections at various levels of analysis. On the surface, they are recognisable things (face validity). They also have some discriminant validity. For example, people in some of the conditions can be treated effectively with drugs that do not work for people in other conditions, and prognoses differ between conditions (predictive validity). That is, when we account for the attributes of a particular condition, we can predict with some accuracy what will happen next. These nine categories might be called clusters of biological and psychological variables, prototype states, or, illustrative mind-body conditions. In any case, my descriptions of them are based on five starting assumptions:

1. The states can occur if no unadulterated reflex, such as immobilisation, has been initiated. The cardiac, pulmonary, and nervous systems producing the states are subject to dynamic control, and have more than zero degrees of decisional freedom in responding to information.
2. Effective stress regulation depends on the alignment between the more or less competent sub-systems: heart, lungs, ANS, brainstem, HPN axis, limbic system, and neocortex.
3. Following Porges (2011), I assume that low levels of RSA range indicate poor dynamic control (e.g., unresponsive or ineffectively responsive to information) and that high RSA range indicates high competence to respond to changing information about stressors.
4. I assume that the nucleus ambiguus, a brainstem nexus for afferent and efferent myelinated vagal nerves, can exchange information with neocortical conceptual areas.
5. Theoretically, any combinations of sympathetic arousal and parasympathetic tone can exist. In practice, certain combinations are more likely than others.

The horizontal axis of Figure 4 depicts a continuous range of low to high sympathetic arousal. In an oversimplification of sorts, I assume that sympathetic arousal increases in a simple linear fashion, analogous to how fuel is delivered into a car engine by pressing on the accelerator. The vertical axis arranges parasympathetic tone from low to high. Respiratory sinus arrhythmia (RSA) is an operational measure of parasympathetic tone. High RSA range indicates the person is capable of inducing a wide range of rates and intensities of heart action within a period of milliseconds. Low RSA range indicates that rates and intensities are constrained within a narrow, relatively unchanging region. Combinations of different levels of parasympathetic tone and sympathetic arousal work, in part, to produce body–brain–mind states ranging from pathological to highly competent.

If heart and lungs are regulated too rigidly (low RSA range), it is hard to think and behave in a complex, sophisticated manner. This is especially so in real and imagined emergencies when sympathetic arousal tends to be high, and the heart and lungs are working consistently hard and fast. Mind–brain and visceral elements are in bidirectional, causal relationships. Calm thoughts can relax the body and a body at ease is a comfort to the mind. Body, brain, and mind are parts of one whole regulatory system. Causal forces (chemical and electric signals) are sent and received by each element.

Ideally, the whole system works to confer knowledge and good feelings to the person and evolutionary advantages to their species. In some sense, the individual's body, brain, mind, and social world are "all in it together". But decisional authority is not distributed equally throughout the person's body, brain, mind, or social environment. In the newborn mammal, few decisions are made in neocortical areas. With development, the system of concepts about the self and external reality, stored in the neocortex, may become authorised to decide how to resolve the person's conflicts. Many, if not all of the patients I have seen in psychotherapy doubt their own authority to override decisions made by some part of their body, mind, or other people.

Interpreting reality with valid concepts promotes good decisions to cope with stressful conflict. Ideally, body, brain, and mind are aligned during control attempts in emergencies. Most people find it difficult to do anything, including thinking, at low levels of sympathetic arousal. Performance on increasingly complex mental tasks improves at moderate or average levels of sympathetic arousal, and performance starts to decline for most individuals at high sympathetic arousal levels. But high arousal tends to facilitate simpler, brutish tasks (e.g., breaking down a door and running like hell). These are the assumptions of the Yerkes–Dodson law (Figure 3). But Yerkes–Dodson is a statistical law. Some individuals can defy the odds and operate very competently at high levels of sympathetic arousal.

High competence and peak experience

People with high parasympathetic tone have somehow learned to regulate heart rate variability (HRV), respiration and the cognitive

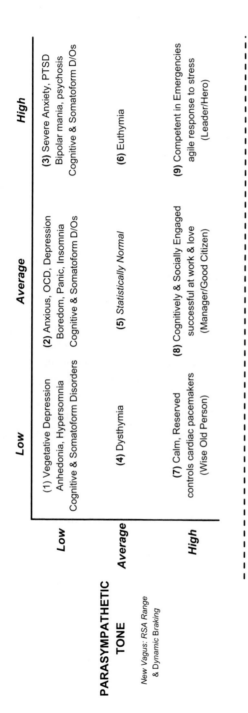

Figure 4.   Thinking, feeling, overt behaviour, and autonomic nervous systems.

operations that depend on well-timed, effective control of sympathetic arousal. Condition 9 in Figure 4 is a state of highly responsive parasympathetic braking *and* high sympathetic arousal. Racing car drivers in such a state, for example, could likely drive very fast on a tortuous road and win the race without being injured. They have the energy, and can quickly gather sensory data to make good decisions constantly about their direction (steering) and speed (braking).

Decisions about where you are going and when and how hard to brake can be made on the basis of instinct and/or learned semantic concepts. To drive safely and fast on a dangerous road depends on the information processing competence of the brain–mind system. The driver must sense quickly (and constantly) distances between objects, and the directions and speeds of objects. Then he must use concepts to interpret the meaning of the data. Specifically, he needs ideas that have implications for predicting the likely amounts and kinds of pains and pleasures one might incur if approaching or avoiding a particular point in time and space.

What the driver really needs is a cognitive system that functions as fast and decisively as the old instinctive one but that has more potential for accurate prediction and control. Of course, if conscious, intentional decision-making processes produce responses that are not better than hard-wired instincts, why bother thinking? The value of neocortical operations like thinking is not speed. Rather, thinking increases the range of response options beyond those offered by the instinctive, subcortical processes.

For example, our racing car driver processes information in order to decide on when and how to adjust speed and direction. If these variables are thought to be in a zero-sum relationship, the driver's only response options are increase speed or increase control. Roughly speaking, primitive instincts operate on the basis of go, no-go logic. The winning driver will be the one who makes the best, most nuanced decisions about how to control all the relevant variables.

There are of course descriptions of athletes and others in flow states or zones in which thinking and moving are performed in uniquely competent and pleasurable ways (e.g., Csikzentmihalyi, 1990). I assume that such states are related to having fast access to the most valid concepts of nature, and that access to valid concepts and the ability to use them gets faster as the conceptual system itself becomes more meaningfully organised (Bernstein, 2011, Chapter Eleven). Being in some sort of uniquely pleasurable and competent zone might depend on access to valid concepts. I think Deci's (1975) idea of *intrinsic reinforcement* involves engaging with concepts and mental processes directly, for the pleasures they yield in the moment. These pleasures of planning or thinking are somewhat separate from the *extrinsic rewards* one experiences upon attainment or consumption of goals (e.g., the pleasures of hunting vs. the pleasures of eating).

Perhaps hungry mammals aroused by threats or appetitive desires can achieve something like flow states. This has to be the same sort of assumption made by people who wish to act instinctively with a feeling of wholeness, like an animal in the wild, or by people who want to go back to being a small child with only a few fanciful ideas. Human infants have a large, essentially concept-free neocortex, and non-human, adult mammals have a neocortex too small to contain many concepts. The relative simplicity of infant and animal minds suggests that babies and cats may be flowing more of the time than adult humans.

In any case, the task of seamlessly integrating instinctive somatic reflexes with inferential decision making to create a state of flow is like what happens in condition 9 in Figure 4. Highly aroused people under threat from a lion are able to differentiate thinking from acting. They can assess relevant self-attributes (e.g., strength, speed, past experience) and situational variables (e.g., lion's strength, speed, and the distance to a protected place). This information leads to consideration of decisional options, and predictions of each option's chance of success. Then, the best option is chosen and enacted.

One needs durable, strong habits of mind to maintain parasympathetic tone when under threat. This is because high sympathetic arousal works to potentiate instinctive immobilisation, flight or fight behaviour. The arousal of such tendencies occurs in mind too. Thinking is strongly influenced by signals coming from subcortical regions of the brain. The instincts have proven useful over evolutionary history. The tension to enact security and appetitive instincts does not disappear in the presence of potent releasers. But fixed action patterns cannot account for all the non-prototypical aspects of one's current situation. This is when one needs an active, concept-using neocortical response.

Ideally, the special competencies of the sympathetically aroused mind and body are co-opted, in part by operations involving the myelinated vagus, for the creation in the neocortex of a sophisticated, custom-made response to a current stress. Sensations of threatening or attractive objects in the world or the brain–mind release adrenergic hormones (e.g., epinephrine) and neurotransmitters (e.g., norepinephrine, dopamine). These chemicals speed reaction time, and increase visual acuity, muscular strength, and endurance. Endogenous opiates are also released under stress to raise pain thresholds. The combination of adrenergic stimulants and opiates is highly pleasurable and enhances the pleasurable feelings that can come from thinking about objects, compared to merely sensing them (e.g., Biederman & Vessel, 2006).

Better than well

People with high parasympathetic control will experience chronic or more changeable levels of sympathetic arousal. Condition 7 in Figure 4 involves high parasympathetic tone and low levels of sympathetic arousal. As people age, adrenergic hormones and neurotransmitter levels tend to fall and with them, energy levels. But if the person is not suffering from some dementias or other brain damage, the lessons learned about parasympathetic braking remain functional. Older, otherwise intact people can ideally use energy very efficiently and effectively. The intrinsic rate of the cardiac pacemaker, unrestricted by parasympathetic braking, is very fast. It makes sense then for everyone, especially older or sick people with limited energy, to coast downhill using minimal vagal breaking to optimise energy usage.

Because everyone loses energy with advancing age, one can use adrenergic stimulants in older patients as a cognitive enhancer and antidepressant (e.g., methylphenidate). Over half of these patients experience improved executive functioning, better mood, and more energy. Some have no clear positive reaction, and a small proportion can regress into anxious or even psychotic states. Over time I have become better at predicting good and bad responders to stimulants in this older group (cf., Amen et al., 2008). Poor responders tend to have less developed personalities and impoverished social relationships. This is consistent with Porges' assumption that high parasympathetic tone potentiates social engagement. Good responders have high parasympathetic tone, and have learned and can activate semantic concepts that explain something about the causes or meaning of visceral sense data. These are wise old people who can be considered better than well.

But I want to emphasise the cognitive causes and effects of parasympathetic tone. Those with poor parasympathetic tone become less competent at processing information when the press of sympathetic arousal increases. They cannot contain, explain, or make good use of the increased energy. Using stimulants in such cases is like blowing air into a rubber balloon. Sometimes the balloon is durable enough to hold the pressure, analogous to maintaining competent thinking, feeling, and overt behaviour. But the balloon breaks if the patient has strong, dominant habits to use invalid concepts to explain events in her own mind and body, and the minds and bodies of other people. Tendencies to enact one's strongest habits, helpful or harmful, increase more as sympathetic arousal increases than do tendencies to express weaker habits (e.g., Hull, 1943; Miller & Dollard, 1941).

So, if a person has strong habits to do stupid things, giving them adrenergic stimulants can work to degrade, rather than enhance, cognitive and social functioning. But it is usually worth trying stimulants in such cases because the potential benefits are so great. If the response is poor, even psychotic, my experience is that the negative effects always cease quickly once the medication is stopped. However, in all such cases one should start patients on low doses to gauge drug effects. In general, I prefer that people use stimulants on an as-needed basis (PRN) rather than as an unchanging, daily regime.[1]

Another type of better-than-well person has high parasympathetic tone and average sympathetic arousal levels (condition 8). They tend to be successful socially and at work because they have better than average habits to use valid concepts. That is, their personalities are effective control systems. But they don't have exceptionally high endogenous, adrenergic tone, especially dopaminergic tone. We can assume that the incentive value or attractiveness of pursuing very high aspirations is average in such cases.

Attempts to perform complex conceptual tasks are driven and controlled by the pleasures underwritten by dopamine and opiates (see Biederman & Vessel, 2006; Bernstein, 2011, p. 49). Without above average dopamine levels, one is unlikely to experience, and subsequently anticipate, feeling the most sublime pleasures from resolving complex conceptual and social tasks. Accordingly, someone in condition 8 is more likely to pursue and be successful in situations calling for using specific, detailed concepts concerning the salient costs and benefits regulating social transactions. Transactional expertise works to maintain social stability.

The motivation to stimulate and lead social, organisational and conceptual change, and tolerate greater risk, is more characteristic of those in condition 9. Leaders, compared to managers, are more incentivised to approach the resolution of complex conceptual and social conflicts and less bothered by the risks (e.g., Burke & Litwin, 1992). More exactly, those in condition 9 enjoy taking risks in order to gain pleasure and success. This is consistent with Freud's (1921) belief that a leader's influence is based on his capacity to have stronger than normal feelings, and an ability to communicate the feelings and their associated ideas to followers. The historian James MacGregor Burns (1978) considered the greatest leaders those who are able to change the thinking of followers. He called this transformational or conceptual leadership.

Normal

By definition, most people, most of the time, have average levels of sympathetic arousal and average levels of parasympathetic tone (condition 5). It is generally recognised that parasympathetic tone is a more important determinant of mental and physical health than sympathetic arousal levels (e.g., Harvey et al., 2010; Nugent et al., 2011). Because parasympathetic tone supports general health and durability, changes in sympathetic arousal occurring with average sympathetic tone, usually produce mental and physical states that are within normal limits.

When average control combines with average sympathetic arousal, you get an average state of mind (condition 5). Average parasympathetic tone with low sympathetic arousal may result in dysthymia, a gloomy feeling that falls short of full-blown clinical depression (condition 4). In contrast, when people with average autonomic, conceptual, and social competence are in a state of high sympathetic arousal, they will feel mostly positive, happy, or euthymic (condition 6). This sort of normal happiness can edge into a more intense happy feeling or hypomania. The assumption that most people like to feel jolly and competent to cope with life is consistent with the increasing, widespread usage of sympathomimetic psychostimulants (e.g., Smith & Farrah, 2011; Swanson et al., 2011), and glutamate agonists like modafinil.

Note

1. In many cases it is a mistake to advise patients that they have a chronic mental condition and that they need to take antidepressants, for example, in the way a diabetic takes insulin. This mistake is rooted in a host of factors.

Recent psychiatric graduates are schooled mostly in neurobiological diagnosis and psychopharmacological treatment methods. They use algorithms to make decisions about drugs on the basis of changes in overt symptoms. There is little attention paid to psychodynamics or to how people learn. Patients themselves feel slighted that doctors show little appreciation of the complexity of their conditions and their potential to learn to better operate their minds. When one has a hammer, everything is a nail: that is, if the doctor knows little about other mental health treatments such as talking psychotherapies, then drugs are his only tool. Other methods that could help people make meaning of their anxieties and depressions and, thereby, move past them, are not used. So, endless daily use of psychotropics occurs.

Before about 1965, most psychiatrists were well trained in psycho-analytic methods. I think the best group of psychiatrists was trained between about 1940 and 1975. They were trained psychoanalysts, experienced with war neurosis, and young enough to learn cognitive methods, and the basics of the new science of therapeutic psychopharmacology. By necessity, the early psychopharmacologists had to be experimentalists with drugs.

Today one still needs to approach each case as an experiment. Biological, psychological, and social interventions need to be tried, their effects observed, and treatments refined in light of the results in each individual case. Otherwise, one gets locked into ridged, unchanging treatment methods based on overt symptoms. Evidence of deeper processes is rarely sought out. Simplistic, descriptive diagnostic taxonomies (e.g., DSM, ICD-10) lead to less than creative use of drugs therapeutically.

Besides deficiencies in medical education, fear of legal authorities affects mental health care. In some parts of the USA, the prescribing behaviour of doctors is under close legal scrutiny. As-needed drug use can, on the surface, resemble recreational drug use, so pharmacologists are reluctant to experiment with unorthodox agents and dosing strategies.

Perhaps the worst constraint on psychiatric practice is Pharmacological Calvinism (Klerman, 1973). This is the belief that using drugs that cause good feelings is morally wrong. The doctor may feel less anxious if mental conditions are defined simply as medical disease entities that need to be cured. Little attention is paid to the complex of biological, psychological, and social causes and effects of mental states. This may help the doctor but not do much for the patient.

CHAPTER TEN

Psychopathology

Sensations, thoughts, and feelings of anxiety can result from being physically ill, or living in stressful, dangerous environments. Our concern here is with people who don't feel well despite being in materially safe situations. Such individuals use repetitively invalid concepts to interpret reality. This usually causes overestimations of threats to security, anxiety, reduced mental competence, and poor decision making. In a smaller proportion of people, the tendency to underestimate risk is the psychopathology.

The theorist working at multiple levels of analysis has the potential to develop strong construct validity (see Campbell & Fiske, 1959). High construct validity involves integration and operationalisation of ideas at multiple levels of analysis. It is, in effect, equal to psychological or conceptual depth. For example, operationalisations of the concept depression are made by experts at three levels:

- biological measurement of pathognomonic brain activity and neuro-transmitter system anomalies
- psychological measurement of chronic mental habits associated with depression such as harsh self-judgements

- social behavioural measures of avoiding pleasures such as social and sexual intercourse.

In my experience, six valid and reliable disease concepts can be used to describe most functional psychopathology. The conditions can occur singly or in various combinations: anxiety, cognitive, somato-form, depression, bipolar, and psychotic (Bernstein, 2011, 2012). Each syndrome can be recognised by words used in everyday speech (face validity). We can specify with some accuracy the predisposing condi-tions and likely course in each case (predictive validity). Characteristic changes in metabolic processing rates in different parts of the brain are peculiar to each disorder, and different neurotransmitter systems are implicated in each syndrome (discriminant validity). In short, the six disease concepts have characteristic somatic, conceptual, and feeling attributes. For example:

1. Anxiety is associated with magnified estimates of danger, increased basal ganglion blood flow, and low parasympathetic tone (Porges, 2011).
2. Depression is associated with guilt feelings (Freud, 1923) and pessimism (e.g., Alloy & Ahrens, 1987). It is correlated with changes in the hippocampus (Massey & Bashir, 2007), the thalamus (Amen, 2003), and neurotransmitters and receptor systems (e.g., Friedman, 1975).
3. In bipolar mood disorders, thoughts and feelings change quickly. Increases in left basal ganglion and limbic blood flow have been observed (Amen, 2003). Grandiose optimism is seen in mania, as well as in creative, fluid states of mind prone to easy distractibility of attentional focus (see Biss et al., 2010).
4. Cognitive problems, such as difficulty focusing attention, are associated with feelings of confusion, increased blood flow to the basil ganglion and deep limbic system, and decreased flow rates in the pre-frontal cortex (e.g., Amen et al., 2008).
5. Somatoform patients with hypochondriasis are always paying attention to their body; chronic fatigue is correlated with decreased caudate nucleus volume (e.g., Hakala et al., 2004).
6. Psychotic conditions present with odd thinking including paranoia and dissociation. In schizophrenia, a chronic psychotic condition, there is extensive loss of neocortical tissue starting in teenage years (e.g., Thompson et al., 2001).

In medical terms, a functional psychopathology is one without apparent organic or structural cause. But we know that every mental event occurs because something has happened in the brain. The brain is an organic entity and it has physical structure. A person experiences some of the activity of her brain consciously, but most of it never enters awareness.

As we have increased the ability to represent the activity of the brain and correlate it with the person's subjective experience, formal scientists and some naïve scientists are able to understand that organic elements affect mental experience and competence. I use the term functional to describe symptoms of psychopathology that are the most potentially reversible by learning. They are problems caused mostly by software that might be rewritten.

Promoting functional mental change

The microanatomy of single neurons, the macroanatomy of groups of neurons (e.g., the entire neocortex), the vasculature, and all the other structures of the brain can change to varying degrees at varying rates. Change is a cause and an effect of physical development, learning, stress, disease, and injury.

Big structures such as the brainstem, limbic system, and cortex represent the gross anatomy of the brain, which is observable mostly via visual inspection. Extensive defects in macroanatomical brain regions might be called hardware problems. They can be due to flawed brain development as in mental retardation, schizophrenia, or autism; and by injuries or diseases like blows to the head, stroke, cancer, and Alzheimer's and vascular dementias.

A person may be able to compensate for hardware defects by creating microanatomical changes through learning. Learning might be thought of as involving software change. But most exactly, learning involves changes in the microanatomy of nerve cells (e.g., Kandel & Schwartz, 1982). For example, after a stroke that disables certain functions such as movement of an arm, patients can learn to use brain regions unaffected by the stroke to regain lost function (e.g., Krakauer, 2005). This involves changing information processing operations, and gives an insight into the brain's ability to regulate itself, especially with help from the mind.

Changing the strength of habits to activate concepts to explain sensory data, and to initiate signals to the musculature, involves microanatomical change. Neuronal microanatomy involves the structures in the very extensive dendritic branches that populate the synapse. This is the tiny space between neurons that is bathed in thousands of types of chemical signalling agents including hormones (e.g., epinephrine) and neurotransmitters (e.g., norepinephrine).

Receptors for these molecules lie upon neurons' highly branched terminal dendrites in the synapse. Changing habits of concept usage involves the up and down regulation of the number and types of synaptic bud-receptors spouting from proximal neurons (e.g., Gonzales et al., 2007).

Behaviourists, and cognitive and clinical psychologists have been the experts in methods for changing the habits of animals coded in software. The software includes specifications regarding habit hierarchies (e.g., Hull, 1943; Spence, 1956). That is, what are the person's dominant habits to use particular concepts to interpret the meaning of sense data? And what less dominant habits, involving activation of better explanations for things, might exist, unused in mind? Both normal development and change aided by psychotherapy involve increasing the strength of more effective habits so they become dominant habits. Old habits don't leave the brain. One can only change their relative likelihood of expression.

Habit strength can be affected powerfully when psychotropic drugs are combined with habit-altering training.

> Antidepressant drugs and psychotherapy combined are more effective in treating mood disorders than either treatment alone ... Combining extinction training with chronic fluoxetine, but neither treatment alone, induced an enduring loss of conditioned fear memory in adult animals. Fluoxetine treatment increased synaptic plasticity, converted the fear memory circuitry to a more immature state, and acted through local brain-derived neurotrophic factor. Fluoxetine-induced plasticity may allow fear erasure by extinction-guided remodeling of the memory circuitry. (Karpova et al., 2011, p. 1731)

Most generally, patients should have access to information about bodily conditions (e.g., bio or neurofeedback) as they are exploring their subjective experience of mind with a therapist. This makes treating mental problems less of a hit or miss affair. By triangulating with events from both body and mind, conflicts can be identified and worked with. Ideally, clinicians should use talk combined with biofeedback (e.g., Porges, 2011), neurofeedback (e.g., Thomas, 2012), and drugs that increase neural plasticity such as Serotonin Reuptake Inhibitors.

Outside the medical context, the availability of computers in cell phones will make data about the conditions of the body and brain available to everyone. This could cause a surge in learning about the relationships between society, body, brain, and mind. Changing many minds is analogous to other strong determinants of evolution such as climate change, volcanoes, and floods. Evolutionary forces affect all the life systems: social, psychological, biological. At what point does a social activity or mental competence call for designating a new type of creature? Perhaps we have to some degree become *homo sapiens imperator*—man who controls knowledge.

Executive functions

The term executive functions has been used to describe processes that control attentional focus, management of items in memory, planning, and other things. These are decision-making processes. At the neocortical level, decisions are affected by both logic and habits of mind. For example, one person may habitually attend to pleasurable sensations or concepts, and another may dwell on unpleasant things. Interestingly, adrenergic stimulants that work to increase attentional control also work to elevate mood.

People are more or less competent at making executive decisions. Sometimes incompetence qualifies the person for a diagnosis of a cognitive disorder such as attention deficit. But attentional control is at the end of a causal chain of innumerable somatic, psychic, and social variables. In short, the ability to regulate attention is the apex of human information processing competence.

A very small number of young children may have attention deficits due to delays in neocortical development. But the most important cause of attentional dysregulation in both children and adults is anxiety. Stimulant drugs can remediate problems with attention regardless of the cause. Ignorance of this fact has caused all sort of fruitless debates about whether adults can have attention deficit disorder and whether they should be treated with stimulants.

Anxiety can be treated with tranquillisers and stimulants. My preference clinically is to use stimulants but mostly on an as-needed basis rather than the prevailing custom to use such drugs in a regular dosing schedule. Not only is that often not necessary, but it makes it difficult for patients to learn the causes of their anxiety and attentional problems.

My ideas about the processing of sensory and conceptual information are consistent with other theories of executive functioning. For example, Banich (2009) imagines a sequential cascade of information processing in neocortical brain regions involved in goal attainment (see also, Baddeley, 1986, 2002). He describes cybernetic test-operate-test-exit processes (TOTE). In his model, the mid-dorsolateral prefrontal cortex (DLPFC) selects a representation of goal attainment. This involves use of a standard or ideal state to represent completion of the task. Decisions about operations to achieve the standard occur in the anterior cingulate cortex (ACC). Then the ACC tests if the standard has been attained. If so, the brain exits the process. The competence of each process is influenced by the competence of the prior processes.

Executive functions occur in the grey coloured part of the neocortex, aided by information from subcortical areas. Myelinated cortical white matter, sitting anatomically between the neocortex and the subcortical regions, is centrally involved in communicating data from below to the neocortex, and from one neocortical area to another. (The myelin gives these neurons a white colour). The phylogenetically newer, myelinated part of the vagal system developed in historical and anatomical relationships with the myelinated white matter in the cortex. Together, they represent adaptations to promote conceptual thought in the grey matter areas of the neocortex.

The grey, non-myelinated neurons in neocortical areas do not have especially prominent long dendrites or axons. But their synaptic arborisations are extensive and complex, containing tens of thousands of signal receptor sites to absorb thousands of signalling molecules. Associative neurons must be critical parts of concept creation and usage. This is consistent with their demonstrated role in learning in simple, sensory-motor networks (e.g., Kandel & Schwartz, 1982).

Remember, concepts are collections of sensory attributes or details of objects. Concepts work to contain and explain the various attributes they contain. So, conceptual processes in the neocortex depend on fast access to raw data, or slightly more processed sensory data (protoconcepts) from all modalities. Also, the conceptual operating system must access its own contents including remembered and current ideas, plus information about how one feels. This suggests that thought and feeling are more or less consciously affected by tendencies to make instinctive responses to sensation. These are "pending decisions" made in subcortical structures. Data about the urgency to act on subcortical decisions must be available to the neocortex.

A central assumption I am making is that the validity of the concept used to contain and explain a sensation or other concepts determines the intensity of pleasure. Logically, pain intensity might either reduce or increase when explained with valid causes. But most of the time anxiety, guilt, and physical pains decrease when one sees things more realistically (e.g., Bion, 1962). This is, in part, because most of the time people use somewhat invalid concepts to understand themselves, usually erring on the side of over-criticism. This was true in Freud's Victorian age and it is today.

Anxiety

The six pathologies in my scheme are all downstream from anxiety in a causal sequence. The more serious pathologies result from chronic failure to control anxiety (e.g., Bernstein, 2011). Anxiety is a normal response to danger. It becomes pathological if the person chronically over- or underestimates the real probabilities of pain and injury. Inaccurate expectations of danger, pleasure, or anything else, stem from holding invalid theories of the self and the external world. Expectations of pleasure and pain are based on the person's theories of how nature and her own self works to cause events.

Sympathetic arousal levels are correlated with anxiety and the ability to think competently is usually related to anxiety in a curvilinear manner (see Figure 3). The most common psychopathologies involve the effects of anxiety on cognition. Cognitive incompetence is a cause and an effect of some inability to tell the difference between feelings of pain stemming from damage to the tissues of the body, and pain stemming from unpleasant thoughts. This leads to somatoform disorders like hypochondria and pain syndromes such as fibromyalgia in which there is no gross tissue damage observable in the body.

Some common and some unique pathognomonic sorts of executive function problems are involved in each six forms of mental illness.

One phenomenon that occurs in all pathology, albeit with somewhat different features, is misattribution of sympathetic arousal.

Misattribution of sympathetic arousal

Misattribution of arousal was studied first by Schachter and Singer (1962). Their two-part theory of emotion was that having an emotion depended on two variables: (1) sympathetic arousal, and (2) an explanation or attribution about the cause of the arousal. (I use the term feeling for what they call emotion.) In the classic experiment to test the theory, subjects were led to believe they were participating in a study of visual acuity, and that they would receive an injection of a drug that would affect their eyesight. Half of the subjects got injections of epinephrine (high sympathetic arousal condition); the other half got a saline placebo injection (average sympathetic arousal condition). Individual subjects then sat in a waiting room in which a confederate of the experimenters acted either angry (angry confederate condition) or euphoric (euphoric confederate condition).

As expected, in the angry confederate condition, subjects with high sympathetic arousal reported feeling more angry than average arousal subjects. Similarly, in the euphoric confederate condition, high arousal subjects reported feeling more euphoric than average arousal subjects. When high arousal subjects were told that the injection they were getting would produce side effects like agitation, jitteriness, and sweating, that is symptoms of sympathetic arousal, they were unaffected by the cues in the social environment and reported feeling no more angry or euphoric than those in the average arousal condition.

Schachter and Singer (1962), Dutton and Aron (1974), Zillmann (1983), and many others have confirmed that what I call feeling results when one uses a concept to interpret the meaning or the cause of sensations in the body. The concepts used can be manipulated in a laboratory, and are influenced every moment in the real world by teachers, doctors, salespeople, potential sex partners, actors on stage and screen, and everyone else (see Zillmann, 2006; Bernstein, 2011, p. 138).

Knowing how one feels is determined by the concepts used to interpret sensations coming to the brain from the external world by way of exteroceptors, from the body by way of autonomic afferent neurons, and from chemical signals carried in the blood by hormones.

Semantic concepts reside somewhere in the neocortical structures and processes of the brain. They are stored in memory and can be developed by the person in real time, as needed. In my view, mental competence depends on: (1) the validity of the concepts used for explaining raw sense data coming from the viscera or the external environment; and (2) the strength of habits to use particular concepts or types of concepts to explain things.

Somatoform disorders represent conceptual incompetence involving attributions of pain. Pain can come from damaged tissue in the body and from thoughts and memories. Somatoform patients largely discount unpleasant thoughts as causes of pain. For example, MRI and other imagining techniques find tissue injury in these patients that is more or less normal for their age. Everyone develops some degree of spinal degeneration with aging. But the usual aches and pains of aging seem particularly severe in fibromyalgia patients. These patients, who are almost all woman with histories of sexual trauma in childhood, tend to attribute all their pain to damage in the back or neck. They usually present first at middle age with back and neck pain, social avoidance, sleep problems, and depression.

Normally, ideas and feelings emerge constantly into consciousness. If one is afraid of one's own memories, awareness of the contents of mind creates a state of emergency. Patients with trauma histories, including fibromyalgia patients, habitually try to avoid thinking about thinking. Memories or ideas associated with their earlier traumas evoke fear and sympathetic arousal. In other words, somatoform patients tend to minimise or not use mental pain as a category of potential sources of pain. This leads them to attribute all or most of their pain to somatic causes and causes all sorts of trouble in living (see the case of Mr K in Bernstein, 2011).

For example, I treated a man with chronic headaches, neck and back pain. He sought medical treatments including opiates, surgeries, and physical therapies. It is not that he had no damage to his head and neck. but the physical therapies were never quite effective. Analysis revealed that he had various mental habits and memories that evoked mental pain including anxiety and sadness. I made a concentrated effort to have him always consider two types of attributions for the pain he felt in his body: mental causes and physical causes. When he began to do this, the subjective sense of the severity of head and back aches lessened. In attribution terms, when two possible causes for an effect are considered (e.g., tissue damage and physic pain), the person discounts the size or importance of any single cause (Kelly, 1967). In this case, merely considering that he might have mental pain caused a reduction in his perception of the amount of physical damage to his body. Having a more complete valid theory of the causes of his pain increased his ability to control pain.

Serious psychopathology

I include both cognitive and somatoform disorders in each of the three low parasympathetic tone situations in Figure 4 (conditions 1, 2, and 3). This is because: (1) the most general, valid concept of the person is *seeker of knowledge*; and, (2) being able to differentiate between sensations, concepts, and feelings that originate from the external world and those coming from inside one's body and mind, are fundamental mental competencies. Accordingly, incompetence in executive functioning involving these distinctions underlies serious psychopathology, and represents the most frustrating, important barriers to self-realisation. Studies of misattribution of the causes of one's feelings are the best operational examples of this problem (e.g., Schachter & Singer, 1962; Zillmann, 1983).

The negative effect of low parasympathetic tone on cognitive competence occurs at all levels of sympathetic arousal. But the degree of arousal influences the nature of the negative effects. Figure 4 illustrates how variations in sympathetic arousal operate to produce different symptoms when parasympathetic control is low (conditions 1, 2, and 3).

In condition 1, there is low parasympathetic tone and low sympathetic arousal. This state is unlike condition 7 where we have assumed that the person can make efficient and effective use of low energy. This could be made possible by means of timely, smart control of the intrinsically energetic sinoatrial cardiac pacemaker. In contrast, condition 1 involves poor control of low energy. They have vegetative depressions characterised by sadness, guilt, hypersomnia, low energy, and weight changes. Vegetative symptoms usually develop after a period of chronic unresolved stress and anxiety. Chronic, unresolved stress causes sympathomimetic, adrenergic neurotransmitters to fall to low levels.

The result is low energy, depressed mood, and declines in executive functioning including dysregulation of attentional focus and memory retrieval processes. Anhedonia, the inability to enjoy the appetitive, gustatory pleasures of life, occurs in condition 1. Most importantly, anhedonia involves a loss of mental competence and, in turn, a reduction in the felt pleasures of thinking. Patients with these symptoms usually do best when given stimulating drugs that increase levels of dopamine and norepinephrine in the synapse. These include bupropion, atomoxetine, and amphetamines. Glutamate agonists such as modafinil are also helpful.

Condition 2 represents low parasympathetic tone plus average sympathetic arousal. This is a more aroused state than condition 1, but control systems are no better. Defences against poorly regulated stress and anxiety involve more energetic obsessions and compulsions, boredom and insomnia. These conditions respond to drugs that elevate synaptic serotonin levels such as the SSRIs fluoxetine and escitalopram. Adrenergic stimulants can be added to a drug regime to help improve cognition and mood. And, of course, drugs that potentiated the activity of the body's main inhibitory neurotransmitter, gamma-amino butyric acid (GABA), can work to reduce felt anxiety. These agents include the minor tranquilizers or benzodiazepines and the minor mood stabilisers such as gabapentin and pregabalin that also work to reduce neuropathic pain.

Condition 3 includes the most severe functional psychopathologies. A system with high, poorly controlled energy is in a most vulnerable state. Overall, mood regulation is poor and feelings can go from very elated to very depressed. These shifts may be more or less rapid. People may be so afraid of being in this condition that they regress to using primitive defences including psychotic delusions, especially paranoid delusions. Paranoia is a particularly useful operation for a very aroused person needing to get some control. This is because the task of cognition is greatly simplified by the paranoid assumption that there is only one thing to fear. That is, a single malevolent force is the cause of all one's problems. This sort of belief can "glue the mind together", albeit at the cost of being able to know reality and, in turn, function effectively in the world.

When psychotic states are induced by trauma, the predominant symptoms involve repetition in waking and dreaming sleep of memories of the traumatic event itself, and associated episodic and semantic memories (e.g., Tulving, 2002; Tulving & Szpunar, 2009). I assume this is because the brain is prompting the mind to attempt to resolve conflicts set in motion by the traumatic event: for example, the chronic, intense stress of conflicts felt by a child injured by a supposedly protective agent such as the parent.

Posttraumatic conditions are so difficult to treat by conventional psychotherapeutic methods because arousal of traumatic memories and associated sensations stimulate the hippocampus and amygdala about two milliseconds before they reach neocortical areas (e.g., Kalivas et al., 1993; LeDoux, 1996). This means that neocortical information processes using semantic concepts to understand visceral and environmental sensations, can begin only after autonomic and hypothalamic responses to avoid pain and fear have gained momentum.

Poor control of mental and autonomic operations causes the worst mental states. The best treatments for a person in condition 1, 2 or 3 is one that promotes learning how to regulate mutually cognition and parasympathetic tone. Drugs affecting cholinergic receptors, especially muscarinic agonists, might have a beneficial effect on parasympathetic tone (e.g., Olshansky et al., 2008). In such cases, all our treatment modalities should be used together: (1) drugs that increase neural plasticity (e.g., serotonin reuptake inhibitors); (2) hallucinogens (e.g., Bouso, 2010; Bernstein, 2011); (3) biofeedback; (4) neurofeedback: and, (5) psychodynamically oriented cognitive therapies.

PART III

CHAPTER ELEVEN

Information processing, mental competence and psychotherapy

Mental experience depends on the brain. The brain depends on the plumbing of the rest of the body to provide oxygen, glucose, and a million other things, and the brain needs the body to help it move around in the external world. Why does the person think and move around? I assume it is to know reality. Why? Because understanding nature and the self by means of the most valid general and specific concepts leads to feelings of great pleasure. Feelings are the result of using concepts to contain and explain the causes of the sensations the person gets from the external world and the body. Body and brain evolve to thrive in their biological and social environments. It seems safe to say that *forms of knowledge of nature are built into the body*, and can be recognized somehow by the nervous system.[1]

The degree of pleasure of feelings is a sort of gauge of the validity of the concepts used to interpret sensory data and other concepts; the primary drive of the person is to experience these feelings. Even if the truth that comes to be known implies that one might experience some pain, the pleasure of recognising nature in the self is more powerful than the motive to avoid learning. Otherwise, there would be no growth of individuals or evolution of species. Of course, things that happen and things that don't happen to the person can result in defensive avoidance of truth and pleasure. The aim of all psychotherapies is to remediate the damages done to the person's competence to process information and experience pleasure in life.

It seems there are multiple barriers to increasing scientific under-standing of the person. Besides the sheer technical complexity of the task, most of the presumed obstacles to advancement represent failures of imagination. It is hard, if not impossible, to overestimate the con-servative nature of most scientific thinking.

For example, the word epigenetic refers to biological and psycho-logical phenomena that are caused by something above or outside the genes. Since evolution is assumed to operate by means of changes in pro-tein coding genes proper, epigenetic influences might seem to present a problem for evolution theory. Until just recently biologists believed that the 98% of the human genome that did not operate directly to syn-thesise proteins was junk DNA. It is now accepted that this epigenetic junk is critically important for regulating the activation of the protein synthesis done by traditional genes (e.g., Pennisi, 2012). The higher-order control function played by the ignored DNA had been outside the focus of genetics theory. Because we lacked until recently technolo-gies to represent what went on in the genome, genetics just ignored this large proportion of DNA.

Things that are hard to reify tend to be ignored by scientists. Freud sensibly turned away from studying the brain because its workings were mostly unknowable in his day. But the underlying realiser is the imagination. In some sense, anything that can be imagined has validity of some sort. It is at least thinkable, and if it has enough validity it might someday be realised materially in time and space, outside the mind of the imaginer. But now we should focus on the more mundane matter at hand, that the competence to know reality varies from very high to very low.

A model of information processing competence (Figure 5) includes consensual assumptions made by neuroscientists about relationships between brain areas and mental functions (Chapter Four, Figure 1). Data from the external world and the body is manipulated in cortical and subcortical brain areas to discern its meaning, and generate expecta-tions about the utility of various possible responses. The neocortical top of the system has potentially the most decisional authority. Assumptions from polyvagal theory (Porges, 2011) are consistent with this model. Myelinated vagal nerves in the brainstem communicate with heart, lungs

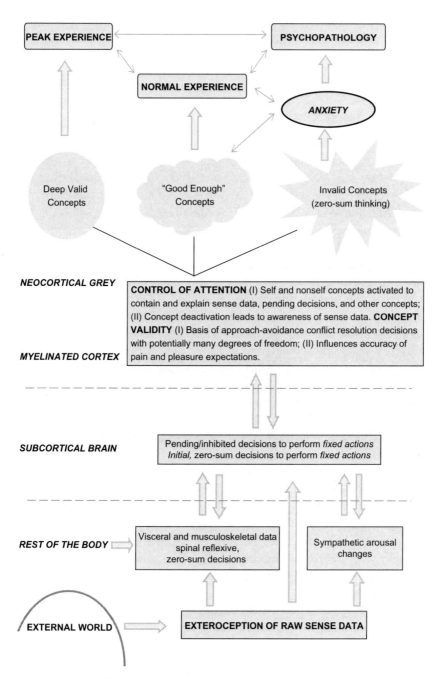

Figure 5. Information processing competence.

and, more or less directly, neocortex. Information about the organs and muscles is received in neocortical semantic processing areas (grey matter) via myelinated neurons (white matter). Decisions made in the neocortex can be transmitted back down into the rest of the brain and body.

Developing parasympathetic and cognitive control

Development of high parasympathetic tone depends on properly myelinated vagal nerves and learning. The learning can occur unconsciously by trial and error (e.g., Thorndike, 1912). Infant and adult brains receive sense data from the viscera. No newborns and perhaps few adults have especially valid, sophisticated semantic-concepts to contain and explain data coming from their own sensory autonomic nerves. Without concepts to capture sense data from the body or external world, consciousness is presented mostly with rather raw sensory data (e.g., Snyder, 2009).

But some interpretation of the sense data is taking place. With few or no semantic concepts in mind, the infant knows the practical meaning of the sense data that qualify as releasers of instinctive motoric and secretory actions to regulate the viscera. Such instincts work to colour sensations with some indication that pleasure and/or pain are to be expected when, for example, one sees or hears "mother" or "cat". As the concepts used by the baby become more valid and articulable, self-control increases dramatically. High mental competence makes it at least possible for an individual to gain control over ANS functions not usually subject to conscious control.

Sense data about the state of the body's organs, including the heart, come to the brainstem via vagal afferents. This sense data becomes associated automatically in mind with contemporaneous changes in thoughts and feelings. Such connections in time between ANS events and more or less conscious neocortical events are stored in episodic memory (e.g., Tulving & Szpunar, 2009). The connections are encoded as semantic concepts. By definition, a concept is a container of object attributes.

The developing infant's self-concepts and concepts of the external world are at the core of the individual's episodic memory. As such, early episodic and procedural memories are the foundations of the mind. The foundational concepts have the most influence on organising the mental field, and establishing ground rules for a lifetime of making sense of things. They are the person's bible. If the earliest episodic memories involve trauma, the person's development will be complicated from the start.

Much has been written from various psychological and biological schools about empathy, that is, the responses one animal makes to sensory data originating from another individual (e.g., Ainsworth & Bowlby, 1965; Bowlby, 1969; Davis, 1983, 1994; Kramer et al., 2010; Schore, 2003a, 2003b). How the early caretakers respond to the infant is especially important in mammalian development. Increased infant stress, in reaction to being inaccurately understood, has been carefully described (e.g., Ainsworth et al., 1978). Logically, the infant must send some data about his bodily state to the caretaker via facial gestures, physical postures, or vocalisations. These gestures release fixed action patterns, and can cause higher-level feeling and conceptual reactions in the parent. Facial expressions (e.g., Emde, 1980; Tronick et al., 1978); mirror neurons (e.g., Decety & Ickes, 2009; Gallese, 2001; Rizzolatti & Craighero, 2004), and *projective identification* (Klein, 1932) have been posited as mediating responses to the internal states of other individuals.

Learning can be made more programmatic by caregivers who know accurately the internal state of the child. The accuracy of judgements one makes about other people is effected by: (1) cognitive empathy, including causal attributions about, for example, why the baby is crying; (2) feeling empathy, or intuitive sensations and feelings mediated by mirror neurons; and (3) scientific concepts of physiology and psychology. These methods are used to diagnose the infant's internal state. This may lead to attempts to increase and decrease sympathetic arousal and to teach the child how to control the parasympathetic brakes. External stressors (e.g., light, temperature) can be raised or lowered; visual, tactile and auditory sensations can be provoked by presenting visual objects, stroking, tickling or singing. Bodily postures or activities that alter energy can be performed (e.g., rocking, lying down). Foods and medicines can be given.

Especially for the infant, the ability to manufacture words and string them together in private thought and public speech depends importantly on the actual presence of another social agent. With self-development, thought can occur in the absence of others. But all people have strong habits to conform in thought and overt behaviour to real or imagined social pressures. Everyone must be able to respond competently to pressures emanating from their own gut, brain, and mind.

Kohut's (1977) idea of optimal empathic failure describes how the parent can regulate tension or sympathetic arousal by presenting goals that are moderately difficult to attain. One holds the spoon at a distance just far enough to motivate approach and grabbing. If goal objects are too hard or too far away to attain, frustration, aggression and eventually avoidance of tasks ensues. If tasks are too easy, little approach energy is aroused. These relations between task difficulty and the arousal and enactment of achievement motives were described thoroughly by McClelland and his group (e.g., McClelland, 1958).

Most importantly the adult can help the baby learn concepts, that is, words that can be used to contain and explain what otherwise would remain unconscious sensations from the body. The best parents are curious about the baby's body and motivated to approach the child and understand it with valid concepts. Parents who are afraid of or disgusted by the child's mind and/or body, will avoid attending to information coming from the child, and avoid focusing on their own sensory, conceptual, and feeling reactions to the child.

At some point in an emergency, anyone can lose parasympathetic tone. Extreme pain or fear from somatic disease, social disaster, or intentional torture can sooner or later cause a degradation of parasympathetic control of the body (e.g., defecation, syncope, catatonic physical immobilisation) and the mind (e.g., confusion, panic, dissociation, psychosis, catatonic immobilisation of thought).

If the person's early or later development is marked by frank trauma, or if caregivers were chronically unable to register competently enough the child's physical and mental states, the person may wind up in psychotherapy. What have people with mental illness failed to learn? Most simply, they have not learned good-enough mental control to satisfy some important need or desire. Mental control or competence depends on: (1) the validity of the concepts used to contain and explain sensations, and other concepts; and (2) habits learned to activate control-relevant concepts at the right times and places. Problems with mental control cause, in turn, problems with controlling everything else, including the viscera, the voluntary muscles, and social relations.

Responses to sense data involve more or less neocortical influence

The neocortex, the site of the most sophisticated brain processors, works largely to inhibit immediate action based on very early, initial information processing and decision making in the subcortical brain.

Thinking works to make decisions to resolve conflicts produced when sensory arrays potentiate both instinctive approach and instinctive avoidance behaviours. Conscious or unconscious use of concepts can produce decisions that might work to, at least, distract the focus of an animal's brain–mind control system from enacting a pending, fixed action (instinct).

It seems obvious that information about fixed actions that are near thresholds of overt enactment can reach the neocortex. Thinking about sensation or pending decisions works, in part, to inhibit muscular action. Temporarily disrupting instinctual urges or gut reactions can give the executive time to attend to and process information. Situations can be analysed. The person might think, "Perhaps semantic concepts should be used to describe this current situation. I'd rather not rely on the statistical validity of the instinct that has been potentiated by this sensory array." Ideally, thinking works to increase control and is worth the bioenergetic costs of intensive information processing. The person may make more accurate estimates of how events will transpire, and can develop strategies and tactics for coping with predicted changes in the internal and external environments.

Distraction of attentional focus is similar to what was called *displacement* by Freud, Kurt Lewin, and ethologists. Momentary displacement, disruption or distraction from a goal or focus of attention might be a necessary component of a more sophisticated defence like *sublimation*. Freud imagined sublimation involved displacing sexual goals with tamer cultural aims like playing the violin.

At any one moment, directing attention is more or less under executive control. And, one has a focus of attention during dreaming. During REM sleep, the mind's eye is controlled somewhat differently from how it focuses during wakefulness. For one thing, REM dreaming depends most probably on the presence of endogenous hallucinogens such as dimethyltryptamine (DMT) (Wallach, 2009). The dreamer observes and interacts with people, landscapes, and events not usually seen or imagined during ordinary wakefulness.

In dreaming sleep, it is as if the executive self observes and often acts in a drama produced and written by non-executive functions of mind. It is the executive's task to make solid predictions and plan effective actions to promote the safety and productivity of the person.

From this perspective, dreams are all attempts to get the attention of the chief executive. The followers, the rest of the mind and body, ask, "What goes on here? Do you know what you are doing up there?" Chronically poor estimates of situations and individuals are made by people deemed mentally ill. Psychiatric disorders usually involve repeated use of invalid concepts for containing and explaining sensation. This produces inaccurate expectations of pain and pleasure, which are poor guides for overt behaviour. Use of both valid and invalid concepts can be habitual and unreflective, or subject to conscious reflection. The psychotherapy patient can only hope that his therapist is at least a little more *compos mentis* than him.[2]

Somatic variables, semantic concepts, and feelings in psychotherapy

A clinician should attempt to make a model of the patient's self-regulatory system. What variables affect the system's competence to control sensations, concepts, feelings, and overt behaviours? All communications made by clinicians of every school are based explicitly or implicitly on assumptions about: (1) the state of the patient's mind; (2) the state that is desired by the patient and/or imagined by the clinician as better than the current state; and (3) how one operates to move the person into the preferred state.

With what we know now, the state of brain and body should, if possible, be accounted for in making diagnostic formulations of the causes of patients' symptoms. Of course, all naïve psychologists are equipped with evolutionarily equipment to somehow register the internal state of the other. This probably involves mirror neurons that stimulate a tendency for one's own body to mimic the overt bodily postures of others (e.g., Gallesse, 2001). Specific overt facial gestures and other bodily postures are causes and effects of specific feelings in all people (e.g., Ekman, 1978; Izard, 1979; Lanzetta & Orr, 1986). Hence, observing another can make one's own feeling responses into valid diagnostic indicators of the feelings of the other person. This is feeling empathy. The other form of empathy involves inferential, cognitive processes. Davis (1983, 1994) named them empathic concern and perspective taking, respectively. These are reliable concepts with face, predictive, discriminant, and construct validity.

But as the psychoanalysts learned, it is quite easy to confuse what the other is feeling and thinking with the self's feelings and thoughts. Transference and countertransference are both examples of the general process of projecting one's own internal state onto the other. The tendency to confuse projection and empathic accuracy was common among formal psychologists until Cronbach (1955) pointed out their methodological errors. There are now reliable methods for validly differentiating between projection and accurate social judgements, and between cognitive and feeling empathy. For example, we showed that perspective taking, but not a feeling of concern for the other, can increase an observer's ability to know how another would like to see himself (Bernstein & Davis, 1982).

The complexities of understanding intrapsychic and interpersonal systems can be reduced by simultaneous approach from biological, psychological, and social angles. Triangulation helps us locate the patient's position in mental space. I think that measures of physiological processes will become increasingly common in clinical psychotherapy and in non-medical contexts. Real-time biofeedback of RSA range to aid learning how to control polyvagal tone has already been used successfully with PTSD patients (e.g., Porges, 2011; Zucker et al., 2009). Neurofeedback is also being used to treat a variety of other mental disorders (e.g., Thomas, 2012).

A therapist might help the patient to recognise how changes in RSA are correlated with changes in feelings and thoughts. Instances of such correlations should be abundant given the tendency to repeat habits that represent poor compromises with reality. In other words, opportunities to understand and influence mental states are plentiful when somatic variables and mental variables are measured and used together in psychotherapy. Biofeedback, neurofeedback, and eye movement therapies qualify as somatic therapies (see Mollon, 1995).

In eye movement desensitization and reprocessing (EMDR) we manipulate a somatic variable (visual focus) while the patient attempts to think about what might be troubling her (e.g., Bernstein, 2011; Mollon, 2005; Shapiro, 2001). At first, many patients find it difficult to do two things at once. That is, think and track the therapist's finger with the eyes. This is a general sort of functional mind–brain incompetence seen in anxiety states. Multitasking is difficult under high arousal (see Figure 3) and patients with posttraumatic stress tend to be highly aroused and anxious.

With practice, patients learn to differentiate movements of the mind's eye from movements of the eyeball. This can work to alter mental habits. Trial and error learning is made more efficient with

EMDR, in part because we are giving the patient more chances (trials) to observe covariations between somatic variables, feelings, and thoughts.

How EMDR affects mental states is complex. In contrast, RSA range seems more simply related to control of thought and feeling. For example, a PTSD patient might note that as she increases her parasympathetic tone with breath control, anxiety too can be more effectively controlled. Low parasympathetic tone and poor anxiety control are proximal causes of dysregulated feeling and thought.

Thinking and learning use data from interoception and exteroception

It is somewhat paradoxical that sensory data about autonomic states already in the person's brain may be recognised more easily via exteroception than interoception. Yoga experts are able to register consciously raw sensory data and somehow use it in learning how to control what are for most people entirely autonomic, unconscious functions. The feats of yogis prove the point that such learning can affect levels of consciousness (e.g., Weil, 1972). And various neurological conditions such as autism work to make usually unconscious sense data available to consciousness (e.g., Snyder, 2009; Snyder et al., 2004).

How do statistically normal individuals think about sensations in the body? Everyone must have some implicit, useful, face valid hypotheses about how their body works. How are these relationships understood unconsciously by people with somatoform and other anxiety disorders? At some point, everyone must experience something like *signal anxiety* (Freud, 1926). This, in turn, stimulates effortful attempts to avoid awareness of truth and pleasure.

Psychodynamic types of models are needed to describe how any particular patient copes with signal anxiety. In the most severe cases, memories of horrible trauma cause chronic and acute anxiety states in these patients, years after the trauma. Explicit hypotheses need to be spelled out about how distorted self- and non-self-concepts work to cause anxiety (Bernstein, 2011, Appendix III). These diagnostic hypotheses should be informed by observations of the relationships between subjective experiences of thoughts and feelings, and real-time somatic measures such as parasympathetic tone, EEG patterns, and other measures.

How does attention shift from interocepted to exterocepted sense data? Are such operations in a zero-sum relationship? It is likely that they are for at least a tiny moment. Snyder (e.g., 2009) thinks that one can be aware of either relatively raw sense data or concepts, and that one can switch attention between these two things rather rapidly, in milliseconds. I imagine that shifts of conscious attention between interoceptive and exteroceptive data channels occur at rates of change similar to shifts between sense data and concepts, and that RSA range changes at similar rates. If these types of variables work together somehow to regulate sensations and feelings, it would make sense that they change at similar rates.

In any case, I think normal citizens equipped with biosensors and computer displays will, with or without a human therapist, learn about their bodily states by attending to external presentations of sense data. For example, they will attend to a cell phone screen containing a graphic representation of changes in sensory data that already is represented somewhere in their nervous system. Wide use of such technologies could cause a marked increase in the average person's ability to control mind and body.

Brain–mind as hedonic calculator

As noted in Chapter Four, I assume that all goals must be hedonically laden to some degree at least. Fast consumption of the most compelling goal objects (e.g., foods, drugs, sex objects, and yes, ideas) causes the greatest pleasure. "We are so constituted that we can gain intense pleasure only from the contrast and only very little from the condition itself." (Freud, 1930) Perhaps the fastest way to obtain contrast between subjective feeling states is to change attentional focus. The next fastest methods may be intravenous or insufflative delivery of certain psychotropic drugs. I use the word consciousness to describe what is in focal attention.

The first step in processing sensory data involves unconscious and/or conscious registration of the data somewhere in the nervous system. Explicit and implicit decisions about what to think about determine, in part, the person's competence to experience pleasure and avoid pain and injury. If attention is under low or no control, consciousness may change from this to that with no apparent rhyme or reason. Most people become ill after some time in a meaningless state of mind. Poor executive control of attention can cause dizziness, nausea, fear, frenzy, immobilisation, and psychosis. The critical point is that the person has to make at least some meaning of sensations and thoughts to not go mad. Meaning is derived from assumptions about the relatedness in time and space between the sensations, semantic concepts, feelings, and overt behaviour of the self and others.

Fundamentally, the meanings of things are based on estimates of the potential pleasure and pain one is likely to experience when interacting with them. These expectations determine to a large degree how a body–brain–mind system orients itself in the physical, mental and social worlds (see Chapter Nine on the semantic differential). Ideas reside in the material machinery of the brain in order to determine the meanings of sensations. Sensations are caused by changes in structures in the world and in the body. I have assumed that accurate conceptual interpretations of sensations lead to more pleasurable feelings than inaccurate interpretations. For example, most people would attribute a sensation of warmth on their face in the morning to the light from the sun. Alternatively, it could be attributed it to the devil setting them on fire. Activating such an invalid concept to explain sensory data from the skin will cause trouble.

Concepts, drugs, and focal brain lesions as causes of brain–mind states

The proximal causes of pleasure and pain are neurotransmitter actions at synaptic receptor sites. Biederman has shown that interpreting visual sense data results in more pleasure than mere sensation of visual stimuli (e.g., Biederman & Vessel, 2006). This is because there are more mu-opioid receptors on neurons in association areas of the visual cortex than in the sensory neurons leading to the conceptual areas. Operationally, habituation to sense data from all modalities results in a reduction in nervous activity in sensory neurons. Continuing to think about the meaning of sensations sets off a cascade of information processes driven by mu-opioid receptor agonism, suppression of GABA (the most prevalent inhibitory neurotransmitter), and further propagation of information processing in the corpus striatum leading to disinhibition of dopaminergic neurons. Opiates can produce euphoria and pain reduction, and dopamine is involved in anticipatory pleasures (e.g., Schultz, 2010).

Endogenous (e.g., DMT) and exogenous hallucinogens (e.g., LSD, psilocybin) raise neuronal habituation thresholds (e.g., Cooper et al., 2003). This implies that when under the influence of hallucinogens, the concepts a person habitually uses to organise sensations are not effective at causing habituation. That is, old habits of thinking do not work to contain and terminate awareness of sensations as they do in more normal states of mind. This motivates attempts to create new or different containing concepts. If the person can generate such novel ways of thinking he may have the highly pleasurable feelings of a good hallucinogenic trip (Bernstein, 2011). If not, a bad trip may result involving anxiety about being overwhelmed by unremitting, inadequately contained sensation. Subsequently, pleasurable, enlightening, or frightening psychotic hallucinations may be activated to control fear.

The central question for Freud in the beginning and for neuroscience now is the same: how do the mind and brain work more or less competently to make good approach pleasure and avoid pain decisions? Certainly, social, psychological, and biological variables determine together the person's mental competence. These variables include those affecting how numerous neurotransmitters interact in all the anatomical structures of the nervous system.

I find it remarkable that Solms and Turnbull (2012) say that studying patients with focal brain lesions is the preferred method of neuropsychoanalysis because:

> it follows directly from where Freud had left off … enabling us to correlate our psychoanalytic inferences with *definite* neuroscientific ones. Structural neurological lesions provide infinitely more precision than do psychopharmacological manipulations, considering all the interactive vagaries of neurotransmitter dynamics. (p. 139)

Kaplan-Solms and Solms (2000) did psychoanalytic therapy with patients who had right parietal-lobe damage. Such lesions have been associated with difficulties in forming whole object representations. They found that after therapy the patients became somewhat less narcissistic and more competent in their object relations. They did not spell out too exactly how the lesions operated as causes of patients' subjective experience or psychological competence.

In contrast, if a person is given a sufficient dose of an opiate, tranquilliser, amphetamine, or hallucinogen we can confidently predict that she will soon experience rather marked changes in thinking and feeling. We can be certain that the particular molecule she ingests has initiated the changes. These are reliable, valid, unambiguous cause and effect relationships that are inconsistent with the idea that using psychopharmacological manipulations to understand the brain and mind is imprecise, vague, and somehow not neuroscientific.

It might appear that Solms and Turnbull (2012) are discouraging the use of drugs as independent variables in mind–brain studies. But they ask in the same paper, "Why do we not have systematic psychoanalytic studies of the manipulations of the different classical neurotransmitters that psychopharmacologists regularly tinker with in conventional psychiatric settings?" (p. 141)[3]

I don't quite understand their answer to the question they pose in the title of their paper: "What is neuropsychoanalysis?" But regardless of Freud's greatness, or what neuropsychoanalysis is, following from where Freud had left off is not a scientific justification for using or not using any particular research method.

To be pedantic, the goal of science is to identify the causes of natural phenomena. Subjective experiences of sensations, concepts, and feelings are causes and effects of biological, psychological and social activity. If a neuropsychological function depends somewhat on a specific brain region being intact, it follows that injury to that area could interfere with the ability to perform the function. But, most generally, brain structures interact with numerous chemical, electric, psychological, and social factors to cause subjective experiences.

Notes

1. This is where epigenetics and psychoimmunology become relevant.
2. Confusion about how to apply neuroscience findings in the clinic is due, in part, to ambiguity in basic mind–brain theories. What should students know before starting clinical training? Which theoretical bibles and traditional methods should be taught? Eclecticism has become a *de facto* school of psychotherapy. This is a compromise solution made to cope with the lack of integrated theory. Many creative clinicians take an idea from here and another from there and develop their own, private, integrative theories. But most psychotherapists could use help to understand more completely what it is they do.

   Increasing knowledge of brain and mind is causing patients, scientists, and clinicians to alter their conceptions of how mental and somatic illnesses are related (e.g., Shorter, 1992). This causes scientific, political, moral, and economic conflicts among medical insurance companies, doctrinaire psychiatrists, medical and non-medical psychologists, religious fundamentalists, and patients seeking help for mind–brain conditions.

The healthcare crisis in America and around the world is due, in large part, to thinking based on acceptance of the hard problem, that body and mind exist in separate ontological worlds. The fact is that all disease affects the body, brain, and mind. Most visits to primary care doctors are caused by chronic, unresolved psychosocial stress (Rosendal et al., 2005; Shaibani & Sabbagh, 1998). The underlying psychological causes of physical disease are rarely treated (for an exception, see Abbass et al., 2010).

3. Some of this important type of work has been done (e.g., Amen et al., 2008).

CHAPTER TWELVE

Authority, self-control, and metatheory

I have assumed that the amount of pleasurable feeling experienced in consciousness is generally indicative of the degree of validity of the concepts used to interpret sensations and other concepts, and that getting valid feedback about the self might be the greatest of the great pleasures of knowing reality. It would follow that people are always motivated to learn about the validity of their own ideas. Such learning about the self is intrinsically rewarding (cf., Deci, 1975).

Michael Young's (1958) idea of a *meritocracy* might describe societies in which those with the most valid ideas become authorities in the minds of others. An individual's authority determines their rank in social dominance hierarchies (e.g., Alcock, 2010; Lorenz, 1963). The pleasures from being recognised as an authority are largely extrinsic rewards in Deci's theory.

The person has more raw data about his own body and mind than about any other aspect of the world. He is connected to himself by about a hundred billion neurons in the brain, and I don't know how many others in the rest of the body. This access to data puts the self in an especially good position to develop valid concepts to explain itself. In the end, we register the external world and the internal world by means of electrochemical events occurring in the structures of the

153

nervous system. Accordingly, nothing can ever be known as exactly as what goes on in one's own brain.

Part of the registration process involves explicit awareness of valid and invalid concepts about oneself, that is, self-consciousness. People vary in the degree to which their self-concepts include the idea that they are somehow authorised to be themself (cf., Winnicott, 1960b). Individuals lacking concepts indicating that they are legitimate interpreters of reality, find it difficult to resolve conflicting tendencies to approach or avoid other people and objects emerging from the external world and the mind itself. Under such conditions, it is difficult to identify self-defining goals and, therefore, practically impossible to realize or actualise one's self-concepts (e.g., Bernstein, 2003).

In the military, a general officer has the most authority to organise and control other soldiers. The manner in which general, self-defining concepts work to regulate the body and mind of an individual is similar to how leaders regulate social systems. And, the system of self-concepts and the habits and rules for activating them are analogous to the operating system of a computer. The self functions as a personal bible that specifies rules for living.

Ideally, self-concepts and society's normative customs and laws are more valid than invalid. Validity in this context is measured by exactly the same criteria used in formal science: face, predictive, discriminant, and construct validity. Foundational, deep self-concepts, and the habits to use them, are at the top of a hierarchy of more specific, operational concepts and habits. The general, foundational self-concepts can determine the use of the more specific concepts.

Developing self-authority

The person's first leaders or teachers are the parents. The empathic competence of parents is the most important factor determining the developmental trajectory of the person (e.g., Ainsworth & Bowlby, 1965; Kohut, 1977). Young children, and all adults to varying degrees, come to regard themselves as others regard them. Social psychological research concerning the effects of leadership behaviour on group members is also somewhat descriptive of the effects of self-concepts on one's own subjective experience and overt behaviour.

Autocratic leaders create social conditions that promote aggression between group members but also high productivity. Democratic leaders tend to have less aggressive and moderately productive groups. Aloof, *laissez-faire* leaders produce the highest levels of aggression and the lowest productivity (e.g., Lewin et al., 1939; Litwin & Stringer, 1968). When group survival is threatened by external dangers or internal chaos, leaders who take unilateral, autocratic control promote survival and achievement more effectively than do friendly, democratic types (Fiedler, 1964).

Autocratic, democratic, and *laissez-faire* parents affect children in the manner that leaders affect social organisations. Very controlling, autocratic parents frustrate the child's impulses. Perhaps the most valid maxim in all of psychological theory is that frustration leads to aggression (e.g., Dollard et al., 1939). The arousal of aggressive feelings and thoughts causes guilt and anxiety in children and adults who fear retribution for violating moral standards (talion dread). Then, obsessive-compulsive rituals and other defensive mechanisms can develop to undo the prohibited feelings, and control anxiety (e.g., Freud, 1909).

But autocratic sorts of parental behaviour of a moderate variety can promote in children conscientiousness, and an ability to organise the mind and behaviour. The idea of optimal empathic failure is relevant here (Kohut, 1977). One tries to not overly frustrate the child but to establish goals that may be just beyond their current grasp. This promotes the ability to tolerate frustration, suppress aggression, and learn how to make order from multiple, conflicting sensations, feelings, and thoughts. Orderly individuals are often successful in their work and social lives. In contrast, distant, unavailable, *laissez-faire* parents produce the most frustration, aggression, and depression, and the least functional citizens (see Seligman, 1975; Tronick et al., 1978; Emde, 1980; Carlson, 2010).

Empathically responsive, democratic parents tend to reduce a child's fear of her own impulses, thoughts, and feelings (e.g., Horney, 1950; Winnicott, 1960a, 1960b). This can promote a child's belief in her own authority to decide how to think and behave overtly.

Social dominance

Relations between individual members of many animal species, including humans, are structured by dominance hierarchies. Social rank or authority depends on the competence to influence others. Influence involves primarily the ability to cause others to experience pleasures that reinforce particular ways of thinking or acting, and/or pains that deter certain thoughts or behaviours (cf., French & Raven, 1959, on social power).

One can be consciously aware of sense data, concepts, or feelings (cf. Snyder & Mitchell, 1999). I define feelings as meaningful sensations, that is, sense data whose meaning is inferred by use of concepts. Rudimentary, initial data processing occurring in subcortical brain areas is enough to determine if sense data indicates something painful or pleasurable. If these sorts of reflexive decisions are not immediately enacted, they become input for subsequent, higher-level review. They can be considered pending decisions, which potentiate specific sorts of responses and, hence, exert pressures on subsequent information processing (see Figure 5).

Executive functioning involves neocortical review of pending subcortical decisions. Semantic concepts contain or inhibit pending fixed actions and are used in processes comparing them to other options. A mental system's "meaningfulness" could be measured quantitatively by assessing the extent to which networks of concepts are primed or used more or less simultaneously. This involves spreading activation—the automatic tendency for concepts associated with sensations or other concepts to go into a state of readiness for activation. Semantic networks riddled with conflicts must operate neurophysiologically differently than less stressed networks. Distinctive EEG states likely underlie the workings of more valid and less valid belief systems.

Social influence

Competent social influence involves taking account of the sophistication and readiness state of the nervous system of influence targets. For example, rats have a rudimentary neocortex and can learn concepts, but they are unlikely to respond to speeches urging them to be reasonable. Compared to humans, other mammals are usually more influenced in the moment by raw sensory data indicating pain and pleasure. Top ranks in the dominance hierarchies of such creatures are usually occupied by the physically strongest and most aggressive individuals. Animals of all species can be influenced by simple sensory pleasures and pains. In primitive human groups such as criminal gangs, physical strength and a willingness to threaten or actually harm others can also determine social rank.

Individuals with advanced information processing competence can be influenced by concepts as well as simple sensations. Appeals to others to alter their behaviour may involve concepts of morality, loyalty, responsibility, peace, love, beauty, patriotism, justice, truth, fairness, practicality, and countless other reasons. Concepts can influence others because every idea has some potential to cause feelings of pain or pleasure. And, to repeat, the deepest valid ideas are the most potent causes of pleasure. If invalid ideas had as much potential as valid ideas to cause pleasure, individuals and cultures would have never developed increased knowledge of nature.

Of course, our knowledge is incomplete and will likely remain so for ever. In the meantime, society needs parents, teachers, doctors, and leaders, and each individual needs self-regulatory concepts. If we take truth as the ultimate authority, all conceptual social systems used to influence people including governments, scientific theories, and individual self-regulatory systems are more or less inauthentic compromises with reality. But as a practical matter we follow a useful maxim: the perfect is the enemy of the good. Life goes on, except for the most immobilised perfectionists (see Winnicott, 1960b).

Metatheory is superfluous

I have equated the depth of concepts with their generality. General ideas organise more specific, concrete, operational concepts. Typically, general ideas are assumed wrongly to be mere abstractions, divorced from material reality. Lewin was famous for saying there is nothing as practical as a good theory. By definition, valid general concepts always work to organise other valid, more specific concepts that ultimately impinge on physical realities of nature. Construct validity is based on the assumption that general concepts can be concretely operationalised, verified experimentally, and connected systematically (Campbell & Fiske, 1959).

The so-called hard problem, which considers mental and physical phenomena to be fundamentally different things, assumes that concepts are mere abstractions without physical manifestations. This belief has motivated the creation of metatheories such as metaphysics and metapsychology. But:

> If metaphysical speculation is a shooting at the moon, philosophers have always begun by shooting at it; only after missing it have they said there was no moon, and that it was a waste of time to shoot at it. Skepticism is defeatism in philosophy, and all defeatisms are born of previous defeats. When one has repeatedly failed in a certain undertaking, one naturally concludes that it was an impossible undertaking. I say naturally, but not logically, for a repeated failure in dealing with

> a problem may point to a repeated error in discussing the problem
> rather than to its intrinsic insolubility. (Gilson, 1937, p. 85)[1]

A case in point was the widely accepted belief of psychologists from 1955 to 1982 that it was impossible to measure objectively observers' accuracy in judging what other people thought and felt. The so-called *rating scale method* had been used for years by psychologists to measure interpersonal accuracy. Then, a withering critique of the method was written by Cronbach (1955). It turned out that the traditional technique did not measure an observer's accuracy in knowing the subjective experiences of actors. Rather, its "accuracy scores" indicated the degree of similarity between observer and actor, plus a tendency for the observer to project his ideas about himself onto the actor. In short, the method had not identified keen psychologists but instead statistically average people who assumed implicitly that everyone else was similar to them.

The embarrassing criticism, combined with an implicit superstition that knowing what was in another's mind might really depend on some magical, metasensory, or extrasensory perception, worked at once to stop all research on this centrally important problem. Instead of merely following the suggestions made in the critiques about how to fix the measuring methods, the field of accuracy in person perception lay dormant for over twenty-five years.

Eventually, research informed by the earlier critiques started (e.g., Bernstein & Davis, 1982; Harackiewicz & DePaulo, 1982) and has flourished ever since (e.g., Friesen & Kammrath, 2011). Such valid methods could have been used the day after the critiques of the old methods were published. But apparently new work on the question had to wait until the old generation of methodological naïfs had retired.

Freud acknowledged freely the methodological limitations of his day. He predicted accurately that it would take about 100 years to develop experimental methods and technologies to make reliable and valid observations of the workings of the brain (Kandel, 2006). In the meantime, he developed theories of mental functioning aided by observations of patients' overt behaviour including their use of words (semantic concepts). The term metatheory, including metapsychology, describes hypotheses imagined to be unamenable to scientific study. The central, dynamic concepts of psychoanalytic theory such as pleasure principle, repetition compulsion, and defence, plus structural ideas like superego, were all considered metapsychological.

But in every branch of science, parts of metatheories have become amenable to scientific study over time. As a result, some ideas get discarded and others are retained and refined by continuing research. I have already described how rough equivalents of Freud's metaconcepts have since been operationalised, tested experimentally, partially validated, and subsequently refined (see Chapter Four).

Most simply, to theorise is to invent concepts to process data and other concepts. It is to do thought experiments. This involves imagining explanatory concepts, using them to process data, judging how well they work to explain the data, and how they might relate to other explanatory concepts. These processes are the defining feature not only of formal scientific theorising, but also of everyday imagining, wondering, and daydreaming. Freud called it "abstract thinking". The concept of metapsychology is superfluous and should be retired along with the concept affect.

Known for his scepticism of religion, Freud attributed his self-defining passion—the competence to think abstractly—to his religious heritage. Edmundson described Freud's thinking on this subject in his review of *Moses and Monotheism* (Freud, 1938):

> Judaism's distinction as a faith comes from its commitment to belief in an invisible God … The ability to believe in an internal, invisible God vastly improves people's capacity for abstraction. "The prohibition against making an image of God—the compulsion to worship a God whom one cannot see," Freud says, meant that in Judaism "a sensory perception was given second place to what may be called an abstract idea—a triumph of intellectuality over sensuality." If people can worship what is not there, they can also reflect on what is not there, or on what is presented to them in symbolic and not immediate terms. So *the mental labor of monotheism* prepared the Jews—as it would eventually prepare others in the West—to achieve distinction in law, in mathematics, in science and in literary art. It gave them an advantage in all activities that involved making an abstract model of experience, in words or numbers or lines, and working with the abstraction to achieve control over nature or to bring humane order to life. (Edmundson, 2007, italics added)

I think "the mental labour of monotheism" describes the workings of a control system in which one's own concepts of reality are invested with authority to control mind and body. The thoughts and actions of individuals and social groups tend to be firmly organised when a singular authoritative agent is in control. This presents a dilemma for the individual and for societies. Competence and authority is a powerful combination. Everything being equal, the person or group might succeed best if authority is based on valid rather than invalid concepts of reality.

Concepts can vary in at least three dimensions: valid-invalid, subjective-objective, and general-specific (see Chapter Three). Generality is more or less the same as depth. I assume that the general and specific self- and non-self-concepts that cause mystical and other peak experiences are more valid than those underlying normal and pathological experiences. Grand, valid visions of reality can be intensely pleasurable and reinforcing. Mystical experience might be considered valid spiritual experience. Like all valid phenomena, they are durable and somewhat controllable.

In contrast, concepts promoting paranoid states are mostly invalid and subjective. The tendency to project aggressive, sexual, and anxious feelings is pathognomonic in paranoia. There is no differentiation between general and specific concepts about the self and the external world. Instead, all levels of understanding are conflated. This creates a feeling of the connectedness of everything. It's all about one thing: "They are out to get me". Every specific event proves the general concept. "I saw him look at me. This proves he is part of the worldwide conspiracy to destroy me." This produces a feeling of knowing the relationship between everything small and large. On the face of it, paranoia may appear to be a valid mystical experience. But, of course, it is a form of pseudo-depth, based on invalid general and specific concepts.

Clinicians are well aware that those in paranoid states can be smugly satisfied with themselves for discovering "the real truth" behind the plots organised against them by the authorities. Of course, this is a rather complete projection of the self's authority. If such projections worked to control subjective experiences as reliably as more valid concepts of causality, the human race would have never developed. Animism would rule the individual and society. There is enough surface similarity between valid extreme experiences and invalid psychotic states, that profound scientific and subjective insights into reality have always been associated with mental illness.

Note

1. This quote came from a good paper on construct validity by John Horan (1995).

CHAPTER THIRTEEN

Moving through space, time, and light

Individuals and groups who learn and remember the most valid concepts about the self and the rest of nature are able to make the best decisions. A system of concepts can be arranged hierarchically, with the most general ideas at the top of the system exerting a pervasive influence on all the more specific, operational decisions made at lower levels. Executive decisions use general concepts.

In addition to generality or depth, a centrally important heuristic for organising brain–mind concepts is the difference between appetitive and consummatory thinking and overt behaviour.

> Today, hierarchical concepts continue to guide behavioural neuroscientists' thinking about motivation. Hierarchy concepts work extremely well for describing large-scale relations between the forebrain and the lower brain. [Various theorists] suggest that the forebrain can usefully be posited to initiate appetitive motivated behaviour by a hierarchical mechanism, whereas the brainstem executes consummatory aspects of motivated behaviour. (Berridge, 2004, p. 204)

For example, one may decide by means of neocortical information processes to attempt to get food or sex. Once the meal or mate is obtained, instinctive brainstem processes become involved with controlling the overt consummatory behaviour (eating, copulating). The anatomical, neurochemical, and autonomic systems regulating appetitive and consummatory functions are related, but different. Considered from a short temporal perspective, getting something always seems to precede consuming it.

The registration of need states in the brainstem can work first to recruit neocortical appetitive decision making and overt hunting for goal objects. Neocortical information processing of semantic concepts involving desires and attempts to satisfy them, and initial processing of sensory data in subcortical regions of the brain indicating somatic needs, are in dynamic, mutually regulatory relationships.

> Historically, learning theorists have often distinguished between the conditioning of relatively general motivational responses and of more specific outcome expectancies to Pavlovian Conditioned Stimuli (CS). However, this traditional distinction confounds two variables, that of the content of learning (specific *vs.* general) and its function ("motivational" *vs.* "cognitive") in the control of behaviour. It is possible that the differential modulation of appetitive and consummatory behaviours reflects the outcome of allostatic processes that have evolved to anticipate rather than react to events … Thus, CS-activation of a representation of food may be accompanied by an induction of appetite that further enhances both food-procuring and consummatory behaviours, allowing an animal to forage and eat beyond its present needs to be prepared for future famine. Well learned cues therefore may potentiate feeding even under conditions of satiation. (Galarce et al., 2007, p. 104)

In other words, without valid semantic concepts to regulate eating and other appetitive desires, the salient, sensory data emanating from goal objects (tasty food, secondary sexual characteristics) play an inordinate role in determining overt appetitive and consummatory behaviour. This can cause obesity, hypersexuality and other problems. Persisting in any behaviour beyond a meaningful point represents a failure to shift attentional focus from the behaviour releasing features of a goal object to different goals, and to semantic concepts explaining the meaning of obtaining and consuming any particular goal. Attention may become fixated for a variety of reasons including motives to avoid attending to other exteroceptive and interoceptive sensory data that might cause anxiety.

Desire, satisfaction, and transcendent experience

Somatic and mental needs and wants vary throughout the day. Discrepancies between the real state of things, and standards for ideal levels of material and mental items, are assessed constantly by cybernetic testing processes performed in various parts of the brain and body. Gaps between real and ideal conditions motivate attempts to achieve ideal or at least adequate levels of somatic and mental articles. The process of attaining standards has been described variously by biologists and psychologists as attempts to maintain homeostasis (e.g., Bernard, 1867; Cannon, 1932), complete tasks (Zeigarnik, 1927), reduce drives (Festinger, 1957; Hull, 1943), and so on. Most simply, living things are busy constantly with desires and attempts to satisfy them.

Buddhism is a religion based on assumptions that are somewhat consistent with the various formal scientific theories of homeostasis and drive reduction. It assumes, in part, that life is characterised by dissatisfaction, and desires to perform behaviours to reduce it. One aspect of Buddhism is the advice to practise some form of meditation. The transcendental meditation movement (TM) promoted a non-secular form of Zen Buddhist meditation. Begun by Maharishi Mahesh Yogi in the 1950s in India, TM spread to the West in the 1960s. The student is advised to sit in a comfortable chair for twenty minutes twice a day, close the eyes and repeat in mind a mantra, a two-syllable euphonious sound like ding-dong. If extraneous thoughts enter consciousness, one is instructed to return attention to the mantra. TM is thus a form of concentrative mediation that differs from mindfulness meditations in which one is instructed to just let thoughts flow as they might. The common element in both types of meditation is that they systematically alter the way conscious attention is deployed.

I enrolled in the TM class during graduate school and began meditating regularly according to their instructions. After a few months of practice, I noticed some of the effects I had been led to expect. These included a general decrease in everyday anxiety and most remarkably, an expansion of the hypnagogic state one typically experiences between waking consciousness and sleep. Everyday awareness and sleep seemed more similar than before the meditation practice had started. This is consistent with the reliable observations that EEG patterns seen in light sleep are similar to those found during meditation (see Kahn & Polich, 2006). But meditation is not exactly sleep. It is more usually character-ised as a state of restful alertness. TM and other meditative methods create an unusually integrated state of mind in which the competencies of both the waking mind and the sleeping mind are present contempo-raneously. This is related to the state of lucid dreaming (e.g., Dresler et al., 2011).

After over a year of everyday practice, I noticed that soon after clos-ing my eyes and starting to repeat the mantra, I had a sensation that my body was ceaselessly going up, up, up. It was a pleasant feeling of being weightless. I imagined I had achieved the state of transcendence, or climbing up from the earth, free of gravity.

This "going up" sensation occurred shortly after I had started to have a particular thought while meditating. I began to wonder when I had actually thought of the mantra. After a year of repeating the sound/word over and over again, intending to activate awareness of the mantra became the dominant mental habit elicited by the medita-tive situation (the mantra, the quiet room, comfortable chair, the times of day). The strength of competing habits to active thoughts other than the mantra must have fallen as the practice itself became effortless and more pleasurable. Hebb's law would predict that the neurons encod-ing procedural and episodic memories of the repeated practice ses-sions would fire and then wire together to build an increasingly large and more complex neural network. Repetitive mantra processing had somehow changed my brain and my subjective experience of doing the task.

The amount of energy used by the brain to operate habits depends on habit strength (e.g., Gailliot, 2007). Strong habits need relatively weak amounts of stimuli to become activated. Sometimes a single experience will change mental habits markedly (e.g., car accident, sexual assault). More usually, repeated experiences strengthen habits that determine the general features of the person's brain and mind.

I imagine that a biological agency operates constantly to increase the efficiency of executive decision-making processes. The brain and all biological systems tend to search for less expensive methods for get-ting and consuming things. In the meditation experience, I had asked myself, "How little effort can I use and still experience the mantra?"

and, "When had the appetitive state of seeking the word, changed into a state of consuming or registering the word?" After repetitive practice and, hence, after the strengthening of the habit to activate the concept of the mantra, one experiences simultaneously bringing the desired concept into being and consuming it. This reminds us of the ancient uroboros image of a snake eating its own tail. The uroboros can symbolise something constantly recreating itself, or a primitive mind state that lacks differentiation (e.g., Neumann, 1949).

Normally, consummatory processes work to terminate appetitive processes. And logically, the executive energy miser's anxiety and efforts should relax after sought objects have been seized (e.g., oxygen, money, food, sex, heroin, eight AAA batteries, lottery ticket, condoms, the latest electronic gadget). But as the habit to think the mantra became more and more automatic, I was led to think of thinking of what I knew I was already thinking. This produced a sensation that can be seen with barbershop mirrors. That is, when the mirrors are lined up just right, you can see an infinite regress of objects in all the mirrors.

My hypothesis is that the transcendent feeling of going up endlessly can be caused by explicit awareness of a ubiquitous or infinite thought, and that this experience is due to altering the relationship between appetitive and consummatory brain and mind processes. After all, if one seems to have automatically what one desires, the usual strivings of everyday existence disappear. There is no gravity, seriousness, urgency, or goals. As a pop song from 1967 suggested, one may float up, up, and away. That a transcendent feeling may result from a lack of goals is likely why the Bible commands believers to observe weekly a day of rest or Sabbath on which no profane goals can be pursued.

Altering mental states and habits

Shortly after learning how to enter reliably a transcendent state, I stopped the practice entirely. Was I afraid of disappearing into infinity? I wasn't consciously aware of being afraid. But most young people are not well prepared mentally to pursue otherworldly things and, for example, should probably avoid non-medical use of hallucinogenic drugs. But after people learn to cope adequately with the demands of living in the world, they should be prepared to experiment safely with different methods of controlling consciousness including meditative practices and drugs. This can promote physical health and more complete appreciation of reality among statistically normal individuals and those with pathological habits of mind.

> A considerable body of research supports the idea that meditative training can mitigate the effects of anxiety and stress on psychological and physiological functioning. The functional plasticity of the CNS affords significant neurophysiological state changes that may evolve into trait effects secondary to the long hours of practice, stylized attentional deployment, reframing of cognitive context, and emotional regulation involved in meditative training. This possibility is consonant with the relationships among increased stress, increased corticosteroid levels, and inhibition of hippocampal neurogenesis. (Cahn & Polich, 2006, p. 201)

As noted in Chapter Eleven, it seems likely that the best therapeutic practices will involve patient and therapist having simultaneous access to real-time physiological data (e.g., biofeedback, neurofeedback) as they engage in social exchange about concepts (e.g., talking together). Serotonin reuptake inhibitors (e.g., Karpova et al., 2011) and hallucinogens (e.g., Bouso, 2010; Wolfson, 1985) might be added beneficially to the mix of biofeedback and social exchange.

Using objective physiological measures in psychotherapy is critical for limiting the extent to which therapists project their own mind states onto patients. It is quite easy for even sophisticated people to confuse their own feelings and thoughts with accurate inferences about the other's feelings and thoughts (see Chapter Twelve). Therapists in the cognitive, self-esteem school might be prone to projecting concerns about their own self-esteem onto patients. Psychoanalytic school clinicians might confuse their own sexual problems with those of their patients.

The best therapists of any school are very aware of how sensory data from the body appears in consciousness. Freud famously thought that sensuality, at some level, was the same as sexuality. Perhaps his most profound dictum was, "Where the id has been, the ego shall be" (Freud, 1932). One can get pleasure and pain from sensations from inside the body (more or less id) and from concepts used in executive functions to interpret sensations (approximately the ego). Of course, the self- and non-self-concepts of therapists, patients, and everyone else are more or less compromises cooked up between the truth, ignorance, and wishes.

Knowing what is true is the most important cause of good feelings and good health (e.g., Bion, 1962). Expanding the range of valid self- and non-self-concepts one can apprehend consciously might be seen as the purpose of development.

Levity, gravity, sublimity, and light

After repeated transcendental meditation practice, my appetitive efforts to find or think or hear the mantra become seamlessly connected to the registration or consummation of it. This experience is not statistically normal. That is, most adults are not usually in such a state. But it is a state that is somehow familiar to everyone. TM seems to restore in the adult the infant's competence to experience things merely imagined as if they were realised physically. It produces what Zen masters call a beginner's mind (Suzuki, 1970), or what Freud (1913) called the omnipotence of thought.

Adults need to practise to regain this natural mental competence because once concepts are learned, it can be difficult to turn them off in order to access raw sensory data from outside and inside the body. This is consistent with the extensive work of Allan Snyder on control of focus of attention in normal and autistic people (e.g., Snyder et al., 2004).

The TM experience of weightlessness, upward movement, and restful alertness is not an ecstatic, mystical experience of complete knowledge or an oceanic feeling of merger with nature (c.f., Freud, 1920). In 1905, William James wrote that there are varieties of religious experience. Today, we might say there are varieties of non-ordinary conscious states involving alterations in the usual, everyday processes controlling attention.

There are various mind–brain states that are more markedly different from usual waking consciousness than are meditative states. As noted above, Freud (1930) assumed that the greatest pleasures are due to the greatest contrasts between states. One sort of high contrast state is caused by sudden, grave threats to life (see Bernstein, 2011, Chapter Four). Looming threats such as predators can quickly stimulate high sympathetic arousal and, ideally, precise parasympathetic control enabling the brain–mind to process information very competently at very high rates (see Figure 4, condition 9). Time seems to slow down in emergencies; decision making is precise, and muscular strength increases.

Such enhanced mental and physical competence increases one's chances of surviving a threat.

Fast brain-state change can not only promote survival but also pleasure. Engaging in any activity that actually or symbolically threatens one's security can work to configure the brain into an emergency state. Such behaviours include skiing, rugby, race driving, skydiving, high stakes gambling, military operations, and sex play involving sadism and masochism. Risky behaviours to attain extreme pleasure act like drugs that quickly reconfigure controls in the brain. For example, inhaling cocaine will suddenly challenge steady state or everyday levels of sympathetic arousal. Stressing homeostatic controls causes a swift response to reinstate baseline levels of autonomic functioning (cf., Northoff, 2011). The up-regulation of arousal itself, and the attempt to re-establish status quo functioning, can be experienced as pleasures or pains.

Also, consciousness can change dramatically in beautiful, safe, natural environments. In such situations, people may experience deep, pleasurable feelings and thoughts about the exquisite organisation of the natural world. These include peak feelings and thoughts of being at one with nature.

We evolved to be alert and ready for trouble in the wild. Today, once dangerous natural areas have been changed into nature reserves or national parks in which the most serious threats to life have been eliminated or controlled. Moreover, technologies such as moveable protective environments (e.g., vehicles), anti-venoms, and weapons work to increase security in raw, natural environments. One can be in such places without much arousal of threat avoidance instincts. Neocortical information processing has many more degrees of freedom when there is little urgency to make and enact threat avoidance decisions. Under such conditions, motivation to approach ideas and objects in the mind and the external world is much greater than the motive to avoid learning. Large discrepancies between approach and avoidance motives characterise non-ordinary states of consciousness.

At this point in history, the person comes into natural environments as a dominant power. One is able to shift attentional focus freely, less inhibited by subcortical tendencies to worry. This comfortable sense of freedom leads one to think of wild environments as home. A place one knows and belongs in biologically. Sensory data seem understandable, exquisitely organised and familiar.

So, one can experience: (1) sublime pleasure and understanding in beautiful natural environments; (2) levitation when tension between appetitive and consummatory orientations disappears; and (3) very competent (fast and accurate) cognition when confronted with serious threats to life. Each of these mind states depends on a unique configuration of control elements in the subcortical and neocortical areas of the brain. This suggests that neuroscience should focus on biological, psychological, and social variables involved in attentional control during approach-avoidance decision making under high and low conflict conditions.

The idea of being up (in physical space) is associated with feeling happy (in semantic conceptual space), and being down is connected to feeling sad (cf., Lakeoff & Johnson, 1980). This means that we can make a map of relations between brain structures and processes that work to determine the person's position in time and space, and those that process semantic concepts. Intriguingly, for example, the hippocampus is involved during non-REM sleep with making spatial maps of important areas visited during the day, and consolidating semantic memories (e.g., Wagner et al., 2004).

Survival is enhanced if animals can remember where and when they encountered important objects such as predators, prey, or potential sexual mates. I have observed in clinical practice that patients who report having forgotten a dream, can at least almost always remember if the dream scenes occurred in a dark setting as if at night, or in the light as if in day time. Just as being up is associated with feeling good so is being in light. Happy dreams tend to occur in light settings. Frightening dreams occur more frequently against a dark background. Dreams in twilight, typical of sunset and sunrise, or those in stark moonlight are often important dreams in which usually conscious thoughts and feelings are mixed with ideas residing mostly outside focal awareness.

Observation of my own dreams and the relations between sensations, cognitions, and feelings suggests an hypothesis regarding dreams of flying and falling. Falling dreams are usually experienced as frightening and flying dreams as pleasurable. Falling involves visual and kinaesthetic sensations that the ground is looming towards one, and expectations that the whole thing will end badly. Flying involves sensations of movement parallel to the ground (tracking), or soaring to the clouds. The ground looms in falling, the clouds loom in flying. That is, the sensory input to flying and falling dreams is quite similar. The concept one uses in the dream to interpret visual and kinaesthetic sense data of looming and tracking determines if they are experienced as happy flying or anxious falling. Sometimes a dreamer finds the right idea in the middle of a falling dream and transforms it into a flying dream.

L'ESPRIT D'ESCALIER

After completing Chapter Thirteen, I read some papers about Pharmacological Calvinism (Klerman, 1973), or the belief that using drugs that cause good feelings is morally wrong. Then I went to sleep and had this dream:

> I was sitting with Ronald Reagan and said to him, "You are really great, or maybe it's just projection". He laughed and in his guile-less manner said, "What's projection?" I explained that sometimes a person denies his own thoughts or feelings and imagines they are properties of another person. In other words, maybe it was me who was great or felt great, not Reagan. He said, "Maybe it's the Prozac they have in the bedrooms here at Buckingham Palace".

Sometimes dreams seem to condense large amounts of information into short lessons or parables. They may distil a problem to its essence. Dreaming is a continuation of thinking about what one had been thinking before falling asleep, the so-called *day residue* (Freud, 1900). A dream is evidence of the brain–mind's attempt to continue working on leftover, residual, incomplete thinking processes. A dream, like all thinking, is in part a product of *spreading neuronal activation*.

171

Moreover, dream thinking is affected by endogenous hallucinogens (e.g., Wallach, 2009) that increase neuronal thresholds of habituation (e.g., Cooper et al., 2003) and thereby must alter somehow the way the brain processes information. Conscious correlates of information processing occurring right before I fell asleep included the idea that I had just completed my book; a pleasurable mood; and thoughts about Pharmacological Calvinism. This dream was largely a product of this book. It was born of the book. So, like a child, it might help to advance its progenitors—the concepts that came before it.

People have tried to discern some meaning in dreams since ancient times. Modern dream analysis started with Freud and Jung. My method for analysing dreams has always involved collecting data about the day residue, associations to items in the dream, and the dreamer's feelings during the dream. This is still essential information to collect from a dreamer. But my thinking about dreams was augmented by a course I took from Robert Boznak at the C. G. Jung Institute, Boston.

Boznak assumes that the "I" in a dream represents the dreamer's usual state of waking consciousness, and that all the other people and objects in the dream represent aspects of the dreamer's mind that are typically outside focal awareness during the day (e.g., Boznak, 1986). In effect, a dream is the experience of an interaction between these more and less conscious aspects of the person's mind. Boznak also assumes that if the "not I" elements of a dream include a god, king, president, capital city, palace, or infant, then the habits of waking mind are interacting with a Jungian sort of self. From a Freudian perspective the dream is an interaction of the day residue (the dream from above) and the state of the person's unconscious mind (the dream from below).

A cognitive, information processing approach to dreams is not inconsistent with either Jungian or Freudian ideas. Dreaming is involved with attempts to encode and store new information into the existing structure of semantic concepts in the brain, and to encode and store procedural habits to activate concepts (e.g., Born & Wagner, 2004; Stickgold, 2005; Wagner et al., 2004). Changes to memory occurring in both waking and dream states involve two general processes of mind: assimilation and accommodation (e.g., Piaget, 1928, 1954). That is, data acquired during the day is more or less altered to fit into the person's memory (assimilation); and the existing memory structures change more or less to help contain the new ideas (accommodation). This might involve an experience of insight into how concepts may be related.

Endogenous and ingested hallucinogens function, in part, by increasing neuronal habituation levels (e.g., Cooper et al., 2003). This suggests that existing concepts encoded by sets of neurons may be insufficient to contain the day residue, and that new concepts, generated in dreams, need to supplant pre-dream concepts. In other words, when habituation of old concepts occurs they are just not as acceptable or pleasurable to the brain and mind as they once were. Ideally, one's brain–mind creates more valid, ample concepts of the self and other things that function to better contain and explain information from the previous day (e.g., Wagner et al., 2004).

So, turning to my dream, I would first attempt to account for the day residue and the feelings in the dream, which we have done already. Next, for this dream it seems most important to describe my existing concepts about Ronald Reagan. A psychoanalyst would say we need to collect my associations to the idea of Ronald Reagan. My thoughts and feelings about Reagan have had a long history.

I first saw Reagan as the host of The General Electric Theater, which came on television on Sunday nights between 1954 and 1962. I was ten years old in 1962 and had I watched this show regularly. I was very impressed by Reagan and liked him very much. He was physically appealing and a convincing orator, at least to me as a child. His positive image had to be a combination of who he tended to be normally and some calculated decisions made by corporate marketing experts. In any case, as a ten-year-old I sort of idolised him, and so did many people. In a 2011 scientific study by Gallup Polling, Reagan was regarded as the greatest United States President by 19% of all American adults. In comparison, Lincoln was thought to be the greatest by 14%, Clinton by 13%, and Kennedy by 11%.

When there is a widespread liking for a person or thing, we can assume that subcortical brain functions are playing an important role. Whereas the neocortex of each individual is modified idiosyncratically by living and learning, subcortical structures change less within a person and between people. In physiology, *consensual actions* are involuntary correlates or causes of voluntary actions, like when the iris constricts after the eyes are opened. If most animals of a species instinctively want to approach or avoid an object, the action has the quality of a reflex. It is not caused by rational analysis. Felt preferences do not (at first) depend on inferences (Zajonc, 1980). Reagan's charms, especially for a small child or unsophisticated adult, worked like biological releasers of fixed, instinctual reactions. For example, animals are drawn to possible mates with attractive secondary sexual attributes. Reagan and others with something like charisma or sex appeal stimulate strongly subcortical brain processes.

As an adult, I did not find his ideas especially compelling. Nonetheless, like most people, I found it hard to dislike him. He framed the problems of the world simply in general terms as a battle between Good and Evil, America vs. Russia. His was a zero-sum, us-or-them theory of reality. Otherwise, his professed beliefs involved adherence to mostly normative social values. And he used humour to signal he was a "red-blooded everyman", not a prude. Of course, he had lived and worked in Sinful Hollywood. His public utterances were more or less consciously crafted to not arouse too much neocortical activity in voters that might inhibit their reflexive positivity toward him. The positive attitudes most people had for Reagan were both causes and effects of the widespread and plausibly valid assumptions that his decision to increase spending for weapons, and his ability to befriend Mikhail Gorbachev and Margaret Thatcher, helped speed the end of the Cold War.

Reagan was described by his biographer, Edmund Morris, and his son, Ron Reagan, in a televised interview (Stahl, 1999). The son said:

> He was a great dad for a very small child. He was a very physical person, so he loved nothing better than to go out and play football with the neighborhood kids ... And the bonding that happened there was significant. But it happened in the physical arena, not sitting down and talking about life. What impressed me most about my father, as well as being troubling about him, is that he treats everybody the same way. Now when you're his kid, of course, that doesn't always work for you. But as you get older you appreciate that he never condescended to anyone. I have never seen him belittle anyone ... I think all his children loved him desperately.

The biographer said:

> He was truly one of the strangest men who have ever lived ... Every person I interviewed, almost without exception, eventually

would say, 'You know, I could never really figure him out'... His only ambition that I can discern up to his college days was to act ... When he became president we were full of self-doubts. The national spirit was at rock bottom. And overnight, there was this mysterious change in the national self-image. It was so quick that it can only be ascribed to him.

He seemed comfortable in his body, instinctive, "natural", with a sense of humour, and was seemingly without guile or pretence. Morris asked, "Did Reagan understand what he understood?" He had to have self-reflective competence of some sort, perhaps a very high level of it. But he had automated habits to act confidently regardless of doubt and he was rather convincing. He was a trained actor after all. He seemed a lovable, loving, humble and heroic character. Many people didn't have this image of him, but they were in the minority.

To decipher my dream, the next pertinent task is to distil these different attributes of Reagan in my memory to answer the question: "What is the essence of my Reagan concept that became conscious and active in the dream?" I think that he represents to me the idea of *genial but radical reductionism*. He is ignorant of psychological processes like projection and emphasises the role of chemical causes of mental states ("prozac in Buckingham Palace bedrooms").

The actual person of Ronald Reagan communicated to his followers that he saw political and moral reality as a choice between one system and another. In other words, that there was immiscibility between two social theories—communism and capitalism—and that they could never be understood as having common underlying roots. From a practical perspective this seems to have been a useful, valid enough way to view the world's problems in the 1980s. Reagan's communication of these concepts worked, in part, to help end the chronic conflict between the two political and economic systems.

But all forms of human social behaviour, including those governed by different normative assumptions about what is good social and economic behaviour, have common, fundamental bases in biology. Capitalism and communism are two species of social organisation. As the writer Philip Roth (1983) has said, in capitalism "everything goes and nothing matters" while in communism "nothing goes and everything matters". Usually, extreme theories of how to control social life and oneself represent pathologies.

My concept of Reagan is similar to how I view theorists who assume a hard problem exists in attempting to integrate theories of physical and mental things. So, I assume that Reagan, whom people followed in no small part on the basis of subcortical reflexes, represents in my dream my concepts of affect theory and my disagreement with the acceptance of a hard, mind-body problem in science.

The relationships between the physical body and the conceptual activity of the mind have been the central concern of this book. My dream reiterated the central problems encountered when attempting to integrate concepts of the body, brain and mind into one whole system. Yet, after Reagan implicitly discounts my theory, I continued to feel positive about him and "me" throughout the dream. This reflects my actual conscious attitude that affect theory is likable, but in a way that Ronald Reagan might be likable.

In the dream, Reagan seemed too dense to know what a thing like projection might be. But a trained actor's business is projection. As clinicians we understand the utility of the imperfect concept of projection. But a scientist may ask rightly, "What is projection, really?" Well, projection like dreaming is a form of information processing. It is thinking. Thoughts are projected on a mental screen of some sort. Specifically, thoughts and feelings are projected on a screen inside one's mind. They are the objects that appear in focal attention.

Usually, people imagine that the thoughts and feelings emerging in their focal awareness have originated from a part of their own mind that had just been outside consciousness. In its psychoanalytic usage, projection describes people imagining that thoughts and feelings they apprehend with their mind's eye are those of another person. Of course, sometimes what emerges from one's own unconscious is consistent with what another person is actually thinking or feeling. For example, a person wanting to deny their own hostility towards others may imagine that others are hostile to him when they are, and also when they are not.

Hostility in one person tends to breed hostility in others, perhaps by means of reflexive, affective responding to the facial and postural gestures of the other. Or, we could invoke a psychoanalytic concept as a cause such as *projective identification*. More concretely, mirror neurons are probably involved. In any case, the paranoid person often appears to be an uncannily accurate judge of others. It is difficult for anyone, naive or formal scientist, to differentiate projections from accurate knowledge of others (see Chapter Eleven). All social interchange involves some combination of accurate attributions about the origin and location of concepts, and inaccurate projection and identification with projections.

Inside my dream, I may be projecting an aspect of myself onto Reagan. If Reagan is my idea of radical reductionism, who am I in my dream? By Boznak's Jungian approach, the agent operating as me in the dream should correspond mostly to my waking mind, something with features of a Freudian ego that interacts in the dream with a Jungian self-representation in the form of a giant authority figure—the President of the United States. But attempting to understand this dream and indeed all the operations of the mind–brain will not be advanced especially by means of old concepts of ego and self. George Northoff has written perceptively about this:

> Concepts of 'self' reveal the same ambiguities as the concept of the ego, because the duality between subjective and objective realms is reinforced rather than being bridged. The concept of self must thus be considered a "conceptual tranquilizer" rather than a true bridge ... How can we build a true bridge between subjective and objective realms in the concept of self without confounding it with the ego? ... Cortical midline structures are involved in what is called self-related processing and these are integrated with subcortical processes to yield an integrated subcortical–cortical midline system ... . Rather than processing each stimulus by itself independent of the others ... the brain may in fact code each stimulus in relation to others (i.e., in terms of the difference between them) ... This means that each incoming stimulus is related to extero- and interoceptive and neural stimuli ... This in turn makes it impossible to clearly isolate and characterize each stimulus by itself independent of the other stimuli. However ... there must be a continuum between self- and non-self-related stimuli and thus between self and other, and this is exactly what can be observed in current imaging studies. (Northoff, 2011, p. 224)

Concepts of self, ego, and affect are fuzzy and, hence, a bit too difficult to operationalise in neuroscientific experiments. In contrast, one can't go entirely wrong using valid, general information processing concepts when starting to investigate mind and brain processes.

In the meantime, can we understand my dream with psychoanalytic concepts? Well, it is a stretch to assume, as might Jung or Boznak, that Reagan, a capital authority, represents the central, organising concept of my mind. More plausibly, "me" in the dream, my waking brain–mind state, seems to be the authoritative, more powerful, controlling agency. I was controlling my reactions to Reagan. I was self-reflective and imagined I may have projected feelings onto him. I was not angered when he contradicted my theories.

But the nature of the day residue of this dream was highly abnormal statistically. One doesn't finish a book on most nights. On the rare day one realises important concepts, perhaps waking consciousness moves to the top of the hierarchy of mental control processes. So perhaps we have to qualify the assumption that the "not me" part of a dream always represents a big Jungian self and that the "me" always represents the smaller, managerial or executive functions of something like a Freudian ego.

On the other hand, I can still imagine that Reagan represented some sort of deep, more important wisdom than my waking mind. His disagreement with my basic premises might be seen as a way for the mind to regulate itself. Jung talked about inflation and deflation of the entire self as the underlying causes of mania and depression respectively. Maybe my dense Reagan was smart to be not too smart. One needs to be brought down some after accomplishing something important to oneself.

The last important element of this dream derives from my bedtime reading of papers on Pharmacological Calvinism, part of the day residue. In the service of regulating my mind's degree of narcissistic love of itself, Reagan was pointing out that "you and I just feel good, or are good because of brain chemistry". Affective Reagan does not seem to be a Pharmacological Calvinist in the dream, just a reductionist. But at bottom, he implies I have done wrong. There is something wrong about my thinking. Of course, something may be wrong in the sense of being untrue or in the sense of involving a sin, or both.

This book began with the idea that the clash between motives to know the truth and the purported sinfulness of knowledge is the centrally important dynamic for understanding the mind and brain. The tendencies to obtain the great pleasures to be derived from knowledge of reality and infinity must be resistible. This does not mean that they must be categorically forbidden. But rather that one must have the means of controlling the pursuit of pleasures. The person's desire and ability to gain pleasure is at once the greatest driver of information processing and the greatest threat to mental stability. For example one can experience infinite expansion of thought or mind as an ecstatic thrill or as a terrifying dissolution of the mind.

The fear of committing original sin can be considered the ultimate default option for discouraging attempts to gain knowledge and its pleasures. Punishment for sinning is disintegration anxiety (e.g., Kohut, 1977) or actual mental collapse. But disintegration of sorts is a prelude to reintegration, which is a great pleasure. More competent minds can tolerate and enjoy changes in status quo thinking and feeling.

Freud (1923) described the relationship between the ego and the libidinous id as that of a rider on a horse. The horse is physically larger and stronger than the man. By entering into a cooperative relationship with the horse, the man can remain the leader. The best riders know what horses need and want, and help them to get enough pleasure so that the animal does not merely allow itself to be led, but yearns to be cared for and guided by the rider. (Reagan, by the way, was a keen horseman.) This sort of relationship between neocortically based executive decision making and subcortical urges characterises the most competent human beings.

Dreaming promotes felicitous alignment between a person's body and mind. Each night the brain enters a state that can inform the person about the state of the union of body and mind. (In America, the president delivers a State of the Union Speech to the nation each January.) Dreaming is in the service of controlling and expanding the validity of thoughts thereby allowing for greater feelings of pleasure in life. Depending on a dreamer's current state, optimal control may call for sympathetic stimulation and/or parasympathetic down-regulation of information processing operations.

Psychosomatics in religion and science

Injurious relationships between the mind and body of the individual have been the focus of psychoanalysis, psychosomatic medicine, neuropsychology, and psychoimmunology. Religions too are concerned with the problem. Christian Scientists say "there is no death without sin". Occasionally, the media reports that a church member has forbidden doctors from administering proven somatic treatments to one of their dying children.

How a religious crank misunderstands body-mind relationships is related, in part, to what inhibits integration of scientific psychology and biology. A very religious person may believe that controlling perfectly thoughts (or intentions), feelings, and behaviours so as not to sin will result in immortality. This seeming over-estimation of the power of the mind can be contrasted with the tendency of some neuroscientists to underestimate the large yet, for most practical purposes, finite effect of neocortical cognitive operations on somatic health.

Cybernetics describes the basic similarity of control operations in biological and psychological systems. Structures in the body's tissues, such as baroceptors, are used in regulating blood pressure; concepts or standards of correct behaviour encoded somehow in brain tissue operate to regulate thinking, feeling and overt behaviour (see Festinger,

1954). As I understand things, a Freudian superego is a semantic concept processing area of the neocortex.

All normal and pathological physical processes involve the nervous system more or less directly, and the brain constantly gets data from and sends signals to all the important somatic systems. Many chemical singling processes and drug actions are common to all types of cells. Understanding the basic processes of neural transmission and how drugs alter these processes is important for integrating pharmacology and psychopharmacology and, more generally, psyche and soma in medicine.

Standards of correct behaviour are based on the person's concepts of what is true and what is good. Such standards are semantic concepts that exist as structures and processes in the brain. More and less valid concepts about nature and religious imperatives, or morals, work to control the person. The wonderful, clean, creative, loving, destructive, stupid, hating, dirty brain and its maddening cousin, the mind, depend on the rest of the body. When everything is going right, a mind populated with valid self and non-self concepts has the most legitimate authority to control itself and the body.

If parts of a controlling apparatus are exposed to unremitting stress or injury, risk of dysfunction and breakdown increases. For example, chronic, unresolved stress can cause depletion of adrenergic neurotransmitters, then alterations in corresponding synaptic receptor sites. This causes somatic and psychic changes that cluster together first in anxiety disorders, and can often proceed to major depression. Similarly, disorders of insulin-producing cells can cause a cascade of changes in all somatic and psychic systems.

Historically, psychosomatic medicine has tried to link certain personality traits to particular somatic diseases. For example, driven, Type-A personalities are thought to get more heart disease than relaxed, B-Type personalities (Freidman & Rosenman, 1959). Personality traits are best thought of as strong habits to activate particular concepts to interpret reality, which in turn has implications for overt behaviour. Habits of the body and mind are supported by underlying, neurochemical processes. Perhaps an ambitious, Type-A person is more loaded with stimulating neurotransmitters than others and at some point the chemicals become cardiotoxic.

No habit of thinking or personality trait is all bad or all good for an individual's health and wealth. But repetition of ways of thinking that do not reduce stress effectively can damage the somatic structures and processes supporting the brain and the entire nervous system. In psychosomatics we should look for distal causes of disease in genetics, in the concept learning history of the individual, and in the neurochemical and microanatomical processes underlying responses to external and internal stressors. Kandel and Schwartz (1982) used ideas and methods from learning theory *and* molecular biology in their classic experiments with sea snails. In mammals, psychosomatic research must include study of the biological and psychological processes that regulate focal attention.

Mental habits can have unintended physical consequences

I assume mental and physical stresses are always due to decisional conflict, specifically approach-avoidance conflict. Anxiety involves ineffective forms of mentation such as obsessive worry and exaggeration of risks to security. Conscious feelings of anxiety may increase when poor decisions are made about how to resolve acute and chronically stressful conflicts. Such decisions can be made with or without the aid of attempts to control focal attention in order to identify the causes of stress, injury, or pain. Now, sometimes avoidance is the best decision (e.g., when one has no chance of controlling a situation). Approach may be better if one has some reasonable chance to rectify a problem.

Habits to avoid or approach thinking about unpleasant, stressful things can represent a form of psychopathology. Byrne (1961) developed a way to measure reliably the strength of a person's habit to avoid or approach thinking about problems. He called those with strong avoidance habits *repressors*, and those with strong tendencies to approach thinking about problems *sensitizers*. Compared to sensitizers, repressors report less felt anxiety. This does not mean that repressors are not processing information about physical and mental stressors outside of focal attention. It only means they tend to be less consciously aware of anxiety than sensitizers. Operationally, repressors use cognitive operations such as denial and dissociation. Sensitizers are more likely to suffer from obsessional disorders. Many scientists have gone on to refine these important ideas and research methods (e.g., Derakshan & Eysenck, 1997).

The more common, non-pathological habit to approach thinking about difficulties is a useful thing. If one knows a few true things about the world, using such ideas while thinking consciously can increase the chances of resolving immediate or long-standing problems. (Remarkably, this idea has been received by more than a few of my patients as a profound revelation!) In the clinical version of the habit, thinking involves ineffective problem solving and decision making. Something gets in the way of effective thinking. A true or untrue thought might just repeat uncontrollably, doing little to remove the cause of the person's anxiety.

But, the neurological and psychological structures and processes that produce both creative and pathological forms of repetitive thinking are fundamentally the same. Changes in relatively easy to observe biological variables (e.g., lesions in the gross anatomy of the brain) can cause changes in information processing. The biological operations of information processing involve difficult to observe microanatomical and neurochemical processes. Evidence of the brain's information processes can appear in the person's focal attention or not. In either case, such processing can affect other parts of the body and mind. For example, chronic, repetitive attempts to resolve a particular sort of conflict could act proximally to wear down parts of the neuroanatomical and neurochemical systems sub-serving the information-processing operation. Or, in a more roundabout way, brain damage can result from making bad decisions to reduce conflict such as hitting oneself in the head with a hammer to rectify an imagined sin. (Readers might need to be reminded that certain patients make such decisions on a regular basis.)

Most doctors, scientists, and patients do not want to be bothered by complex causal explanations. It would just be simpler and nicer for everyone if all diseases and everything else were caused by one sort of thing. Science has a reductionist bias to consider biological or obviously material causes of diseases rather than social and psychological causes. Religious extremists like to focus on social psychological variables like morality to explain everything. Regardless of such biases in thinking, one can say with certainty that reality is complex, it operates simultaneously on biological, psychological, and social levels, and is sometimes frightening and painful to consider.

For example, most people would prefer to avoid thinking about amyotrophic lateral sclerosis (ALS) or motor neurone disease. ALS was described first in 1865 by Charcot, one of Freud's most influential teachers. Patients are usually over 45 and come in initially with motor dysfunction of the feet and hands. This progresses within about three years to motor paralysis extending to the chest and head. Conscious mental life is left largely unaffected. About 80% of patients die within five years of diagnosis. The overall incidence of ALS is small (1 in 50,000 people). Only 15% of cases have a familial genetic origin. Males get ALS at about twice the rate of females. The disease has been described as "mind imprisoned in body".

The general tendency to avoid thinking about unpleasant topics can be overcome by motives to approach the integration of basic scientific theories that can support development of treatments for disease. In the end, ALS is just one of a million things that can and will kill you and everyone else. But ALS might be especially important for understanding how biological, psychological, and social systems interact.

Perhaps the most remarkable thing about ALS is that a personality trait of patients, obvious to every clinical neurologist, has never been described in any scientific publication as even a partial, possible cause of the disease. ALS is known widely by neurologists as "nice guys disease". The only paper I could find that mentions ALS in the same breath as psychosocial factors makes no suggestion of psychological causation (Rana et al., 2008). Campbell's Psychiatric Dictionary (2004) says ALS "develops as *a pure motor syndrome*" (italics added).

No one seems reluctant to say that hard driving, aggressive people are more likely to get heart disease than other people. Why do scientific writers avoid mentioning the rather striking correlation between niceness and ALS? Well, most people would like not to imagine that being nice could have anything to do with damaging health. It just wouldn't be nice.

In America, ALS is called "Lou Gehrig's Disease" after the great baseball player who was diagnosed when 38 years old. Gehrig was known to be exceedingly nice, and as a courageous "iron man" who played in a record number of games regardless of pain or injury. In 1939, at a Yankee Stadium ceremony to mark his retirement from sport (and his coming death), he famously told 60,000 people, "Today, I consider myself the luckiest man on the face of the earth". This was a deep remark to make in such a situation, and it still evokes strong, complex feelings.

Of course, any attempt to find a connection between niceness and ALS depends on making some assumptions about what it is to be nice. The dictionary indicates that nice means pleasant, kind, friendly, considerate, respectable, or of an acceptable social or moral standard. Logically, a person can be chronically nice for at least two reasons. First, they may not know of, or be unmotivated to do, "not nice" things. For example, patients with Down's syndrome tend to be friendly and nice. Their genetic defect (Trisomy 21) and the resultant mental retardation probably makes it hard for them to learn or to activate concepts that are not instrumental for satisfying the social attachment needs of immature, dependent individuals. This might be called low-conflict niceness.

In otherwise healthy adults who develop ALS, I think niceness involves high levels of chronic conflict. An adult must be able to use and control aggressive and sexual ideas and behaviours to function in the world. This means they must use concepts specifying what many, or most, (or all) people consider "not nice". When an impulse to violate a standard of niceness is stimulated in or out of focal attention, the nice person inhibits the impulse. The especially nice person is involved in more arousal and inhibition of not nice thoughts, feelings and behaviours than normal.

A plausible hypothesis is that this chronic stress involves a dysregulation of glutamate, the major excitatory neurotransmitter in the mammalian central nervous system.[1] There is now no doubt that derangements in glutamate metabolism can cause the death of motor neurons by a variety of mechanisms (LeVerche et al., 2011; see also Xie et al., 2013). Riluzole, a glutamate system modulator, is the only medicine ever shown to have even a modest ability to slow the progression of ALS. Nonetheless, no one has ever suggested that mental conflict is in any way involved in the causation of this disease. I think this ostensible mistake made by neuroscience is rooted in a fundamental religious idea:

> The carnal mind is not subject to the law of God ... So then they that are in the flesh cannot please God. (Bible, Romans 8:8)

ALS is considered one of the most horrible diseases occurring in man: "An intellectually preserved human being in a motionless body" (LeVerche et al., 2011, p. 3). In short, it is a version of hell. But the Bible suggests that a functioning body with its sinful, "not niceness" is fundamentally at odds with God. By this logic one might imagine that a person with ALS is closer to God and heaven than to hell. Such a proposition highlights the hardest problems for science, medicine, religion and the individual person.

Note

1. This suggests adding a third dimension to the scheme of nine psychosomatic types depicted in Figure 4, Chapter Nine. That is, we might account for something like "glutamenergic tone" together with sympathetic arousal and parasympathetic tone. This would produce a 3 x 3 x 3 scheme resulting in 27 psychosomatic types, which could more completely capture the sorts of variation observed in human competence.

REFERENCES

Abbass, A., Campbell, S., Hann, S., Lenzer, I., Tarzwell, R., & Maxwell, D. (2010). Cost savings of treatment of medically unexplained symptoms using intensive short-term dynamic psychotherapy by a hospital emergency department. *Archives of Medical Psychology,* 1(2): 34–43.

Ainsworth, M., & Bowlby, J. (1965). *Child Care and the Growth of Love.* London: Penguin.

Ainsworth, M., Blehar, M., Waters, E., & Wall, S. (1978). *Patterns of Attachment.* Hillsdale, NJ: Erlbaum.

Alcock, J. (2005). *Animal Behaviour: An Evolutionary Approach.* Sunderland, MA: Sinauer Associates.

Alloy, L. B., & Ahrens, H. (1987). Depression and pessimism for the future: Biased use of statistically relevant information in predictions for self versus others. *Journal of Personality and Social Psychology,* 52(2): 366–378.

Amen, D. G. (2003). *Healing Anxiety and Depression.* New York: Berkley.

Amen, D. G. (2008). Predicting positive and negative treatment responses to stimulants with brain SPECT imagining. *Journal of Psychoactive Drugs,* 40(2): 131–138.

Anderson, J. R. (1983). A spreading activation theory of memory. *Journal of Verbal Learning and Verbal Behaviour,* 22(3): 261–295.

187

Aronson, E. (1969). The theory of cognitive dissonance: A current perspective. In: L. Berkowitz (Ed.), *Advances in Experimental Social Psychology* (pp. 1–34). New York: Academic Press.

Aronson, E. (1992). The return of the repressed: Dissonance theory makes a comeback. *Psychological Inquiry, 3*: 303–311.

Aronson, E., & Carlsmith, J. M. (1963). Effect of the severity of threat on the devaluation of forbidden behaviour. *Journal of Abnormal and Social Psychology, 66*(6): 584–588.

Aronson, E., & Mills, J. (1959). The effects of severity of initiation on liking for a group. *Journal of Abnormal and Social Psychology, 59*: 177–181.

Baddeley, A. D. (1986). *Working Memory*. Oxford: Clarendon.

Baddeley, A. D. (2002). Fractionating the central executive. In: R. T. Knight & D. T. Stuss (Eds.), *Principles of Frontal Lobe Function* (pp. 246–260). Oxfordshire: Oxford University Press.

Bakan, D. (1966). *The Duality of Human Existence: An Essay on Psychology and Religion*. Chicago: Rand McNally.

Banich, M. T. (2009). Executive function: The search for an integrated account. *Current Directions in Psychological Science, 18*(2): 89–94.

Bard, P. (1928). A diencephalic mechanism for the expression of rage with special reference to the sympathetic nervous system. *American Journal of Physiology, 84*: 490–516.

Barratt, B. B. (2013). Free-associating with the bodymind. *International Forum of Psychoanalysis, 22*(3): 161–175.

Baumeister, R., & Bushman, B. J. (2010). *Social Psychology and Human Nature* (2nd edn). Illinois: Wadsworth.

Beach, F. A., & Jordan, L. (1956). Sexual exhaustion and recovery in the male rat. *Quarterly Journal of Experimental Psychology, 8*: 121–133.

Beck, A. T. (1967). *Depression: Clinical, Experimental and Theoretical Aspects*. New York: Harper & Row.

Beck, A. T., Rush, J., Shaw, B. F., & Emery, G. (1987). *Cognitive Therapy for Depression*. New York: Guilford Press.

Benabou, R., & Tirole, J. (2003). Intrinsic and extrinsic motivation. *Review of Economic Studies, 70*: 489–520.

Bernard, C. (1865). *An Introduction to the Study of Experimental Medicine*. First English translation (1927). London: Macmillan.

Bernstein, W. M. (1984). Denial and self-defense. *Psychoanalysis and Contemporary Thought, 7*: 423–457.

Bernstein, W. M. (1995). On integrating cognitive and motivational explanations in psychology. In: A. Oosterwegal & R. A. Wicklund (Eds.), *The Self in European and North American Culture: Development and Processes*: 159–168. The Netherlands: Kluwer Academic.

Bernstein, W. M. (2001). Alternating patient posture. *Psychoanalysis and Contemporary Thought, 24*(3): 309–334.

Bernstein, W. M. (2003). Empowerment: A task for the self not the organization. *Organization Development Journal, 21*(1): 75–79.

Bernstein, W. M. (2011). *A Basic Theory of Neuropsychoanalysis*. London: Karnac.

Bernstein, W. M. (2012). Diagnosing mental illness. *Archives of Medical Psychology, 3*(2): 45–59.

Bernstein, W. M. (2014). A basic and applied model of the body-mind system. In: G. H. E. Gendolla, S. Koole, & M. Tops (Eds.), *Biobehavioral Foundations of Self-Regulation* (pages in preparation). New York: Springer.

Bernstein, W. M., & Burke, W. W. (1989). Modeling organizational meaning systems. In: R. W. Woodman & A. A. Passmore (Eds.), *Research in Organization Change and Development*: 117–159. Greenwich, CT: JAI Press.

Bernstein, W. M., & Davis, M. H. (1982). Perspective-taking, self-consciousness and accuracy in person perception. *Basic and Applied Social Psychology, 3*: 1–20.

Bernstein, W. M., Stephan, W. G., & Davis, M. H. (1979). Explaining attributions for achievement: A path analytic approach. *Journal of Personality and Social Psychology, 37*: 1810–1821.

Bernstein, W. M., Stephenson, B. O., Snyder, M. L., & Wicklund, R. A. (1983). Causal ambiguity and heterosexual affiliation. *Journal of Experimental Social Psychology, 19*: 78–92.

Berridge, K. C. (2004). Motivation concepts in behavioural neuroscience. *Physiology & Behaviour, 81*: 179–209.

Bickler, P. E., & Buck, L. T. (2007). Hypoxia tolerance in reptiles, amphibians, and fishes: life with variable oxygen availability. *Annual Review of Physiology, 69*: 145–170.

Biederman, I., & Vessel, E. A. (2006). Perceptual pleasure and the brain. *American Scientist, 94*: 249–255.

Bion, W. R. (1961). *Experiences in Groups*. London: Tavistock.

Bion, W. R. (1962). The psychoanalytic study of thinking. *International Journal of Psycho-Analysis, 43*: 306–310.

Born, J., & Wagner, U. (2004). Awareness in memory: Being explicit about the role of sleep. *Trends in Cognitive Science, 8*: 242–244.

Bouso, J. C. (2010). MDMA-assisted psychotherapy using low does in a small sample of women with chronic post-traumatic stress disorder. *Journal of Psychoactive Drugs, 30*(4): 371–379.

Bowlby, J. (1969). *Attachment and Loss*. New York: Basic Books.

Boznak, R. (1986). *A Little Course in Dreams*. Boston: Shambhala.

Braak, H., & Braak, E. (1996). Development of Alzheimer-related neurofibrillary changes in the neocortex inversely recapitulates cortical myelogenesis. *Acta Neuropathologica, 92*(2): 197–201.

Braak, H., & Del Tredici, K. (2009). Neuroanatomy and pathology of sporadic Parkinson's disease. *Advances in Anatomy, Embryology and Cell Biology, 201*: 1–119.

Brady, J. V. (1958). Ulcers in executive monkeys. *Scientific American, 199*(4): 95–100.

Burke, W. W. (1986). Leadership as empowering others. In: S. Srivastva (Ed.), *Executive Power: How Executives Influence People and Organizations*: 63–77. San Francisco: Jossey-Bass.

Burke, W. W. (2010). *Organization Change: Theory and Practice* (3rd edn). Los Angeles: Sage.

Burke, W. W., & Litwin, G. H. (1992). A causal model of organizational performance and change. *Journal of Management, 18*(3): 523–545.

Burns, J. M. (1978). *Leadership*. New York: Harper & Row.

Byrne, D. (1961). The repression-sensitization scale: rationale, reliability, and validity. *Journal of Personality, 29*(3): 334–349.

Cahn, B. R., & Polich, J. (2006). *Psychological Bulletin, 132*(2): 180–211.

Campbell, D. T., & Fiske, D. W. (1959). Convergent and discriminant validation by the multitrait-multimethod matrix. *Psychological Bulletin, 56*: 81–105.

Campbell, R. J. (2004). *Campbell's Psychiatric Dictionary* (8th edn). Oxford: Oxford University Press.

Cannon, W. B. (1927). The James-Lange theory of emotions: A critical examination and an alternative theory. *The American Journal of Psychology, 39*: 106–124.

Caplan, G. (1970). *The Theory and Practice of Mental Health Consultation*. New York: Basic Books.

Carlson, N. R. (2010). *Psychology: The Science of Behaviour*. Toronto: Pearson.

Carter, C. S., & Keverne, E. B. (2002). The neurobiology of social affiliation and pair bonding. In: D. W. Pfaff (Ed.), *Hormones, Brain and Behaviour* (pp. 299–337). San Diego: Academic Press.

Carver, C. S., & Scheier, M. F. (1981). *Attention and Self-Regulation: A Control Theory Approach to Human Behaviour*. New York: Springer-Verlag.

Clark, R. A. (1956). The relationships between symbolic and manifest projects of sexuality with some incidental correlates. *Journal of Abnormal Social Psychology, 50*: 327–334.

Cohen, P. (1989). *Undergångens Arkitektur* (trans. Architecture of Doom). Documentary film. Sweden: Poj Filmproduktion AB.

Collins, A. M., & Loftus, E. F. (1975). A spreading activation theory of semantic processing. *Psychological Review, 82*: 407–428.

Cooper, J. R., Bloom, F. E., & Roth, R. H. (2003). *The Biochemical Basis of Neuropharmacology* (8th edn). New York: Oxford University Press.

Crestani, F. (1997). Application of spreading activation techniques in information retrieval. *Artificial Intelligence Review, 11*(6): 453–482.

Creswell, J. D., Myers, H. F., Steven, W., Cole, S. W., & Irwin, M. R. (2009). Mindfulness meditation training effects on CD4+ T lymphocytes in HIV-1 infected adults: A small randomized controlled trial. *Brain Behaviour Immunology, 23*(2): 184–188.

Cronbach, L. J. (1955). Processes affecting scores on "understanding others" and "assumed similarity". *Psychological Bulletin, 52*: 177–193.

Damasio, A. (1994). *Descartes' Error: Emotion, Reason, and the Human Brain.* New York: Putnam Publishing.

Damasio, A. (2003). *Looking for Spinoza: Joy, Sorrow and the Feeling Brain.* Orlando: Houghton Mifflin Harcourt.

Dana, R., Carney, D. R., Jost, J. T., Gosling, S. G., & Potter, J. (2008). The secret lives of liberals and conservatives: Personality profiles, interaction styles, and the things they leave behind. *Political Psychology, 29*(6): 807–840.

Davis, M. H. (1983). Measuring individual differences in empathy. *Journal of Personality and Social Psychology, 44*: 113–126.

Davis, M. H. (1994). *Empathy: A Social Psychological Approach.* Madison, WI: Westview Press.

Dawkins, R. (1976). *The Selfish Gene.* New York: Oxford University Press.

de Rios, M. D. (2003). The role of music in healing with hallucinogens: Tribal and western studies. *Music Therapy Today, 4*(3): 1–6.

Decety, J., & Ickes, W. (Eds.) (2009). The Social Neuroscience of Empathy. Cambridge, MA: MIT Press.

Deci, E. L. (1975). Effects of externally mediated rewards on intrinsic motivation. *Journal of Personality and Social Psychology, 36*(3): 71–100.

Derakshan, N., & Eysenck, M. W. (1997). Interpretive biases for one's own behavior and physiology in high-trait-anxious individuals and repressors. *Journal of Personality and Social Psychology, 73*(4): 816–825.

Deutsch, M. (1969). Socially relevant science: Reflections on some studies of interpersonal conflict. *American Psychologist, 24*(12): 1076–1092.

DeWied, D. (1971). Long-term effects of vasopressin the the maintence of a conditioned avoidance response in rats. *Nature, 232*: 58–60.

Diamond, D. M., Campbell, A. M., Park, C. R., & Halonen, A. (2007). The temporal dynamics model of emotional memory processing: A synthesis on the neurobiological basis of stress-induced amnesia, flashbulb and traumatic memories, and the Yerkes–Dodson Law. *Neural Plasticity, 33.* doi: 10.1155/20.

Dollard, J., Doob, L. W., Miller, N. E., Mower, O. H., & Sears, R. R. (1939). *Frustration and Aggression.* New Haven: Yale University Press.

Dresler, M., Koch, S. P., Wehrle, R., Spoormaker, V. I., Florian Holsboer, F., Steiger, A., Sämann, P. G., Obrig, H., & Czisch, M. (2011). Dreamed movement elicits activation in the sensorimotor cortex. *Current Biology,* Published online 28 October DOI: 10.1016/j.cub.2011.09.029.

Dutton, D. G., & Aron, A. P. (1974). Some evidence for heightened sexual attraction under conditions of high anxiety. *Journal of Personality and Social Psychology, 24:* 285–290.

Duval, T. A., & Wicklund, R. A. (1972). *A Theory of Objective Self-Awareness.* New York: Academic Press.

Edmundson, M. (2007). Defender of the faith? *New York Times, 9* September.

Edwards-Stewart, A. (2012). Using technology to enhance empirically supported psychological treatments: Positive activity jackpot. *Archives of Medical Psychology, 3*(2): 60–66.

Egan, L. C., Santos, L. R., & Bloom, P. (2007). The origins of cognitive dissonance: Evidence from children and monkeys. *Psychological Science, 18*(11): 978–983.

Ekman, P. (1973). Darwin's compassionate view of human nature. *Journal of the American Medical Association, 303*(6): 557–558.

Ekman, P. (1978). Facial Action Coding System: A Technique for the Measurement of Facial Movement. Palo Alto CA: Consulting Psychologists Press.

Eldredge, N., & Gould, S. J. (1972). Punctuated equilibria: an alternative to phyletic gradualism. In: T. J. M. Schop (Ed.), *Models in Paleobiology* (pp. 82–115). San Francisco: Freeman Cooper.

Emde, R. N. (1980). Emotional availability: A reciprocal reward system for infants and parents with implications for prevention of psychosocial disorders. In: P. M. Taylor (Ed.), *Parent–Infant Relationships* (pp. 88–115). New York: Grune & Stratton.

Erikson, E. H. (1973). *Childhood and Society.* New York: Penguin.

Festinger, L. A. (1954). A theory of social comparison processes. *Human Relations, 7:* 117–140.

Festinger, L. A. (1957). *A Theory of Cognitive Dissonance.* Stanford: Stanford University Press.

Fiedler, F. E. (1964). A contingency model of leadership effectiveness. In: L. Berkowitz (Ed.), *Advances in Experimental Social Psychology* (pp. 149–190). New York: Academic Press.

Fink, G. (2010). *Stress of War, Conflict and Disaster*. Oxford: Academic Press.

Fiske, S. T., & Taylor, S. E. (2008). *Social Cognition: From Brains to Culture*. New York: McGraw-Hill.

Foushee, H. C., Davis, M. H., Stephan, W. G., & Bernstein, W. M. (1980). The effects of cognitive and behavioral control on post-stress performance. *Journal of Human Stress, 6*(2): 41–48.

French, J. R. P., & Raven, B. (1959). The bases of social power. In: D. Cartwright (Ed.), *Studies in Social Power* (pp. 150–167). Ann Arbor: Institute for Social Research.

Freud, S. (1900a). *The Interpretation of Dreams. S. E., 4–5*. London: Hogarth.

Freud, S. (1905d). *Three Essays on the Theory of Sexuality. S. E., 7*: 135–243. London: Hogarth.

Freud, S. (1912). *Totem and Taboo. S. E., 13*: 1–161. London: Hogarth.

Freud, S. (1920g). *Beyond the Pleasure Principle. S. E., 18*: 7–64. London: Hogarth.

Freud, S. (1921c). *Group Psychology and the Analysis of the Ego. S. E., 17*: 67–143. London: Hogarth.

Freud, S. (1923b). *The Ego and the Id. S. E., 19*: 3–66. London: Hogarth.

Freud, S. (1926d). *Inhibitions, Symptoms and Anxiety. S. E., 20*: 77–174. London: Hogarth.

Freud, S. (1927c). *The Future of an Illusion. S. E., 21*: 5–56. London: Hogarth.

Freud, S. (1930a). *Civilization and its Discontents. S. E., 21*: 75–312. London: Hogarth.

Freud, S. (1933a). *New Introductory Lectures on Psycho-Analysis. S. E., 22*: 1–182. London: Hogarth.

Freud, S. (1939a). *Moses and Monotheism. S. E., 23*: 7–137. London: Hogarth.

Friedman, M., & Rosenman, R. (1959). Association of specific overt behaviour pattern with blood and cardiovascular findings. *Journal of the American Medical Association*, (169): 1286–1296.

Friedman, M. J. (1975). Depression and hypertension. *Psychosomatic Medicine, 39*(2): 124–142.

Friesen, C. A., & Kammrath, L. A. (2011). What it pays to know about a close other: The value of if-then personality knowledge in close relationships. *Psychological Science, 22*(5): 567–571.

Fromm, E. (1966). *You Shall Be As Gods: A Radical Interpretation of the Old Testament and its Traditions*. New York: Holt, Rinehart and Winston.

Gailliot, M. T., Baumeister, R. F., DeWall, C. N., Marner, J. K., Plant, E. A., Tice, D., Brewer, L. E., & Schmeichel, B. J. (2008). Self-control relies on glucose as a limited energy source: Willpower is more than a metaphor. *Journal of Personality and Social Psychology, 92*(2): 325–336.

Galarce, E. M., Crombag, H. S., & Holland, P. C. (2007). Reinforcer-specificity of appetitive and consummatory behaviour of rats after Pavlovian conditioning with food reinforcers. *Physiology and Behaviour,* 16(91): 95–105.

Gallese, V. (2001). The shared manifold hypothesis: From mirror neurons to empathy. *Journal of Consciousness Studies*: 33–50.

Gilson, E. (1937). Being and realism. In: R. Beck (Ed.), *Perspectives in Philosophy*: 85–89. New York: Holt, Rinehart, & Winston.

Glass, D. C., & Singer, J. E. (1972). *Urban Stress: Experiments on Noise and Social Stressors.* New York: Academic Press.

Gould, S. J., & Eldredge, N. (1977). Punctuated equilibria: the tempo and mode of evolution reconsidered. *Paleobiology, 3*(2): 115–151.

Green, E., & Green, A. (1977). *Beyond Biofeedback.* Oxford: Delacorte.

Grossenbacher, P. G., & Lovelace, C. T. (2001). Mechanisms of synesthesia: Cognitive and physiological constraints. *Trends in Cognitive Science, 5*(1): 36–41.

Haggard, M. (1979). *Are the good times really over for good.* SONY BMG Music.

Hakala, M., Karlsson, H., & Kurki, Z. (2004). Volumes of the caudate nuclei in women with somatization disorder and healthy women. *Psychiatry Research: Neuroimaging, 131*: 71–78.

Harackiewicz, J. M., & DePaulo, B. M. (1982). Accuracy of person perception: A component analysis according to Cronbach. *Personality and Social Psychology Bulletin, 8*(2): 247–256.

Harvey, S. B., Hotopf, M., Øverland, S., & Mykletun, A. (2010). Physical activity and common mental disorders. *British Journal of Psychiatry, 197*: 357–364.

Heider, F. (1958). *The Psychology of Interpersonal Relations.* New York: Wiley.

Heise, D. R. (2010). *Surveying Cultures: Discovering Shared Conceptions and Sentiments.* Hoboken NJ: Wiley.

Hobson, J. A. (2004). Freud returns? Like a bad dream. *Scientific American,* 290(5): 89.

Hobson, J. A., & McCarley, R. (1977). The brain as a dream state generator: an activation-synthesis hypothesis of the dream process. *American Journal of Psychiatry, 134*: 1335–1348.

Horan, J. J. (1995). Paradigms for establishing experimental construct validity in counseling and psychotherapy. Paper presented at the Annual Meeting of the American Psychological association, New York.

Horney, K. (1950). *Neurosis and Human Growth.* New York: Norton.

Huitt, W. (2003). The affective system. *Educational Psychology Interactive.* Valdosta, GA: Valdosta State University.

Hull, C. L. (1943). *Principles of Behavior.* New York: Appleton.

Huxley, A. (1954). *The Doors of Perception.* London: Chatto & Windus.

Izard, E. W. (1979). *The Maximally Discriminative Facial Movement Coding System*. Newark: University of Delaware.

Jaensch, E. R. (1938). *Der Gergentypus*. Leipzig: J. A. Barth.

James, W. (1903). *The Varieties of Religious Experience: A Study of Human Nature*. London: Longmans, Green & Company.

James, W., & Lange C. G. (1922). *The Emotions*. Baltimore: Williams & Wilkins.

Jarcho, J. M., Berkman, E. T., & Liberman, M. D. (2011). The neural basis of rationalization: cognitive dissonance reduction during decision-making. *Social Cognitive and Affective Neuroscience, 6*(4): 460–467.

Jarvis, M. (2004). *Psychodynamic Psychology: Classical Theory and Contemporary Research*. London: Thomson Learning.

Johnson, B. D. (2012). *The Cybernetics of Society: The Governance of Self and Civilization*. Jurlandia Institute. http://www.jurlandia.org/cybsoc.htm

Jones, E. E., & Berglas, S. (1978). Control of attributions about the self through self-handicapping strategies: The appeal of alcohol and the role of underachievement. *Personality and Social Psychology Bulletin, 4*: 200–206.

Jones, E. E., & Nisbett, R. W. (1971). *The Actor and The Observer: Divergent Perceptions of the Causes of Behavior*. Morristown NJ: General Learning Press.

Jung, C. G. (1940). Answer to Job. In: *Collected Works of C. G. Jung, 11*. Princeton: Bollingen.

Jung, C. G. (1948). The psychology of the transference. In: *Collected Works of C. G. Jung, 16*. Princeton: Bollingen.

Kalivas, P., Churchill, L., & Litneck, M. (1993). The circuitry mediating the translation of motivational stimuli into adaptive motor responses. In: P. Kalivas & C. Barnes (Eds.), *Limbic Motor Circuits and Neuropsychiatry* (pp. 391–419). New York: CRC Press.

Kandel, E. R. (2006). *In Search of Memory: The Emergence of a New Science of Mind*. New York: Norton.

Kandel, E. R., & Schwartz, J. H. (1982). Molecular biology of an elementary form of learning: Modulation of transmitter release of cyclic AMP. *Science, 218*: 433–443.

Kaplan-Solms, K., & Solms, M. (2000). *Clinical Studies in Neuro-Psychoanalysis*. London: Karnac Books.

Karpova, N. N., Pickenhagen, A., Lindholm, J., Tiraboschi, E., Kulesskay, N., Agustdottir, A., Antila, H., Popova, D., Akamine, Y., Sullivan, R., Hen, R., Drew, L. J., & Castren, F. (2011). Fear erasure in mice requires synergy between antidepressant drugs and extinction training. *Science, 334*(6063): 1731–1734.

Katz, D., & Kahn, R. L. (1973). *The Social Psychology of Organizations*. New York: Wiley.

Kelly, H. H. (1967). Attribution theory in social psychology. In: Levine, D. (Ed), *Nebraska Symposium on Motivation* (pp. 192–238). Lincoln: University of Nebraska Press.

Klein, M. (1932). *The Psychoanalysis of Children*. London: Hogarth.

Klerman, G. L. (1972). Psychotropic hedonism vs. pharmacological Calvinism. *Hastings Center Reports, 2*(4): 1–3.

Kohut, H. (1977). *The Restoration of the Self*. Madison CT: International Universities Press.

Krakauer, J. M. (2005). Arm function after stroke: From Physiology to recovery. In: K. L. Roos (Ed.), *Seminars in Neurology, 25*(4): 385–395.

Kramer, U. M., Mohammadi, B., Doiamayor, N., Samii, A., & Munte, T. F. (2010). Emotional and cognitive aspects of empathy and their relation to social cognition: An *f*MRI-study. *Brain Research, 1311*: 110–120.

Lakeoff, G., & Johnson, M. (1980). *Metaphors We Live By*. Chicago: University of Chicago Press.

Langer, E., & Rodin, J. (1976). The effects of choice and enhanced personal responsibility for the aged: A field experiment in an institutional setting. *Journal of Personality and Social Psychology, 34*(2): 191–198.

Larson, S. K., & Porges, S. W. (1982). The ontogeny of heart period patterning in the rat. *Developmental Psychobiology, 15*: 519–528.

Lazarus, R. S. (1982). Thoughts on the relations between emotions and cognition. *American Physiologist, 37*(10): 1019–1024.

Leary, T., Litwin, G., & Metzner, R. (1963). Reactions to psilocybin administered in a supportive environment. *Journal of Nervous and Mental Disease, 137*: 561–573.

LeDoux, J. (1996). The Emotional Brain: *The Mysterious Underpinnings of Emotional Life*. New York: Touchstone.

LeDoux, J. (2000). Cognitive-emotional interactions: Listen to the brain. In: R. D. Lane, L. Nadel, & G. Ahern (Eds.), *Cognitive Neuroscience of Emotion* (pp. 120–155). New York: Oxford University Press.

LeDoux, J. (2012). A Neuroscientist's Perspective on Debates about the Nature of Emotion, *Emotion Review, 4*(4): 375–379.

Lerner, J. S., & Keltner, D. (2000) Beyond valence: Toward a model of emotion-specific influences on judgment and choice. *Cognition and Emotion, 14*(4): 473–493.

LeVerche, V., Ikiz, B., Jacquier, A., Przedborski, S., & Re, D. B. (2011). Glutamate pathway implication in amyotrophic lateral sclerosis: what is the signal in the noise? *Journal of Receptor, Ligand and Channel Research, 4*: 1–22.

Levin, J. D. (1995). *Introduction to Alcoholism Counseling: A Bio-Psycho-Social Approach*. Washington DC: Taylor & Francis.

Levinson, H. (1976). *Psychological Man*. Cambridge: Levinson Institute.

Lewin, K. (1946). Action research and minority problems. *Journal of Social Issues, 2*(4): 34–46.

Lewin, K., Lippit, R., & White, R. K. (1939). Patterns of aggressive behaviour in experimentally created social climates. *Journal of Social Psychology, 10*: 271–301.

Lieberman, M. S., & Eisenberger, N. I. (2004). Conflict and habit: A social cognitive neuroscience approach to the self. In: A. Tesser, J. Wood, & D. A. Stapel (Eds.), *Building, Defending and Regulating the Self* (pp. 77–102). New York: Psychology Press.

Likert, R. (1932). A technique for the measurement of attitudes. *Archives of Psychology, 140*: 1–55.

Liston, C., McEwen, B. S., Casey, B. J. (2009). Psychosocial stress reversibly disrupts prefrontal processing and attentional control. *Proceedings of the National Academy of Science, 106*(3): 912–917.

Litwin, G. H., & Stringer, R. A. (1968). *Motivation and Organizational Climate*. Boston: Harvard Business School Publications.

Lorenz, K. (1963). *On Aggression*. Vienna: Verlag Dr Borotha-Schoeler.

Luhmann, N. (1995). *Social Systems*. Stanford: Stanford University Press.

Lukianoff, G. (2012). *Unlearning Liberty: Campus Censorship and the End of the American Debate*. New York: Encounter Books.

Lupien S. J., Maheu F., Tu, M., Fiocco, A., & Schramek, T. E. (2007). The effects of stress and stress hormones on human cognition: Implications for the field of brain and cognition. *Brain and Cognition, 65*: 209–237.

Mairesse, F., Walker, M. A., Mehl, M. R., & Moore, R. K. (2007). Using linguistic cues for the automatic recognition of personality in conversation and text. *Journal of Artificial Intelligence Research, 30*: 457–500.

Manuck, S. B., Marsland, A. L., Marsland, M. A., Kaplan, J. R., & Williams, J. K. (1995). The pathogenicity of behavior and its neuroendocrine mediation: An example from coronary artery disease. *Psychosomatic Medicine, 57*: 275–283.

Marcel, A. (1980). Conscious and preconscious recognition of polysemous words: Locating the selective effects of prior visual contexts. In: R. S. Nickerson (Ed), *Attention and Performance, 8*: 435–457. Hillsdale, NJ: Lawrence Erlbaum Associates.

Maslow, A. (1954). *Motivation and Personality*. New York: Harper.

Massey, P. V., & Bashir, Z. I. (2007). Long-term depression: Multiple forms and implications for brain function. *Trends in Neuroscience, 30*(4): 176–84.

Mather, M., & Lighthall, N. R. (2012). Risk and reward are processed differently in decisions made under stress. *Current Directions in Psychological Science, 21*(1): 36–41.

McClelland, D. C. (1955). *Studies in Motivation*. New York: Appleton.

McClelland, D. C. (1958). Methods of Measuring Human Motivation. In: J. W. Atkinson (Ed.), *Motives in Fantasy, Action and Society* (pp. 12–13). Princeton NJ: Van Nostrand.

McClelland, D. C., Atkinson, J. W., Clark, R. A., & Lowell, E. L. (1953). *The Achievement Motive*. Princeton NJ: Van Nostrand.

McNamara. T. P. (2005). *Semantic Priming: Perspectives from Memory and Word Recognition*. New York: Taylor & Francis.

Mead, G. H. (1934). *Mind, Self and Society*. Chicago: University of Chicago Press.

Meier, C. A. (Ed.) (2001). *Atom and Archetype: The Pauli/Jung Letters, 1932–1958*. Princeton NJ: Princeton University Press.

Metcalfe, J., & Mischel, W. (1999). A hot/cool-system analysis of delay of gratification: dynamics of willpower. *Psychological Review, 106*(1): 3–23.

Metin, I., & Camgoz, S. M. (2011). The advances in the history of cognitive dissonance theory. *International Journal of Humanities and Social Science, 1*(6): 131–136.

Meyer, D., & Schvanevelt, R. (1971). Facilitation in recognizing pairs of words: Evidence of dependence between retrieval operations. *Journal of Experimental Psychology, 41*(1): 126–131.

Milgram, S. (1963). Behavioural study of obedience. *The Journal of Abnormal and Social Psychology, 67*(4): 371–378.

Miller, G. A., Galanter, E., & Pribram, K. (1960). *Plans and the Structure of Behaviour*. New York: Holt, Rinehart and Winston.

Miller, N. E. (1944). Experimental studies of conflict. In: J. Hunt (Ed.), *Personality and the Behavior Disorders* (pp. 431–465). New York: Ronald Press.

Miller, N. E., & Dollard, J. (1941). *Social Learning and Imitation*. New Haven: Yale University Press.

Miles-Brenden, P. (2013). Reciprocity, Complementarity and Interdependence. Unpublished manuscript.

Modell, J. H., Idris, A. H., Jose, A., Pineda, J. A., & Silverstein, J. H. (2004). Survival after prolonged submersion in freshwater in Florida. *Chest, 125*(5): 1948–1951.

Mollon, P. (2005). *EMDR and the Energy Therapies: Psychoanalytic Perspectives*. London: Karnac.

Mroczek, D. K., & Spiro, A., III. (2007). Personality change influences mortality in older men. *Psychological Science, 18*: 371–376.

Najmi, S., & Wegner, D. M. (2008). The gravity of unwanted thought: Asymmetric priming effects in thought suppression. *Consciousness and Cognition, 17*: 114–124.

Neely, J. (1977). Semantic priming and retrieval from lexical memory: the role of inhibitionless spreading activation and limited capacity attention. *Journal of Experimental Psychology: General, 106*: 226–254.

Neisser, U. (1976). *Cognition and Reality.* San Francisco: Freeman.

Neumann, E. (1995). *The Origins and History of Consciousness.* Bollingen series XLII: Princeton University Press. [Originally published in German in 1949]

Norman, D. A., & Shallice, T. (1976). Attention to action: Willed and automatic control of behaviour. In: D. L. Shapiro & G. Schwartz (Eds.), *Consciousness and Self-Regulation: Advances in Research* (pp. 1–14). New York: Plenum Press.

Northoff, G. (2011). *Neuropsychoanalysis in Practice: Brain, Self and Objects.* New York: Oxford University Press.

Nugent, A. C., Bain, E. E., Thayer, J. F., Sollers, J. J., & Drevets, W. C. (2011). Heart rate variability during motor and cognitive tasks in females with major depressive disorder. *Psychiatry Research: Neuroimaging, 191*(1): 1–8.

Obrist, P. A., Black, A. H., Brenner, J., & DeCara, L. (2009). *Cardiovascular Psychophysiology: Current Issues in Response Mechanisms, Biofeedback and Methodology.* New Jersey: Transaction Publishers, Rutgers University.

Olshansky, B., Hani, N., Sabbah, H. N., Hauptman, P. J., & Colucci, W. S. (2008). Parasympathetic nervous system and heart failure: Pathophysiology and potential implications for therapy. *Circulation, 118*: 863–871.

Oren, L., & Possick, C. (2010). Is ideology a risk factor for PTSD symptom severity among Israeli political evacuees? *Journal of Traumatic Stress, 23*(4): 483–490.

Osgood, C. E., Succi, G. J., & Tannenbaum, P. H. (1957). *The Measurement of Meaning.* Urbana: University of Illinois Press.

Palensky, B. (2008). *From Neuro-Psychoanalysis to Cognitive and Affective Automation Systems.* Berlin: VDM Verlag.

Panksepp, J. (1998). *Affective Neuroscience.* New York: Oxford University Press.

Panksepp, J. (2011). Review of Antonio Damasio's "Self Comes to Mind": Constructing the conscious brain. *Neuropsychoanalysis, 13*(2): 205–219.

Panksepp, J., & Wright, J. S. (2012). Response to commentaries on Wright & Panksepp. *Neuropsychoanalysis, 14*(1): 59–75.

Pavio, A. (1971). *Imagery and Verbal Processes*. New York: Holt, Rinehart & Winston.

Pennebaker, J. W. (1982). *The Psychology of Physical Symptoms*. New York: Springer-Verlag.

Pennebaker, J. W., & Chung, C. K. (2011). Expressive writing and its links to mental and physical health. In: H. S. Friedman (Ed.), *Oxford Handbook of Health Psychology* (pp. 417–437). New York: Oxford University Press.

Perls, F. (1969). *Gestalt Therapy Verbatim*. Moab UT: Real People Press.

Peterson, C., Seligman, M. E. P., & and Valliant, G. E. (1988). Pessimistic explanatory style is a risk factor for physical illness: A thirty-five year longitudinal study. *Journal of Personality and Social Psychology, 55*: 23–27.

Piaget, J. (1928). *Judgment and Reasoning in the Child*. London: Routledge & Kegan Paul.

Piaget, J. (1954). *Construction of Reality in the Child*. New York: Basic Books.

Porges, S. W. (1983). Heart rate patterns in neonates: A potential diagnostic window to the brain. In: T. M. Field & A. M. Sostek (Eds.), *Infants Born at Risk: Physiological and Perceptual Responses* (pp. 3–22). New York: Grune & Stratton.

Porges, S. W. (2011). *The Polyvagal Theory: Neurophysiological Foundations of Emotions, Attachment, Communication, and Self-Regulation*. New York: Norton.

Rana, S. S., Schramke, C. J., Sangha, A., & Karpinski, A. C. (2009). Comparison of psychosocial factors between patients with benign fasciculations and those with amyotrophic lateral sclerosis. *Annuals of Indian Academy of Neurology, 12*(2): 108–110.

Reich, W. (1933). *Character Analysis*. New York: Farrar, Straus & Giroux.

Rieke, F., Warland, D., Ruyter, R., van Steveninck, W., & Bialek, S. (1997). *Exploring the Neural Code*. Boston: The MIT Press.

Rizzolatti, G., & Craighero, L. (2004). The mirror-neuron system. *Annual Review of Neuroscience, 27*: 169–192.

Rosendal, M., Olesen, F., & Fink, P. (2005). Management of medical unexplained symptoms. *British Medical Journal, 330*: 4–5.

Roth, P. (1983). Quote. *New York Times Book Review*, 30 October.

Rude, S. S., Gortner, E., & Pennebaker, J. W. (2004). Language use of depressed and depression-vulnerable college students. *Cognition and Emotion, 18*(8): 1121–1133.

Russ, T. C., Stamatakis, E., Hamer, M., Starr, J. M., Kivimäki, M., & Batty, G. D. (2012). Association between psychological distress and mortality:

Individual participant pooled analysis of 10 prospective cohort studies. *British Medical Journal, 345*: e4933.

Samtaney, R., Silver, D., Zabusky, N., & Cao, J. (1994). Visualizing features and tracking their evolution. *Computer, 27*: 20–27.

Schachter, S., & Singer, J. (1962). Cognitive, social, and physiological determinants of the emotional state. *Psychological Review, 69*: 379–399.

Schore, A. N. (2003a). *Affect Dysregulation and Disorders of the Self*. New York: Norton.

Schore, A. N. (2003b). *Affect Regulation and the Repair of the Self*. New York: Norton.

Schultz, W. (2010). Dopamine signals for reward value and risk: basic and recent data. *Behaviour and Brain Function, 6*: 24.

Seligman, M. E. P. (1975). *Helplessness: On Depression, Development, and Death*. San Francisco: W. H. Freeman.

Selye, H. (1936). A syndrome produced by diverse nocuous agents. *Nature, 138*: 32.

Shaibani, A., & Sabbagh, M. N. (1998). Pseudoneurologic syndromes: Recognition and diagnosis. *American Family Physician, 15*; 57(10): 2485–2494.

Shapiro, F. (2001). *Eye Movement Desensitization and Reprocessing* (2nd edn). New York: Guilford Press.

Shapiro, S. J., Bloomsmith, M. A. & Laule, G. E. (2003). Positive reinforcement training as a technique to alter nonhuman primate behaviour: Quantitative assessments of effectiveness. *Journal of Applied Animal Welfare Science, 6*(3): 175–187.

Siegel, D. J. (2012). *The Developing Mind: How Relationships and the Brain Interact to Shape Who We Are* (2nd edn). New York: Guilford Press.

Silva, P. J., & Duval, T. S. (2001). Objective self-awareness theory: Recent progress and enduring problems. *Personality and Social Psychology Review, 5*: 230–241.

Smith, M. E., & Farah, M. J. (2011). Are prescription stimulants "smart pills"? The epidemiology and cognitive neuroscience of prescription stimulant use by normal healthy individuals. *Psychological Bulletin, 137*: 717–735.

Snyder, A. W. (2009). Explaining and inducing savant skills: Privileged access to lower level, less processed information. *Philosophical Transactions of the Royal Society of London B, 364*: 1399–1405.

Snyder, A. W., & Mitchell, D. J. (1999). Is integer arithmetic fundamental to mental processing: The mind's secret arithmetic. *Proceedings of the Royal Society of London, Biology, 266*: 587–593.

Snyder, A. W., Bossomaier, T., & Mitchell, D. J. (2004). Concept formation: Object attributes dynamically inhibited from conscious awareness. *Journal of Integrative Neuroscience, 3*: 31–46.

Snyder, M. L. & Wicklund, R. A. (1981). Attribute Ambiguity. In: J. H. Harvey, W. Ickes, & R. F. Kidd (Eds.), *New Directions in Attribution Research* (pp. 197–221). Hillsdale NJ: Erlbaum.

Snyder, M. L., Stephan, W. G., & Rosenfeld, D. (1978). Attributional egotism. In: J. H. Harvey, W. Ickes, & R. F. Kidd (Eds.), *New Directions in Attribution Research* (pp. 91–117). Hillsdale NJ: Erlbaum.

Solms, M. (2000). Dreaming and REM sleep are controlled by different brain mechanisms. *Behavioural and Brain Sciences, 23*(6): 843–850.

Solms, M. (2004). Freud returns. *Scientific American, 290*(5): 83–88.

Solms, M., & Panksepp, J. (2012). The id knows more than the ego admits: Neuropsychoanalytic and primal consciousness perspectives on the interface between affective and cognitive neuroscience. *Brain Sciences, 2*: 147–175.

Solms, M., & Turnbull, O. H. (2011). What is neuropsychoanalysis? *Neuropsychoanalysis, 13*(2): 133–145.

Spence, J. T., & Helmreich, R. L. (1978). *Masculinity and Femininity: Their Psychological Dimensions, Correlates, and Antecedents*. Austin TX: University of Texas Press.

Spence, K. W. (1956). *Behavior Theory and Conditioning*. New Haven: Yale University Press.

Stephan, W. G., Bernstein, W. M., Davis, M. H., & Stephan, C. (1979). Attributions for achievement: Egotism vs. expectancy confirmation. *Social Psychology Quarterly, 17*(5): 443–458.

Stickgold, R. (2005). Sleep dependent memory consolidation. *Nature, 437*: 1272–1278.

Suzuki, S. (1970). *Zen Mind, Beginner's Mind*. New York: Weatherhill.

Swanson, J. M., Wigal, T. L., Volkow, N. D. (2011). Contrast of medical and nonmedical use of stimulant drugs, basis for the distinction, and risk of addiction: Comment on Smith and Farah (2011). *Psychological Bulletin, 137*(5): 742–748.

Tart, C. T. (1969). *Altered States of Consciousness: A Book of Readings*. New York: Wiley.

Thomas, J. L. (2012). Neurofeedback: A new modality for treating brain problems. *Archives of Medical Psychology, 3*(1): 21–35.

Thompson, P. M., Vidal, C., Giedd, J. J., Gochman, P., Blumentahl, J., Nicolson, R., Toga, A. W., & Rapoport, J. L. (2001). Mapping adolescent brain change reveal dynamic wave of accelerated gray matter loss in very early-onset schizophrenia. *Proceedings of the National Academy of Science, 98*(20): 650–655.

Thorndike, E. L. (1913). *The Psychology of Learning*. New York: Teachers College.

Tinbergen, N. (1951). *The Study of Instinct*. London: Oxford University Press.

Tompkins, S. S. (1962). *Affect Imagery Consciousness I: The Positive Affects*. Leipzig: Springer.

Tompkins, S. S. (1963). *Affect Imagery Consciousness II: The Negative Affects*. Leipzig: Springer.

Tronick, E. Z., Als, H., Adamson, L., Wise, S., Brazelton, T. B. (1978). The infants' response to entrapment between contradictory messages in face to face interaction. *Journal of the American Academy of Child Psychiatry, 17*: 1–13.

Tulving, E. (1972). Episodic and Semantic Memory. In: E. Tulving & W. Donaldson (Eds.), Organization of Memory (pp. 381–403). New York: Academic Press.

Tulving, E., & Szpunar, K. K. (2009). Episodic memory. *Scholarpedia, 4*(8): 3332.

Ulrich-Lai, Y. M., & Herman, J. P. (2009). Neural regulation of endocrine and autonomic stress responses. *Nature Reviews: Neuroscience, 10*: 397–409.

Van Veen, V., Krug, M. K., Schooler, J. W., & Carter, C. S. (2009). Neural activity predicts attitude change in cognitive dissonance. *Nature Neuroscience, 12*(11): 1469–1474.

Wagner, U., Gais, S., Haider, H., Verleger, R., & Born, J. (2004). Sleep inspires insight. *Nature, 427*(6972): 352–355.

Walach, H., Schmidt, S., & Jones, W. B. (Eds.) (2011). *Neuroscience, Consciousness and Spirituality*. New York: Springer.

Wallach, J. V. (2009). Endogenous hallucinogens as ligands of the trace amine receptors: A possible role in sensory perception. *Medical Hypotheses, 72*(1): 91–94.

Weil, A. (1972). *The Natural Mind: An Investigation of Drugs and the Higher Consciousness*. Boston: Houghton-Mifflin.

Weil, A. (1980). *The Marriage of Sun and Moon: Dispatches from the Frontiers of Consciousness*. New York: Houghton Mifflin.

Wertheimer, M. (1923). Untersuchungen zur Lehre von der Gestalt (Laws of organization in perceptual forms). *Psychologishe Forshung, 4*: 301–350.

White, T. (2007). *In Defense of Dolphins: The New Moral Frontier*. New York: John Wiley.

Wicklund, R. A. (1975). Objective self-awareness. In: L. Berkowitz (Ed.), *Advances in Experimental Social Psychology, 8* (pp. 233–275). New York: Academic Press.

Wicklund, R. A. (1990). *Zero Variable Theories and the Psychology of the Explainer*. New York: Springer.

Wicklund, R. A., & Brehm, J. W. (1976). *Perspectives on Cognitive Dissonance*. Hillsdale NJ: Lawrence Erlbaum.

Wicklund, R. A., & Gollwitzer, P. M. (1982). *Symbolic Self-Completion*. Hillsdale NJ: Erlbaum.

Wiener, N. (1948). *Cybernetics, or Communication and Control in the Animal and the Machine*. Cambridge MA: MIT Press.

Wilson, E. O. (1975). *Sociobiology: The New Synthesis*. Cambridge MA: Harvard University Press.

Wilson, E. O. (1984). *Biophilia*. Cambridge: Harvard University Press.

Wilson, E. O. (1998). *Consilience: The Unity of Knowledge*. New York: Vintage Books.

Winnicott, D. W. (1960a). The theory of the parent–infant relationship. *International Journal of Psychoanalysis, 41*(6): 585–595.

Winnicott, D. W. (1960b). Ego distortion in terms of true and false self. In: *The Maturational Processes and the Facilitating Environment* (pp. 140–152). Madison CT: International Universities Press.

Winnicott, D. W. (1975). *Playing and Reality*. London: Routledge.

Wolfe, T. (2000). *Hooking Up: What Life Was Like at the Turn of the Second Millennium: An American's World*. New York: Farrar, Strauss and Giroux.

Wolfson, P. E. (1985). Testimony of Philip E. Wolfson, M.D. In the Matter of MDMA Scheduling. Docket No. 84–48. United States Department of Justice, Drug Enforcement Administration.

Wright, J. S., & Panksepp, J. (2012). An evolutionary framework to understand foraging, wanting, and desire: The neuropsychology of the SEEKING system. *Neuropsychoanalysis, 14*(1): 5–39.

Xie, L., Kang, H., Xu, Q., Chen, M. J., Liao, Y., Thiyagarajan, M., O'Donnell, J., Christensen, D. J., Nicholson, C., Iliff, J. J., Takano, T., Deane, R., & Nedergaard, M. (2013). Sleep drives metabolite clearance from the adult brain. *Science, 342*(6156): 373–377.

Yerkes, R. M., & Dodson, J. D. (1908). The relation of strength of stimulus to rapidity of habit-formation. *Journal of Comparative Neurology and Psychology, 18*: 459–482.

Young, M. (1958). *The Rise of the Meritocracy, 1870–2033: An Essay on Education and Equality*. London: Transaction Publishers.

Zajonc, R. B. (1968). Attitudinal effects of mere exposure. *Journal of Personality and Social Psychology, 9*(2): 1–27.

Zajonc, R. B. (1980). Feelings and thinking: Preferences need no inferences. *American Psychologist, 35* (2): 151–175.

Zajonc, R. B. (2001). Mere exposure: A gateway to the subliminal. *Current Directions in Psychological Science, 10*(6): 224–228.

Zaleznik, A. (1989). *The Managerial Mystique: Restoring Leadership in Business.* New York: Harper & Row.

Zeigarnik, B. (1927). Uber das Behalten von erledigten und unerledigten Handlungen (On finished and unfinished tasks). *Psychologishe Forschung, 9:* 1–86.

Zhang, J. (2004). Memory process and the function of sleep. *Journal of Theoretics, 6:* 6.

Zhang, J. (2005). Continual-activation theory of dreaming. *Dynamical Psychology.*

Zillmann, D. (1983). Transfer of excitation in emotional behavior. In: J. T. Cacioppo & R. E. Petty (Eds.), *Social Psychophysiology: A Sourcebook* (pp. 215–240). New York: Guilford Press.

Zillmann, D. (2006). Dramaturgy for emotions from fictional narration. In: J. Bryant & P. Vordere (Eds.), *Psychology of Entertainment* (pp. 215–238). Mahwah NJ: Erlbaum.

Zucker, T. L., Samuelson, K. W., Muench, F., Greenberg, M. A., & Gevirtz, R. N. (2009). The effects of respiratory sinus arrhythmia biofeedback on heart rate variability and posttraumatic stress disorder symptoms: a pilot study. *Applied Psychophysiological Biofeedback, 34*(2): 135–43.

INDEX

207